DONALD MACKINNON'S THEOLOGY

T&T Clark Studies in English Theology

Series editors
Karen Kilby
Michael Higton
Stephen R. Holmes

DONALD MACKINNON'S THEOLOGY

To Perceive Tragedy Without the Loss of Hope

Andrew Bowyer

LONDON • NEW YORK • OXFORD • NEW DELHI • SYDNEY

T&T CLARK
Bloomsbury Publishing Plc
50 Bedford Square, London, WC1B 3DP, UK
1385 Broadway, New York, NY 10018, USA

BLOOMSBURY, T&T CLARK and the T&T Clark logo are trademarks of Bloomsbury Publishing Plc

First published in Great Britain 2019
Reprinted 2019

Copyright © Andrew Bowyer, 2019

Andrew Bowyer has asserted his right under the Copyright, Designs and Patents Act, 1988, to be identified as Author of this work.

For legal purposes the Acknowledgements on p. vii constitute an extension of this copyright page.

Cover design: Terry Woodley
Cover image © iStock

All rights reserved. No part of this publication may be reproduced or transmitted in any form or by any means, electronic or mechanical, including photocopying, recording, or any information storage or retrieval system, without prior permission in writing from the publishers.

Bloomsbury Publishing Plc does not have any control over, or responsibility for, any third-party websites referred to or in this book. All internet addresses given in this book were correct at the time of going to press. The author and publisher regret any inconvenience caused if addresses have changed or sites have ceased to exist, but can accept no responsibility for any such changes.

A catalogue record for this book is available from the British Library.

Library of Congress Cataloging-in-Publication Data
Names: Bowyer, Andrew D., author.
Title: Donald MacKinnon's theology : to perceive tragedy without the loss of hope / Andrew Bowyer.
Description: 1 [edition]. | New York : T&T Clark, 2019. | Series: T&T Clark Studies in English Theology ; 5 | Includes bibliographical references and index.
Identifiers: LCCN 2019007740 | ISBN 9780567681249 (hardback) | ISBN 9780567681287 (epub)
Subjects: LCSH: MacKinnon, Donald M. (Donald MacKenzie), 1913-1994. | Church of England–Doctrines.
Classification: LCC BX5199.M147 B69 2019 | DDC 230/.3092–dc23
LC record available at https://lccn.loc.gov/2019007740

ISBN: HB: 978-0-5676-8124-9
ePDF: 978-0-5676-8125-6
eBook: 978-0-5676-8128-7

Typeset by Deanta Gobal Publishing Services, Chennai, India
Printed and bound in Great Britain

To find out more about our authors and books visit www.bloomsbury.com and sign up for our newsletters.

CONTENTS

Acknowledgements	vii
List of abbreviations	viii
AN INTRODUCTION TO DONALD MACKINNON	1

Chapter 1
MACKINNON'S 'THERAPEUTIC' METHOD — 5
Introduction	5
MacKinnon's 'therapeutic' methodology	8
The focus and end of MacKinnon's philosophical therapy	14
MacKinnon as a Kantian moral theologian	17
MacKinnon contra modernist theology	26
Moral realism	32
Conclusion	42

Chapter 2
BEYOND KANT AND BACK AGAIN: FURTHER INFLUENCES ON MACKINNON — 45
Introduction	45
A. E. Taylor	46
W. R. Sorley	54
The analytical awakening	62
Options for the theologian in light of the analytical turn	75

Chapter 3
MACKINNON'S MORAL CHRISTOLOGY — 81
Introduction	81
MacKinnon on incarnation and revelation	85
MacKinnon on atonement	98
Transition from atonement theology to trinitarian ontology	107
Excursus: *Alter Christus*? MacKinnon on Lenin	114
Conclusion	120

Chapter 4
MACKINNON AND THE LITERARY IMAGINATION   121
Introduction   121
A moral realist reads literature   122
    On scripture as literature   129
MacKinnon and tragic literature   138
Conclusion   150

Chapter 5
MACKINNON, WITTGENSTEIN AND MORAL REALISM   151
Introduction   151
On Wittgenstein and ethics   151
MacKinnon's response to Wittgenstein   161
MacKinnon's unsystematic proposal for moral philosophy: Intuition *and* natural law   173
Conclusion   181

Chapter 6
OVERALL CONCLUSION: CONSIDERING MACKINNON'S PROJECT IN RETROSPECT   183

Bibliography   191
Index   202

ACKNOWLEDGEMENTS

I thank my PhD supervisors, Professor David Fergusson and Dr Fergus Kerr OP, for accompanying me through the process of writing the thesis that prefigured this book. Their encouragement and perceptive criticisms are responsible for whatever is valuable in what follows. I am also indebted to friends and colleagues at Trinity College, Cambridge, who offered unfailing support as I prepared the manuscript for publication.

ABBREVIATIONS

MacKinnon's works

BT   *Borderlands of Theology, and Other Essays by Donald M. MacKinnon.* edited by George W. Roberts and Donovan E. Smucker Eugene: Wipf and Stock, 2011. 1968.

ET   *Explorations in Theology.* London: SCM, 1979.

TT   *Themes in Theology: The Three-Fold Cord; Essays in Philosophy, Politics and Theology.* Edinburgh: T&T Clark, 1987.

PM   *The Problem of Metaphysics*, Gifford Lectures, Cambridge: Cambridge University Press, 1974.

SET   *A Study in Ethical Theory.* London: A. & C. Black, 1957.

AN INTRODUCTION TO DONALD MACKINNON

Stanley Hauerwas once made the offhand comment that 'MacKinnon saved British theology'.[1] Here was an endorsement of Donald MacKinnon's attempt to reframe theology in light of a rejection of 'constantinianism' and the 'Christendom project', his suspicion of popular theological modernizers and liberals of the early to mid-twentieth century and his willingness to see Barth as providing a timely word on theology's true ground and method. Rowan Williams, Nicholas Lash, Brian Hebblethwaite, Fergus Kerr and David Fergusson all cite MacKinnon as an indispensable influence on their thinking, as does his long-time friend, the literary critic George Steiner. Additionally, a number of prominent female moral philosophers who emerged from war-time Oxford, including Mary Midgley, Mary Warnock, Philippa Foot and Iris Murdoch, came under his influence to various degrees.

Donald MacKinnon (1913–94) can be counted among the most influential Anglican theologians in the British context in the second half of the twentieth century. His writings reveal a restive and unsystematic thinker, yet there is a good case to be made that a series of reoccurring questions – 'obsessions' might better suit MacKinnon's temperament – appear throughout. These relate to the demands of moral realism, the tensions between the philosophical positions of realism and idealism and the perennially disruptive presence of Christ, whose redemptive significance cannot be fully appreciated apart from a tragic ascription.

Under the heading, 'Is there an intuition of being? MacKinnon and Lash on analogy in Aquinas', DeHart notes,

> In many ways this story, like much that is most interesting in recent theology in England, begins with Donald MacKinnon. The towering, eccentric Scotsman (no Presbyterian but rather member of the Episcopal Church of Scotland [sic], and a catholic in ecclesial and theological outlook) held the Norris-Hulse chair in Cambridge for almost twenty years (1960–78). As he threaded his life's path of agonizingly self-aware dissent over the course of the blood-soaked twentieth century, he launched one attempt after another toward a contemporary retrieval of the implicit ontology of Nicaea and Chalcedon, always faithful to a creatively Kantian ethics of the limits of cognition, and deeply colored by his bruisingly intimate feel for the irredeemability of historical suffering. This (for its time) highly atypical theological stance challenged and intrigued any

---

1. He made this comment to the author at Durham University in 2012.

number of independent thinkers, especially at Cambridge, as did his tireless recommendations of Barth and Balthasar in a period of Anglican theology when the first was far from popular and the second hardly known.[2]

While MacKinnon has appeared as a conversation partner in a number of academic monographs in the decade after his death, the most important shift in interest coincided with the onset of the twenty-first century, particularly with the emergence of PhD research projects that have focused on MacKinnon in his own right. The most significant contribution has been that of André Muller, whose doctoral thesis has provided a detailed intellectual biography of MacKinnon up until 1959, with a second volume now being prepared.[3] Timothy Connor has also provided an incisive analysis of the interactions between ecclesiological and Christological themes of MacKinnon's various writings, placing them in the wider context of contemporary Anglican ecclesiastical polity, in his 2011 book *The Kenotic Trajectory of the Church in Donald MacKinnon's Theology: From Galilee to Jerusalem to Galilee*.[4] In addition to these, concerted attempts to edit and reissue MacKinnon's now out-of-print publications have occurred, which are indicative of a new generation that perceives the enduring value of his contribution. In this vein, McDowell has produced a 'Donald MacKinnon Reader',[5] a new edition of *Borderlands* has been reissued[6] and a collection of MacKinnon's contributions to the 'signposts' series has been published (*God the Living and True* and *The Church of God*), together with *The Stripping of the Altars*.[7]

What follows is a work that is sympathetic to MacKinnon, perhaps too much so. A focus on his signal achievements is warranted, however, because they have often been obscured by his own difficult style, by the fact that it was impossible to establish any discrete and enduring school of thought in his name, and by the fact that he was so immersed in the particular theological and political controversies of

---

2. Paul DeHart, *Aquinas and Radical Orthodoxy: A Critical Enquiry* (Oxford: Routledge, 2012), 38.

3. André Muller, 'Donald M. MacKinnon: The True Service of the Particular, 1913-1959.' Unpublished PhD Thesis, University of Otago, 2010.

4. Timothy G. Connor, *The Kenotic Trajectory of the Church in Donald Mackinnon's Theology: From Galilee to Jerusalem to Galilee* (London: T&T Clark, 2011).

5. D. M. MacKinnon, *Philosophy and the Burden of Theological Honesty: A Donald MacKinnon Reader*, ed. John C. McDowell (London: T&T Clark, 2011).

6. D. M. MacKinnon, *Borderlands of Theology, and Other Essays by Donald M. MacKinnon*, ed. George W. Roberts and Donovan E. Smucker (Eugene, OR: Wipf and Stock, 2011).

7. Scott A. Kirkland, Ashley J. Moyse and John C. McDowell, ed., *The Church in Dispossession: The Ecclesiological Writings of Donald M. MacKinnon* (Minneapolis, MN: Fortress Press, 2016).

his day that it is tempting to see his work as speaking exclusively to a past epoch.[8] An attentive reading of MacKinnon's oeuvre results in two further convictions. First, that there has been insufficient attention as to the way his commitment to moral realism appears over the disparate writings, providing a point of connection between his theological and philosophical interests. Second, that more must be said about MacKinnon's methodology beyond such labels as 'deliberately unsystematic'. I address this latter concern with the proposal that MacKinnon's method has a distinctly 'therapeutic' character. The issue of MacKinnon's moral realism and call for metaphysical renewal are interlocking themes across this whole study. It is a realism that seeks to contemplate suffering borne of evil unflinchingly, together with the presence of Christ, who (for MacKinnon) is always the crucified messiah of history *and* the mystical body of the Catholic Church at every time.[9] MacKinnon's moral intensity and concern for a post-positivist metaphysics comes to bear on his appreciation of Kant and Wittgenstein, and plays a decisive role in his engagements with literature, Marxism and the person of Jesus.

What becomes evident in exploring these dimensions of MacKinnon's thought is a deep engagement with philosophy. Classics was a core focus of the school curriculum at Winchester and an interest in Plato and Aristotle never left him, no doubt encouraged by his study of the 'Greats' at Oxford and his early close proximity to figures such as A. E. Taylor. Yet it was Kant who had the greatest impact and Janz has argued that MacKinnon's nuanced reading of the Enlightenment master has received something of a vindication in the wake of the fading influence of Strawson's commentary; a reading that led many British theologians to view Kant as *the* enemy. In this context MacKinnon was a minority voice for holding Kant as an indispensable ally for theology. This is certainly a point on which he and Hauerwas would disagree and which, as I will examine in Chapter 5, becomes the greatest source of Milbank's complaint against him. For MacKinnon, the purgation Kant effected in the realms of metaphysics and theology forms a 'point of no return', and the way Kant set up a perennial tension between idealism and realism, freedom and necessity, as unavoidable dimensions of human reason stayed with him as he moved beyond Kant to engage with other interlockers. This point, I think, was crucial for MacKinnon's reluctance to join others in a full embrace of the Wittgensteinian trajectory, although, as my final chapter shows, MacKinnon's reluctance emerged from a perceptive reading of Wittgenstein rather than any indictable avoidance or neglect.

---

8. Janz speaks about MacKinnon as one 'whose illuminating and highly relevant contributions to [the philosophical problem of anti-realism and realism] have been all but lost in contemporary treatments and whose insight opens the debate to theological problems in enormously productive ways'. Paul D. Janz, *God, the Mind's Desire: Reference, Reason, and Christian Thinking* (Cambridge: Cambridge University Press, 2004), 52.

9. For an early affirmation of this sentiment read D. M. MacKinnon, *The Church of God*, Signposts (London: Dacre, 1940).

The first chapter proposes a new lens through which MacKinnon's project may be viewed. It will characterize his work as a form of 'therapeutic' philosophy that combines a call for intense interiority *and* moral realism in a way that sees these notions as mutually involved and reinforcing. As the chapter progresses the extent to which Kant lies behind much of MacKinnon's therapeutic language of 'purgation' and 'illumination' will become clear. So too the fact that moral realism becomes, both the end of a certain therapeutic discipline and a commitment that shapes MacKinnon's engagement with philosophy and theology at every level. It characterizes a 'form of life'. MacKinnon never sets out a *systematic* defence of moral realism nor for his insistence that the tension between idealism and realism is at once (a) something crucial for theologians to confront explicitly, (b) a tension that necessarily exists and remains perennially unsolved, and (c) results in the continued need for a language of metaphysics. Yet, these ideas occur again and again throughout his corpus. They emerge as philosophical inevitabilities from within the task of continued description and re-description of human experience in all its historical particularity.

An examination of the key influences on MacKinnon follows in Chapter 2, and it is here we can detect one of the sources of MacKinnon's restiveness as he seeks to adopt insights from a confident moral apologetic theology of the previous generation, while at the same time respecting the ways in which the analytical turn had highlighted the impossibility of such projects. The remainder of the study is taken up by exploring the various domains in which MacKinnon's therapeutic moral realism comes to the fore. These include his engagements with kenotic Christology (Chapter 3), his convictions as to the indispensability of good literature for moral philosophy and realist theology (Chapter 4), and his response to Wittgenstein as he sought to articulate a post-Kantian position (Chapter 5).

The picture of MacKinnon that emerges in the pages to follow suggests a figure who invites an initiation into a purgative form of therapy that fashions the theologian, and the wider church, as animators of a renewed Catholic humanism with an uncompromising commitment to moral realism. For MacKinnon, Kant was an ally for this project, while for the likes of Milbank, he is what the Catholic humanist must be saved *from*. Some of MacKinnon's critics certainly hit their mark, as the final chapter will show, but there is also room for riposte. In what follows, I seek to shine a light on an original thinker, whose mark on British theology continues to be felt and whose attentiveness to the problem of metaphysics and call for moral seriousness, which were for him, two sides of a coin, remains pressing.

Chapter 1

MACKINNON'S 'THERAPEUTIC' METHOD

Introduction

In an introduction to a book entitled *Wittgensteinian Fideism?*, Szabados speaks about 'a family of writers' 'reading in the borderlands' whose

> line of thinking was fideistic in the sense that they believed in order to understand, that they endorsed the attitude '*Credo ut intelligam*'. This is an attitude to the activity of philosophizing that sees acceptance of rooted practices and ways of life as a given. Such an acceptance is not some peculiar and wilful act of belief, but an expression of reverence and a sense of wonder. This attitude takes what is given seriously. In contrast to traditional philosophy, which employs the method of sceptical doubt as a road to knowledge, fideist thinkers take an attitude of trust as fundamental to action, understanding and appreciation. They aim to do justice to what there is by overcoming forms of thought that distort and by providing perspicuous descriptions.[1]

While claiming that it would be wrong to attribute to this 'family' a 'common essence', Szabados thinks that they do share a 'central concern to leave room for faith by exposing the abuses and pretensions of reason involved in bad philosophy and the scientism of the age'.[2] The invocation of 'fideism' here obscures more than illumines, yet all that follows will indicate that MacKinnon was a sympathetic fringe dweller of the 'family' about which Szabados speaks; a fringe dweller because he continued to see immense purgative potential in the 'sceptical doubt of traditional philosophy'.

Attempts to bring the philosophical and theological output of MacKinnon under the discipline of a single organizing principle is a fraught enterprise, not least because MacKinnon himself admitted that there was nothing particularly organized about the way he thought and wrote. He never claimed to have reconciled the different strands of his thought.[3] The continually shifting,

---

1. Béla Szabados, 'Introduction', in *Wittgensteinian Fideism?*, ed. K. Nielsen and D. Z. Phillips (London: SCM Press, 2005), 14.

2. Ibid.

3. 'I don't pretend that my philosophy and theology hang together. I wish they did. They impinge on each other; but there are many very dark places.' MacKinnon, in L. Macintyre 'Thinking Legend Still in Search of Answers', *Glasgow Herald*, 7 November 1989.

open-ended and interrogative nature of his work indicates as much. Regarding theology, MacKinnon discounts the possibility of synthesis as a factor that arises necessarily from within the discipline itself:

> If 'synthesis' is not to be the lot of Christians in the twentieth century that will be because it is less a theological act than an act of God, a putting together of fragmentary lives and efforts in the resurrection of the dead.[4]

In regard to his philosophical commitments, MacKinnon was too aware of the early-twentieth-century positivist turn in philosophy to align himself with particular forms of idealism fading in its wake, or any analogous approach that lent itself to ambitious exercises in system building.[5] It is not only the idealist tradition, however, that MacKinnon sought to move beyond. He also articulated dissatisfaction with positivist reductionism, concerned that when one submits to its premises and methods, inevitably there will be violations against the manifold complexity of the human subject and 'an expulsion of the poets'; a refusal of some modes of imaginative discourse that are essential in any effort to apprehend history and moral subject.[6] This is despite his lifelong admiration for positivism (and the whole empiricist pedigree) because of its commitment to 'realism' and what he perceives as its purgative intellectual rigour. Perhaps it is the case that – loosely analogous to figures of the early German romantic movement in their own time and context – MacKinnon feared that the atomistic drive of empiricism and its positivist offshoots of the interwar period ended up placing costly limits on the very realism empiricists nonetheless held as an absolute commitment. It is the rigour of the empiricist's drive to capture objective knowledge of the world as it stands independent of specific subjective constructs that is at once the greatest contribution of the empiricist school *and* the source of its most crippling blind spots.

It is no surprise that MacKinnon looked upon the progression of J. S. Mill's thinking with sympathy in as far as the latter affirmed the necessity and usefulness of empirical realism, but alongside a growing conviction that Benthamite epistemological rigour could undermine the realist's receptivity to reality in ways that demanded redress, supplementation and the expansion of terms.[7] The most telling test case in any manifestation of this dispute, and certainly between the likes of Bentham and Mill, is whether poetic forms of speech can constitute knowledge of some sort, or whether they must be rejected or exposed to reductive

---

4. D. M. MacKinnon, 'Some Reflections on the Summer School', *Christendom* 14 (1945): 111.

5. D. M. MacKinnon, 'Revelation and Social Justice', in *Burden*, ed. John McDowell (London: T&T Clark, 2011), 144–5.

6. D. M. MacKinnon, *The Problem of Metaphysics*, Gifford Lectures (Cambridge: Cambridge University Press, 1974), 46–52.

7. Ibid., 46–7.

analysis in order to uncover underlying 'facts'.[8] In MacKinnon's case, and unlike Mill, the resources drawn upon for this critical engagement with empiricism lies less with any specific forms of romanticism and more with Kant, Christian existentialism, Collingwood's historicism and phenomenological approaches to moral action mediated through literature. Closer to MacKinnon's era was Isaiah Berlin: MacKinnon's tutor at Oxford and one whose relationship with positivist philosophy has resonance with features of Mill's biography as described above.[9] Berlin was deeply committed to the positivist turn in British philosophy in the early twentieth century, yet without renouncing a commitment to 'empirical seriousness' spent much of his latter life examining the history of romanticism and defending the notion of freedom within political liberalism.[10]

MacKinnon resisted projects of idealist metaphysics *and* positivist realism in as far as they were judged to distort or limit apprehension of the subject's particular place in history and compromise moral self-apprehension. As intimated above, he saw much more promise in the second although he did posit a qualified re-engagement with Kant as a possible avenue by which to repair some of its deficiencies.[11] Kant is *the* great philosophical figure of modernity for MacKinnon, separating yet holding together the realms of 'nature' and the autonomous rational subject's freedom, while seeking to posit renewed possibilities for speaking about morality, aesthetics and religion.[12]

One important aspect of MacKinnon's project was that of bringing what he saw to be the clarifying rigour of the early-twentieth-century positivists into conversation with Kant. To this conversation he added an abiding commitment to a realist orthodox Christian theology. Given the disparity of these interests and the way that they oppose each other, it is not surprising that his efforts were deliberately and self-consciously unsystematic. MacKinnon preferred to express himself in essays, lectures and short books – mediums that are better at raising questions and probing possibilities than delivering anything by way of definitive solution or 'knock-down' argument.[13] While allowing for creativity and subtlety the openness of texture can be frustratingly obtuse.

---

8. This is a question that MacKinnon often references in relation to Plato. On the philosophical status of the poetic form, see for instance: D. M. MacKinnon, *On the Notion of a Philosophy of History: Lecture Delivered on 5 May 1953 at King's College, London*, Hobhouse Memorial Trust Lecture, 23 (Oxford: Oxford University Press, 1954).

9. Muller, 'True Service', 251–2.

10. D. M. MacKinnon, *A Study in Ethical Theory* (London: A&C Black, 1957), 207–9.

11. *BT*, 55–81.

12. Pamela Sue Anderson and Jordan Bell, *Kant and Theology*, Philosophy and theology (London: T&T Clark, 2010), 11–25.

13. Steiner notes that MacKinnon 'shares this preference with modern logicians …, but also, I would like to imagine, with the pre-Socratics'. George Steiner, 'Tribute to Donald MacKinnon', *Theology* 98, no. 781 (1995): 5.

What kind of a picture is emerging about the peculiarities, risks and priorities of MacKinnon's programme? Indispensable is a conviction regarding the importance of philosophy for the theologian and the centrality of morality to the whole methodology. In the first instance, MacKinnon holds that theology can only remain true to its vocation if it engages with philosophy, not in an apologetic mode but rather as one discipline undergoing testing and refinement at the hands of another. In his inaugural lecture as the Norris Hulse Professor at the University of Cambridge, MacKinnon noted that 'apologetic concern, as Karl Barth (the one living theologian of unquestionable genius) has rightly insisted, is the death of serious theologizing, and I would add, equally of serious work in the philosophy of religion'.[14] Yet, in contrast to Barth's programme, MacKinnon more explicitly emphasizes the way theologians might avoid illusion and resist temptation in as far as they expose their ideas to the sceptical gaze of the modern philosopher. In his context, it is clear that the advent of analytical philosophy in Britain, with its positivist and empiricist dimensions and its tendency to underwrite forms of utilitarianism, provides a worthy provocation or purgation of Christian temptations towards anthropomorphism, as well as voluntarism and abstraction in moral theology. The same could be said for the various trends in Marxist theory with which MacKinnon engaged.

One will search MacKinnon's writing in vain for an equally strong sense that philosophers need to open themselves up to the purgative insights of theology.[15] Beyond an ever-deepening apprehension of revealed knowledge, which can only ever be a scandal to the philosopher, theology's task is to give witness to the irreducibility of personhood's moral dimension and to defend the unique spiritual dignity of men and women in the face of all temptations to reductionism. Further, it can note the way in which moral experience continually raises questions that expose limits and reinforce the poverty of anthropomorphism.

MacKinnon's 'therapeutic' methodology

Claiming that MacKinnon was an 'unsystematic' thinker could be taken as a rebuke. It might suggest a scattered mind that could never quite pull the threads together:

---

14. *BT*, 28. The early influence of Neo-Orthodoxy on MacKinnon is evident in one of his more accessible works: D. M. MacKinnon, *God the Living and the True*, Signposts (London: Dacre Press, 1940).

15. MacKinnon's work does not reflect the characteristic pattern which Insole identifies as typical of (what was to become) the Radical Orthodox movement in which 'there is the usual description of "secular" approaches, reliant upon a mythos or "original violence"; then there is the invocation of the peaceful, analogical Christian mythos that understands the secular better than the secular understands itself; finally there is an invocation of a certain theological position to answer definitively a wider social/philosophical problem'. Christopher J. Insole, *The Realist Hope: A Critique of Anti-Realist Approaches in Contemporary Philosophical Theology* (Aldershot: Ashgate, 2006), 170.

never attaining an acceptable level of coherence, resolution or a convincing response to detractors. MacKinnon knew that he could be obscure, fragmented and tortured in his writing. Yet, a patient examination of MacKinnon's *oeuvre* suggests that he was developing something of a therapeutic method. Approaching his project through this lens helps us to appreciate that the struggle for clear expression flows from the conceptual tensions he was trying to hold and is integral to the perceptiveness achieved.[16] The opening lines of John Wren-Lewis's review of SET, in which exasperation is evident, captures the difficulty in accounting for MacKinnon's method:

> This is a curious book, which at least one reader has gone through carefully twice without being able to grasp quite what the author is trying to say or indeed to achieve. The one thing that can be said with certainty is that it is a study in the different ways that ethical language can be used, written somewhat in the style of a 'novel of atmosphere', bringing out various subtle differences of *nuance* and highlighting the tensions that occur in different situations. Professor MacKinnon studies a number of writers on ethics more or less at random: H. A. Pritchard, Mill and the Utilitarians, Kant, Isaiah Berlin, Bishop Butler, Hegel and St. Paul each serve to illustrate one aspect of his subject, one mood, as it were, in which ethical language may be used. If he makes no reference whatever to the ethical teaching of Jesus, Buddha or Plato, or even of Aristotle or Confucius, it is hard to know whether he can be criticised for omitting them or not: it is scarcely possible to criticise a playwright's use of character when you are not clear just what plot he has in mind.[17]

Wren-Lewis was right to detect a theatrical impulse and the influence of a literary sensibility in MacKinnon's style. In Chapter 4, I will show that MacKinnon was acutely aware of the way plays and novels of realist intensity can invite approaches that are helpfully different to those demanded by modernist philosophers who attempt to prevent flights of fancy by fixating on mimicking the natural sciences or mathematics in key aspects of method. Where Wren-Lewis misses the mark is his claim that MacKinnon chooses his subjects 'more or less at random' and this is a representative case in which the therapeutic ascription is helpful for a defence of MacKinnon. Wren-Lewis *suspects* something more is at play in SET but he can only explain it in terms of the inaccessibility of an artistic temperament. MacKinnon begins the book with a focus on the controversy that dominated modernist moral philosophy; the debate between utilitarians and deontologists, and then proceeds to invoke a number of figures whose work provides a series of

---

16. Murray was the first to associate MacKinnon's project with the 'therapeutic' label. Paul D. Murray, 'Reason, Truth and Theology in Pragmatist Perspective: A Study in the Theological Relevance of Postfoundationalist Approaches to Human Rationality with Particular Reference to the Work of Richard Rorty, Nicholas Rescher and Donald MacKinnon' (University of Cambridge, 2003), 15, 169–73.

17. J. Wren-Lewis, 'A Study in Ethical Theory', *Modern Churchman* 3, no. 2 (1960): 145.

distinctive purgative and reparative resources orientated towards two interrelated goals. The first involves enabling the reader to look beyond the terms of the debate as they had been set (in this vein at least, there is a similarity with Wittgenstein's project), and the second: to convince the reader that part of their 'healing' comes with the acceptance of a form of rigorous, historically grounded realism. If this were MacKinnon's intention then an unhelpful criticism would point to a lack of breadth, comprehensiveness and systematic resolution, while an astute critic would point to the ways in which he has misdiagnosed the problem, sought therapeutic remedies from the wrong sources or missed potential resources altogether.[18]

Regarding the writings of St. Paul, MacKinnon made an observation that could well apply to himself:

> If Paul writes sometimes as a man in pain, the very depth of his perplexity gives a certain purity to his words; for he writes not as if he would provide a solution, but rather as if he would lay the texture of a problem bare.[19]

There is an acknowledgement of unresolved perplexity, a drive towards 'purer' expression, and an emphasis on an open-ended need for diagnosis and 'treatment'. To call MacKinnon 'unsystematic' is to evoke a famously restless and eccentric personality, but also to point to deeply held convictions about the nature of rationality itself and his acute sensitivity to the problem of scepticism. Yet this is not to say that MacKinnon was blind to the benefits of attempts to systematize, whether they emerged from the pen of Barth and Balthasar, or from Russell or Moore. Nor is it to say common threads or carefully developed arguments cannot be found in MacKinnon's various writings. Indeed, the conviction that propels this study is that MacKinnon's project *does* have a central theme, into which all the tributaries of his various thoughts flow; that of moral realism and the perennial dialectic of idealism and realism which warrants the retention of a recall to metaphysics. By his own admission the place MacKinnon found himself was the 'borderlands', where one is caught in an open-ended conversation between philosophy and theology and such liminal spaces proved to be a crucible. In the early to mid-twentieth century, the trend in Britain was towards a revelatory positivism that sought sanctuary from the fires of hostile philosophical trends or alternatively, the abandonment of realist claims for theology in order to make a bid for greater philosophical credibility. MacKinnon refused both options.

To say that MacKinnon is undertaking a type of philosophical therapy means, I contend, looking at his work through an analogous lens to that which Stanley Cavell looks upon the later works of Wittgenstein. Cavell argues that it is unhelpful to characterize Wittgenstein simply as an unsystematic thinker full of radical provocations and half-formed propositions for a non-foundationalist linguistic

---

18. See, for instance, Cornelius Ernst, 'Ethics and the Play of Intelligence', *New Blackfriars* 39, no. 460–1 (1958): 325.

19. *BT*, 156.

philosophy, properly appraisable from an 'objective distance'. Of course, one *can* remain at a distance, but what Wittgenstein sought was to invite us to observe and participate in something that can only be described with an analogy to spiritual disciplines of contemplation and purgation. On exploring the relationship between analytical philosophy and existentialism, a relationship that could also be said to have characterized MacKinnon's borderland wanderings too, Cavell argues that

> in both [Wittgenstein and Kierkegaard], the cure is for us to return to our everyday existence. It will be obvious that this emphasis on diagnosis and cure continues the early image of the philosopher as the physician of the soul, and it also aligns these writers with the characteristic effort of modern thought to un-mask its audience, its world, an effort as true of Marx and Nietzsche and Freud as it is of Kierkegaard and Wittgenstein. And the effort to un-mask requires a few masks or tricks of its own. Traditional forms of criticism, of logical refutation pre-eminently, are unavailing. Our new problems do not arise through inconsistency or falsehood; they are worse than false, and they are all too consistent. What one must do is to alter the terms and the ground upon which the whole argument rests.[20]

The analogy I wish to draw between *our* apprehension of MacKinnon's method and Cavell's 'therapeutic' reading of Wittgenstein's is not without grounding; a point developed in Chapter 5, where MacKinnon's reading of Wittgenstein comes into sharper focus. Indeed, to the extent that they both take up a version of post-Wittgensteinian therapy, Cavell and MacKinnon occupy the same borderland. They approach the boundary from opposite directions; one as a philosopher who is intrigued by the linguistic excesses of theology in a way that potentially marginalizes him among peers; the other, a restive Christian intellectual engaged deeply with philosophy in a way that was isolating. Yet both converge in their efforts to articulate 'realist' moral perspectives after having learnt key lessons from Kant, Wittgenstein and the organized brutality of the twentieth century.

The point here is to draw MacKinnon out of isolation posthumously, placing him among kindred spirits who share some of his intuitions and practices on questions of method. MacKinnon may have been an independent and original thinker, but he was not alone in his attraction to a therapeutic style, just as Cavell is not alone in speaking of Wittgenstein's project in such terms.[21] Roger Shiner has argued that with the exception of Cavell no interpreter of Wittgenstein since Wisdom has

---

20. Stanley Cavell, 'Existentialism and Analytical Philosophy', *Daedalus*, no. 3 (1964): 959.

21. Thompson observes that for Wittgenstein 'religion in relation to the problems of life, is manifestly concerned not with the manipulation of the world but with the transformation of the self, with the state of a person's soul. And Wittgenstein himself was clearly interested in the possibility of such a transformation and with the power of religion to bring it about.' Caleb Thompson, 'Wittgenstein, Augustine and the Fantasy of Ascent', *Philosophical Investigations* 25, no. 2 (2002): 1.

understood the 'ambivalence of the image of philosophy as therapy'; a tantalizing claim given that MacKinnon read and commented appreciatively upon Wisdom's philosophy on a number of occasions.[22] Caleb Thompson, Cora Diamond, James Conant, Thomas Ricketts, Kevin Hector join Peterman and Cavell in advocating 'therapeutic' interpretations of the Wittgenstein's later works. Each in their own way attests to Wittgenstein's restless, vividly self-conscious explorations of various problems in philosophy that are not, in fact, simply 'problems' but 'illusions' and 'temptations', calling for a 'confessional' response by which

> the interlocutors must acknowledge what they actually believe and not just enter in the conversation in a merely academic way. [Peterman calls] this the requirement of confession to emphasize that such acknowledgments made in a therapeutic context often will require recognition that the acknowledged beliefs are mistaken and must be overcome.[23]

Such a style of philosophy plunges interlockers into processes of self-examination and renunciation where sifting illusions and self-deceptions become the focus for a life that integrates intellectual and moral striving. In MacKinnon's terms, such efforts are weighted towards 'reception' of what *is* rather than 'construction', which is to say that philosophical (and theological) method is to be driven by a realist imperative. Works such as Augustine's *Confessions*, Wittgenstein's *Philosophical Investigations*, MacKinnon's SET and PM, and Cavell's *Little Did I Know* could all be said to display this methodological disposition in the broadest sense. In each case 'therapy' necessitates a move from various illusions, unhelpful abstractions and dangerous flights to innocent and de-historicized vantage points, to greater immersion in the concrete, the historical, the 'ordinary' with which the subject must grapple. Variously, it may ground the human being before a God who becomes incarnate in history (Augustine) or before a realization of our 'situatedness' within particular communities of language users (Wittgenstein), or before another soul who I may acknowledge or fail to do so (Cavell), or some combination of all of these (MacKinnon). Realizing the limitations of human apprehension becomes a core epistemic discipline and humility a core moral virtue for the reader joining the confessing author in therapeutic purgation.

Other types of therapy are available – ones informed by the assumptions of radical scepticism, emotivism and anti-realism, for instance. The methodical disposition identified in Wittgenstein, Cavell and MacKinnon, however, aligns itself to the insights of empiricism, moderate scepticism or agnosticism and versions of

---

22. Ibid., 53. See also D. M. MacKinnon, 'John Wisdom's Other Minds & Philosophy and Psycho-analysis', *Aberdeen University Review* 35 (Spring 1954): 271–3.

23. James F. Peterman, *Philosophy as Therapy: An Interpretation and Defense of Wittgenstein's Later Philosophical Project* (New York: State University of New York Press, 1992), 5–9.

moral realism.[24] Such a claim demands unpacking, but at this point we can at least note that it is not a novel line of argument. Thompson, for instance, makes the following observation in relation to what he sees as the analogous concerns of Augustine and Wittgenstein:

> Wittgenstein like Augustine feels his problem as real disturbances, as 'deep disquietudes' [*tiefe Beunruhigungen*] (§111). But more than that, each is deeply concerned with his separation from and connection with reality. Each is deeply interested in language as a medium in which one is brought to or led away from what is real. Consequently, each is exhibiting for us a linguistic activity which can perhaps secure for one presence in the reality and limitations of human existence. For each that activity involves an attention to the details of human life and language, details in which meaning is in the end found to reside.[25]

Cavell and MacKinnon join Augustine and Wittgenstein in this therapeutic drive towards a form of confessional realism, an ascription that becomes particularly resonant in their respective writings on the nature of moral knowledge. As already noted, MacKinnon was a moral thinker with an almost obsessive zeal to critique theologians in the thrall of abstracting forms of idealism, but he did not find the versions of realism proffered by key figures of his British empiricist and positivist milieu as providing anything more than an important corrective.[26] It may be fair to say that some exposure to Wittgenstein, together with the influence of Wisdom, helped MacKinnon towards an embrace of this particular type of dissatisfaction. Discussing Wittgenstein in SET, MacKinnon states that 'if the conception of a reconstruction of human knowledge upon a sure and certain foundation is an illusion, yet like other illusions it may tell us much of the men who attempted it; it can even be regarded sometimes as a specially revealing chapter in their autobiography'.[27] While MacKinnon does not adopt Wittgenstein's substantive proposals to Cavell's extent, particularly on the possibility of employing the language

---

24. It is a rejection of the 'existentialist and Anglo-Saxon heirs of Kant (such as Sartre in France and R.M. Hare in England) [who] make the human will the creator of value, which was previously seen as inscribed in the heavens'. J. E. Hare, *God's Call: Moral Realism, God's Commands, and Human Autonomy* (Grand Rapids, MI: Eerdmans, 2001), 12.

25. C. Thompson, 'Wittgenstein's Confessions', *Philosophical Investigations* 23, no. 1 (2000): 23–4.

26. As noted above, MacKinnon rejected positivist realism and emotivist non-realism and here there is a parallel with Cavell. D. M. MacKinnon, 'Ayer's Attack on Metaphysics', *Royal Institute of Philosophy Supplement* 30, no. 1 (1991): 27–34; D. M. MacKinnon, 'Kant's Agnosticism', in *Philosophy and the Burden of Theological Honesty: a Donald MacKinnon Reader*, ed. John C. McDowell (London: T&T Clark, 2011). See also his review of Ryle's influential monograph: D. M. MacKinnon, 'The Concept of Mind (Book Review)', *Philosophical Quarterly* 1, no. April (1951): 248–53.

27. *SET*, 157.

of metaphysics, this excerpt would suggest that he does share Wittgenstein's sense of the illusory nature of modernist foundationalism and the conviction that the task of curing ourselves may require a much deeper purgation. A confessional confrontation with unsettling forms of self-knowledge edges its way into the realm of philosophical discourse, demanding more from us than standard logical refutations, and opening a way by which, contra Plato, the tragic ascription returns from its former banishment. It also suggests an approach to moral realism that, in an idiom inspired by Wisdom, is less like adding new information to the world, but rather training ourselves to contemplate what is already there with ever-greater perceptiveness.

The focus and end of MacKinnon's philosophical therapy

To examine MacKinnon's therapeutic programme more forensically will mean examining his aversion to anthropomorphism, his embrace of agnosticism (of a kind) and commitment to moral realism, and the way these relate to the perennial tension between realism and idealism. It will be important to take a step back from the focus on Cavell and Wittgenstein to see the more pervasive influence of Kant, who MacKinnon saw as a master exemplar of how this tension could be held and explored. Attuned to the ambition and breadth of Kant's aims, he notes that

> in the first half of the *Critique of Pure Reason*, [Kant] was both trying to give as satisfactory account as he could of our ultimate conceptual scheme, and … as part of the same enquiry, to give an inventory of the fundamental structural features of the world in which we find ourselves.[28]

The articulation of this inventory involves encountering limits: 'The pervasive features of an experienceable world' and an admission that 'our point of view as experients is the human point of view, our world a world marked by the conditions under which alone experience is possible for us'.[29] The outworking of this is a critique of inherited metaphysical projects and the adoption of an agnostic stance described in therapeutic terms by MacKinnon, as is the necessary transition to

---

28. *PM*, 1.
29. *BT*, 254. *PM*, 9. Anthropocentrism and agnosticism seem to be mutually reinforcing in MacKinnon's reading of Kant: 'Kant writes part of the time as if fulfilment of the Socratic imperative – know thyself – would by itself preserve men from the pretension to penetrate the secrets of the unconditioned. Where such emphasis predominates, Kant certainly emerges innocent of the charge sometimes brought against him: that of supposing that we could ferret out the fundamental laws of nature by a kind of specialized introspection; he appears rather as an agnostic, whose delineation of the most pervasive features of the objective world is but a propaedeutic study to the definitive recognition of our ineradicable intellectual limitation.' *BT*, 253.

an emphasis on practical reason in the second Critique.[30] There 'is much both in Kant's criticism of metaphysics and, indeed, in his treatment of the nature of ethical discourse which is congruous with modern logical procedure'. Yet MacKinnon goes on to highlight discontinuities, including that 'Kant will not concede that logical disentanglement is something carried on apart from the subject's immediate presence to, and involvement with, what is being disentangled'.[31] Here we see a subject acutely aware of the limitations under which they labour: a grappling with the problem of scepticism, which also preoccupied Wittgenstein, as well as a commitment to realism. MacKinnon argues that for all of 'Kant's painstaking work in the philosophy of perception … [he] never abandons his underlying loyalty to the common-sense conviction that in coming to know we do not construct a world of our own fashioning, but compel that which is given to us to yield its secrets in ways admitting of our assimilation'.[32] As Strawson noted, and MacKinnon recognized, this insight must be kept in mind when considering the idealistic components of Kant's Copernican revolution:

> All concepts, and with them all principles, even such as are possible a priori, relate to empirical intuitions, that is, to the data for a possible experience. Apart from this relation they have no objective reality (B298). Of the most general of concepts, the categories, Kant says that they 'allow only of empirical employment and have no meaning whatsoever when not applied to objects of possible experience, that is, to the world of sense'. (B724)[33]

This tension between realism and idealism stands at the heart of Kant's agnosticism, which pertains not only to knowledge of God 'in himself' but of all external objects independent of our perception. It is also the point at which the therapeutic ascription comes most clearly to the fore in MacKinnon's reading of Kant. Inspired by him in this regard, MacKinnon uses the term 'agnosticism' to describe a characteristic feature of a person who has undergone therapy and the stance from which further therapy should take place. Additionally, he uses the term 'anthropomorphism' to denote that which obfuscates the realist task and

---

30. 'Temptation' and 'illusion' are terms which evidence the presence of a therapeutic sensibility, and it is relevant to my case that MacKinnon argues in the following terms: 'No one could accuse Kant of taking the issue of temptation lightly; it is an experience which, it might be said, for him comes near disclosing the heart of the human situation'. The temptation is to look for the unconditioned in the wrong place – being caught in the net of the 'transcendental illusion' – and it is also to fail to apprehend the unconditioned when it is manifest in the only place where it can: the practical domain of moral obligation. *SET*, 119.
31. Ibid., 122.
32. *PM*, 7.
33. P. F. Strawson, *The Bounds of Sense: An Essay on Kant's Critique of Pure Reason* (London: Routledge, 1989), 16.

from which we need deliverance.³⁴ Presumably with the *Critique of Pure Reason* A640/B668 in mind, MacKinnon notes that Kant's agnosticism is something which

> has a certain kinship with the *via negativa* of the classical theology, a purification of our concepts from every taint of anthropomorphism, to the intent that we may at least see what it is that, in our attempted use of these concepts to scrutinise the unconditioned, we are attempting. [MacKinnon goes on to argue that if] ... a man sets down Kant's first Critique and calls himself in its sense an agnostic, the position he adopts is something at once similar to and different from the agnosticism of those who have not undergone the same discipline; it is something to be understood in the end in terms of a new self-consciousness concerning the nature of conceptual thinking as such, and it is something which provides supremely the context within which the evident and transcendent authority of the moral law, and the realm of ends, can be grasped.³⁵

Incidentally, the same concern is also evident in MacKinnon's engagement with Plato when he notes,

> We must be on guard [Plato] implies, against the pervasive temptation of anthropomorphism. We must see that that way lies inadmissible contradiction; we must learn and relearn the purgative effect of such recognition, making our own the lesson that in speculation the last enemy is anthropomorphism rather than agnosticism, yet sustained always by a sense that the underlying insights of which the theory of forms is an exploration are significant and important, and that the proper mode for the expression of this theory is always or nearly always dialogue rather than treatise.³⁶

Many of the characteristics of philosophical therapy noted above are evident in these two extracts, including language of purgation, confession, conversion (i.e. reference to 'a new self-consciousness') and a move towards realism which is thought to derive from a deliverance from anthropomorphism.

For MacKinnon, 'anthropomorphism' stands as a representative term for the key temptation of 'idealism'. This is not to be confused with the notion of 'anthropocentrism', however, which is a far more neutral term for MacKinnon, related to his commitment to a form of ethical humanism. As noted above, he speaks of Kant's anthropocentrism in relation to a proper acknowledgement of limitation – something which MacKinnon saw in the comparison between God's knowledge (or any 'ideal' knowledge) and human knowledge in the third

---

34. D. M. MacKinnon, *Themes in Theology: The Three-Fold Cord; Essays in Philosophy, Politics and Theology* (Edinburgh: T&T Clark, 1987), 12–13.
35. *SET*, 90.
36. Ibid., 99.

Critique.[37] An acute awareness of this limitation drives MacKinnon to see links with the tradition of negative theology, to embrace the restlessness of a dialectical style and to see something essential for philosophy and theology in the notion of tragedy.[38] Yet it does not drive him to relativism, non-realism or radical scepticism in epistemology, ethics or theology.

For MacKinnon, forms of agnosticism, anthropocentrism and realism can be mutually reinforcing and this conviction becomes a point of contact, bringing together his theological and philosophical concerns. The revelation of Christ within history, apprehended (with Barth) as the 'objective' presence of God reinforces the fact of human limitation while giving us access to the 'real', as does the apprehension of metaphysical notions such as substance and causality, as does the apprehension of absolute moral imperatives. 'Thrusting against the limits of language' is the Wittgensteinian phrase that MacKinnon invokes to capture the confrontation with knowledge's limits from which a realist affirmation springs, rather than to herald the ultimate triumph of scepticism.[39]

MacKinnon as a Kantian moral theologian

Modern theologians have been perennially divided as to whether Kant should be counted as a friend or foe.[40] As noted above, Kantian agnosticism played a decisive role for MacKinnon, evidenced further by a close reading of the final chapter of SET.[41] Essays such as 'Kant's influence on British Theology' and 'Kant's Philosophy of Religion' are also instructive.[42] Kant's attempt to banish traditional arguments for God's existence and then to revive the notion of God as a 'postulate of practical reason' was a move that captivated MacKinnon.[43] So too the way Kant's critique goes deeper than just dispatching particular arguments for theism; Kant undermined the possibility of 'God' as knowable while promoting scepticism

---

37. *PM*, 7.
38. *BT*, 22.
39. *PM*, 17. See also *BT*, 21.
40. Christopher Insole, 'A Metaphysical Kant: A Theological Lingua Franca?', *Studies in Christian Ethics* 25, no. 2 (2012): 206–8. Milbank bemoans the impact of Kantian agnosticism on subsequent generations of theologians. For Milbank, the sheer contingency of the critical turn implies its arbitrariness, undermining the assumption that all subsequent philosophy and theology are somehow obligated to pass through the Kantian prism. By taking this turn for granted, post-Kantian theologians reveal their own blindness to the contingent construction of the very object of their admiration. Gordon E. Michalson, 'Re-reading the Post-Kantian Tradition with Milbank', *Journal of Religious Ethics* 32, no. 2 (2004): 364.
41. *SET*, 233–77.
42. D. M. MacKinnon, 'Kant's Influence on British Theology', in *Kant and his Influence*, ed. G. MacDonald Ross and Tony McWalter (Bristol: Continuum, 1990). See also *TT*, 29–30.
43. *PM*, 53–72.

regarding the traditional sources of rescue, such as revelation, religious experience and doctrines of analogy. [44]

Kant's agnosticism is demonstrated in his conviction that God cannot 'make up an item of intuition, of awareness or *Anschauung*, as do other objects that become part of the intuitional content of our mental lives'.[45] Knowledge is limited to those objects that we experience, or that which we could in principle experience. 'Thoughts without content are empty' (A51/B75) and Kant maintains that there cannot be an intuition of God that would provide such content (A638/B666).[46] The structure of our conceptual apparatus determines what intuitions are received and how they are understood, and space and time are considered – in qualified terms that have attracted no end of controversy – in some ways inseparable from that cognitive apparatus.[47] It follows that God, being posited as transcending the confines of space and time, cannot be experienced *on principle* and cannot be known by means of the operation of Kant's notions of understanding and reason *on principle*.[48] Yet, as Strawson noted,

> Kant was not content merely to draw this general negative conclusion about the impossibility of transcendent metaphysics. He thought that the propensity to think in terms of ideas for which no empirical conditions of application could be specified was not merely a philosopher's aberration, but a natural and inevitable propensity of human reason. It was even, in some ways, a beneficial propensity. Certain ideas which had in themselves no empirical application or significance nevertheless inevitably arose in the course of scientific inquiry, and might even serve a useful function in stimulating the indefinite extension of empirical knowledge.[49]

---

44. Terry F. Godlove, *Kant and the Meaning of Religion: The Critical Philosophy and Modern Religious Thought* (London: I. B. Tauris & Co., 2014), 48. Kant states, 'I maintain that all attempts to employ reason in theology in any merely speculative manner are altogether fruitless and by their very nature null and void, and that the principles of its employment in the study of nature do not lead to any theology whatsoever. Consequently, the only theology of reason which is possible is that which is based upon moral laws or seeks guidance from them' (A636/B664). Immanuel Kant, *Kritik der reinen Vernunft* [Critique of Pure Reason], 2nd ed. (London: Macmillan, 1933), 528.

45. Ibid.

46. Godlove seeks to articulate 'the very plausible claim that Kant's "rational faith" not only rules out knowledge that God exists but that it disallows even straightforward belief – that it permits only the belief that it is really possible that God exists'. Godlove, *Kant and the Meaning of Religion*, 6, 151–78.

47. Strawson, *The Bounds of Sense: An Essay on Kant's Critique of Pure Reason*, 62–4. MacKinnon discusses the issue and provides a critical defence of Kant's intention on the matter. D. M. MacKinnon, *Explorations in Theology* (London: SCM, 1979), 40–50.

48. Peter Byrne, *The Moral Interpretation of Religion* (Edinburgh: Edinburgh University Press, 1998), 3.

49. Strawson, *The Bounds of Sense: An Essay on Kant's Critique of Pure Reason*, 17.

The postulation of an *ens realissimum* may be one example.[50] Another is the notion of God, but only insofar as it has been uncoupled from any dubious identification with the *ens realissiumum*. While it is not possible to speak about God as a result of the application of reason to nature, or with reference to the logical features of the concept of God analytically (A635/663ff.), Kant does maintain its inevitability and utility in providing coherence in the moral sphere that alternative non-theistic options lack (A634/B662).[51]

MacKinnon appreciates the point that for Kant the ultimate can never be the subject of referential or descriptive statement. He also acknowledges the place Kant allows for continuing language of special revelation, even though it is never strictly necessary for 'pure religion'.[52] Perhaps in the same vein, Insole sees Kant as a modern representative of a long-running tradition of 'intellectualist theology' and Byrne joins MacKinnon in finding some similarities between Kant's agnosticism and question 13, 8 of the *prima pars* of the *Summa*. Here we can observe a minimal notion of God as the ground of a moral teleology about whom it can also be said: 'The source of all things, above all things and distinct from all things.'[53] Yet the fact that we can know *that* God is does not mean we can know *what* God is in any more substantive way, only what God is not.[54] Kant is seen to take this approach to the limits of agnostic doubt, while MacKinnon stays within Thomas's orbit in the

---

50. Henry E. Allison, *Kant's Transcendental Idealism* (New Haven: Yale University Press, 2004), 405–10. And Lawrence Pasternack, 'The *ens realissimum* and Necessary Being in "The Critique of Pure Reason"', *Religious Studies* 37, no. 4 (2001): 467–70.

51. According to MacKinnon, he can still be counted in the tradition of 'negative theology' because 'in the end Kant … can neither accept a religious faith that presupposes a divine self-revelation nor completely subordinate the entertainment of its possibility to morality as an instrument that serves the effective extension of the latter's authority' *TT*, 29.

52. *TT*, 30. MacKinnon refuses any simplistic claim pertaining to Kant's apparent reduction of revelation to morality; a point that remains undeveloped but is made evocatively by noting a resonance between Kant's Christology and that of John's gospel. *TT*, 33–4. On Kant and revelation, see J. E. Hare, *The Moral Gap: Kantian Ethics, Human Limits, and God's Assistance* (Oxford: Clarendon Press, 1996), 42.

53. Byrne, *The Moral Interpretation of Religion*, 64.

54. The link is implicit when MacKinnon draws attention to Kant's identification of the limits of analogy when moving from the sensible to the supersensible. *TT*, 34. The link is more explicit elsewhere: 'The schoolmen admit a critical problem where speech concerning the ultimate is concerned. By what authority do we describe God in these terms or in those terms? It was Aquinas himself who insisted that of God we knew that He was, what He was not and what relation everything else had to Him. It was a modern Thomist who spoke of the ways in which we name God as like the runways of the Clyde which issue ships on the ocean. The ways in which we speak of God issue us out on what Boethius called the ocean of His being; but whereas the runways of a Clyde contain the waters of the ocean at high tide, our names, and I suppose the thought which on a traditional view somehow corresponds with them, contain nothing of that which they name; they are runways and nothing more.'

end.⁵⁵ MacKinnon reiterated the point that the metaphysical expression, together with related moral and religious discourses, properly belong outside the realm of 'pure reason', but remain vital:

> Because Kant believed he had established the frontiers of the objectively conceivable, while allowing a highly significant role, for instance, to the idea of a total comprehension of the world in which we found ourselves (the so-called regulative use of the Ideas of Reason), he had set himself free to appreciate the suggestive power of the mythological. It could, as in the example taken from *Religion Within the Limits of Reason Alone*, sustain and deepen our purchase hold on that unconditioned with which we were all the time in commerce, and whose authority we could only gainsay at the cost of denying our own rational nature.⁵⁶

For Kant, practical reason or the realm of freedom and duty arising within concrete experience is the locus of a qualified renewal of mythical and metaphysical expression, which in turn are taken to be essential to the 'health' of rationality itself in as far as they put us in touch with the 'unconditioned'.⁵⁷ In this vein, he is

---

BT, 210–11. MacKinnon often spoke about an echo of Thomas's 'agnosticism' in the work of Joseph Butler. *PM*, 55.

55. MacKinnon: 'Here … Thomas allows the use of the concept of causality, as it were, to launch our thoughts towards the deeps of the divine. He is agnostic, sophisticatedly so; but his agnosticism is qualified … whereas Kant would seem to have established a veto on every attempt to give sense to the ways in which we conceive the relation of the familiar to the transcendent, even (and this is crucial) to the bare statement that such ontological derivation obtains.' MacKinnon, *PM*, 55. Byrne concurs, 'Where [Kant] departs from the tradition [i.e. Aquinas's 'agnostic' caution] is in his denial that there is either a metaphysically given or revealed order which enables us to discern a relationship between the divine and the human, such that we can then be sure that certain human-rooted perfection terms are true of the divine nature. Kant's realism remains too agnostic to allow such positive predications of the divine. … That divine-human relationship is too thin to allow a positive theology; theology remains an anthropocentric exercise in image construction.' Byrne, *The Moral Interpretation of Religion*, 64–5. Elsewhere MacKinnon also notes the key difference in terms that resonate with his own project: 'The opposition between Thomas and Kant lies in the conviction of the former that the 'existential' thinking which religion demands, does not preclude the fertilization, as distinct from the mere criticism, by religion of man's intellectual insight into reality'. D. M. MacKinnon, 'How Do We Know God? [Book Review]', *Journal of Theological Studies* 46 (April 1945): 110.

56. MacKinnon, 'Kant's Influence on British Theology', 350.

57. This is an insight that MacKinnon took from Strawson: 'At the centre, then, of Kant's achievement, according to Strawson, lies this metaphysic of experience and its corollaries; the delineation of the conditions of a characteristically human experience, especially on the objective side, establishing the illusions both of a dogmatic empiricism and of a confident

given credit for developing the 'moral argument for the existence of God' out the wreckage of the alternative proofs he had demolished.[58] While the God postulated from reflection on the moral order is 'the traditional notion of God as the supreme personal agent possessing the "omni" properties, it is not known as an independent reality external to human subjectivity and the needs of practical reason' (5:125-6).[59] This affirmation has given rise to constant debate as to whether Kant is a realist or a non-realist when it comes to the object of his religious language.[60] The notion of God-as-lawgiver in the realm of practical reason seems non-realist; the result of free, self-conscious human agents, and yet the demand for language of this kind is derived from a reasonable apprehension of the world as it presents itself to us.[61] Further, the claims of religion amount to far more than construction, popular

claim to offer theoretical answers concerning a supposedly transcendent origin and destiny of the world, and its nature, which ignore the duty of assigning sense to our concepts within and not without the framework of our experience.' *BT*, 251.

58. Byrne, *The Moral Interpretation of Religion*, 61. Any such ascription could be misleading if not taken together with the observations already made regarding Kant's rigorous agnosticism. MacKinnon: 'It is a pity that some of those who write on his so-called "moral argument for the existence of God" do not pay more attention to [Kant's] writing on religion. It is clear from the argument of the Dialectic in the first *Critique* that he did not regard the kinds of proposition we might suppose the yield of such an argument as intelligible.' *TT*, 26.

59. Immanuel Kant, 'Critique of Practical Reason', in *Practical Philosophy: The Cambridge Edition of the Works of Immanuel Kant*, ed. Mary J. Gregor (Cambridge: Cambridge University Press, 1999), 204–41.

60. Byrne, *The Moral Interpretation of Religion*, 60. See also Godlove, *Kant and the Meaning of Religion*, 50–68. Stern has challenged what he sees to be the 'traditional orthodox reading' of Kant, by which he is interpreted as an idealist who considered individual human subjectivity as determinative in producing the content of moral imperatives. Rawls defends such a view, for instance. At the heart of the discussion is Kant's identification of a paradox pertaining to the fact that while there may be a concept of good and evil prior to the moral law, it does not serve as a foundation for the moral law, but emerged and is defined 'after and by means of the law'. Robert Stern, *Understanding Moral Obligation: Kant, Hegel, Kierkegaard* (Cambridge: Cambridge University Press, 2011), 36. The tension Kant is exploring lies between the 'is' and 'ought'; the relationship between moral principles and empirical observation, subjective preference, interest and reference to pleasure or pain. The constructionist tends to mount an argument based on Kant's commitment to the subject's autonomy; the realist tends to highlight the way in which Kant desires basic moral principles that are the result of an 'unsullied' exercise of reason. I suspect that the reason MacKinnon is attracted to Kant is that he perceives a refusal to take either option, but to forge an unresolved mediating position.

61. Byrne, *The Moral Interpretation of Religion*, 62. See also Roger M. White, *Talking about God: The Concept of Analogy and the Problem of Religious Language* (Surrey: Ashgate, 2010), 105–34.

consensus or outright fancy, but in their purest form they give expression and motivate adherence to the moral order which, for Kant, could not be otherwise.[62]

What Kant does *not* do is enlist God as the agent of a divine command theory of ethics or as a transcendent 'foundational' support for moral realism.[63] It is the free self-legislating human agent that is the source of the absolute moral 'ought' of which Kant speaks and it is the demand of reason alone that compels one to act dutifully. The most important postulate undergirding the possibility of morality is freedom, by which a person finds it possible to engage in a mode of reflection and decision-making that is not locked into a fixed chain of causation.[64] Apprehension of the self-conscious rational individual in possession of a will is the locus whereby a language beyond naturalistic determinism becomes necessary.[65] A moral philosopher admired by MacKinnon put the matter thus:

> For Kant, nature is a closed and self-consistent system; so is morality. Neither therefore proves God; but he is needed to weld them together; and the moral reason demands their ultimate harmony. Hence God is a postulate of the moral or practical reason.[66]

God is adopted into the argument as a means to ensure that we may retain some confidence in the ultimate coordination of virtue and happiness; a coordination which Kant takes as self-evidently constitutive of the good (5:123-32).[67] This is an approach that works from the conviction that our moral lives are rational in as far as they generate certain ends and that these ends can be achieved.[68] Such ends include the fulfilment of duty *and* the attainment of happiness on the part of moral agents. Indeed, for Kant it would be irrational to posit a moral order where partial or intermediate goods are acknowledged without the possibility

---

62. Godlove, *Kant and the Meaning of Religion*, 52. The tension here is related to a much wider issue that Insole discusses in relation to 'one and two realm interpretations' of Kant's transcendental ideal and Janz's insistence that it is only bad readings of Kant that will try to force him into realist or idealist moulds. I will return to this issue in Chapter 5. Insole, *Realist Hope*, 110–15. See also Janz, *God, the Mind's Desire*, 136–8.

63. This becomes abundantly clear in Kant's distinction between 'natural' and 'revealed' religion. Godlove, *Kant and the Meaning of Religion*, 46.

64. Immanuel Kant, *Groundwork of the Metaphysics of Morals*, trans. Mary J. Gregor and Jens Timmermann, Cambridge Texts in the History of Philosophy (Cambridge: Cambridge University Press, 2013), 57–8. And Insole, 'A Metaphysical Kant: A Theological Lingua Franca?', 212–13.

65. Christopher J. Insole, 'Kant's Transcendental Idealism, Freedom and the Divine Mine', *Modern Theology* 27, no. 4 (2011): 610–12.

66. W. R. Sorley, *Moral Values and the Idea of God* (Cambridge: University Press, 1918), 339.

67. Kant, 'Critique of Practical Reason', 239–46. And *TT*, 27.

68. Byrne, *The Moral Interpretation of Religion*, 61.

of a perfect good (5.111ff).[69] Furthermore, the attainment of such moral ends is only possible if 'natural order and causality are part of an overarching moral order and causality'.[70] It must be possible that moral ends may be realized despite the natural limitations, frustrations and divisions of human life. Ultimately, Kant believed that such moral striving and such a resolution is only possible if both the soul's immortality and God are posited to ensure ultimate fairness, coherence and fulfilment.[71] This qualified teleology constitutes 'Kant's eschatology' according to MacKinnon, by which Kant takes 'his treatment of personal immortality into areas sometimes nearer to Paul's vision of the redemption of the created universe than to the metaphysical traditions associated with Plato on the one hand and Aristotle on the other'.[72]

While MacKinnon will deviate from Kant on the crucial question of the irreducibility of special revelation, he sees Kant as having provided essential purgative resources for the task of theology going forward. MacKinnon notes that

> the sharpest influence of Kant's thought on British theologians of the Reformed tradition lay in the demand it made on them to rethink the crudities of their theology of grace, to find room for human responsibility in their scheme of man's redemption, to seek a place for an authentic autonomy that would yet not altogether forget Luther's words: *Non Deus revivificat, nisi per occidendum*.[73]

It is also clear that along with figures such as Maritain, it was Kant who most inspired MacKinnon's commitment to a form of humanism:

> It was through Kant's influence that the spirit of the *Aufklärung* was effectively baptized into Christ. And this was a conversion that the theological tradition that was to receive it urgently needed. It was not only that the crudities of solifidianism and the debasement of Catholic sacramentalism into the idea of a grace-energy impersonally transmitted through appointed channels demands required correction; it was also necessary that the claim of the Churches to override the rich, fragile stuff of our humanity in the wake of a dogmatic orthodoxy, guarded and enforced by an alleged *Heilsanstalt*, should be effectively resisted.[74]

Following his one-time mentor A. E. Taylor, MacKinnon gave priority to Kant's legacy over Hegel's in the task of therapeutic purgation and clarification, chiefly

---

69. Kant, 'Critique of Practical Reason', 228–31. And Byrne, *The Moral Interpretation of Religion*, 70–2.
70. Peter Byrne, 'Moral Arguments for the Existence of God', http://plato.stanford.edu/archives/spr2013/entries/moral-arguments-god/.
71. *TT*, 26. See also Hare, *Moral Gap*, 54–5.
72. MacKinnon, 'Kant's Influence on British Theology', 354.
73. Ibid., 352.
74. Ibid., 360.

because he thought that the former better managed to encapsulate the 'seriousness' of the moral struggle and the problem of evil.[75] A common view is that Hegel reacted negatively to Kant in as far as he held Kant to posit a dualistic view of the will and an alienating conception of our relationship to rational moral duty.[76] Rather than counting against Kant, MacKinnon found resonance with this focus on the perennially divided self and the perpetual moral struggle of the free agent grappling with scepticism, holding that it constituted a promising sign of authenticity and an indication that Kant may be the more faithful ally of the 'realist'. MacKinnon was not blind to the purgative resources within Hegel's writings, however, evident in the way reference to the 'philosophy of history' and the tragic become core concerns.[77] Yet it is Hegel's legacy in (what became) the moral vision of British idealists that most blinded MacKinnon to potential resources in Hegel's system: it magnified the incompatibilities between Hegel and Kant on the notion of freedom and forced a choice between them.[78]

Kant remained indispensable in as far as he could help Christians revive aspects of their own account of moral agency and purge shaky philosophical supports for theism. In SET, Kant, Butler and St Paul are gathered within a very broadly conceived deontological frame, or what MacKinnon labels the *Gesinnungsethik*.[79] MacKinnon was of the view that the latter two figures could provide examples as to the resources available to advance beyond Kant's restrictive moral formalism. The fact that Christians insist on doing ethics in conversation with particular lives, whether they be Jesus or the saints, and in conversation with robust literary traditions (the focus of Chapter 4) is something to be retained in the wake of Kantian purgation.[80] Hence MacKinnon's positive evaluation of Bishop Butler's

---

75. MacKinnon, 'Kant's Agnosticism', 27–8. This impression is moderated elsewhere. In referring to Hegel's interpretation of Antigone, MacKinnon notes that his 'approach to the problems of the individual in society could not be understood apart from the underlying kinship between his dialectic and the tragic element in human life as he understood it'. MacKinnon adds that 'we must appreciate the insight he displays into the extent to which men are caught and destroyed not by their weaknesses, but by their achievement'. *SET*, 237.

76. Stern, *Understanding Moral Obligation: Kant, Hegel, Kierkegaard*, e-book.

77. Muller notes that 'MacKinnon's reading of recent work by the French Hegel scholars Jean Hyppolite and Jean Wahl suggested to him that some of that [Kierkegaard's and Forsyth's] polemic was … unfair'. Muller, 'True Service', 341.

78. D. M. MacKinnon, 'Moral Freedom', in *Burden*, ed. John C. McDowell (London: T&T Clark, 2011), 83–90.

79. Ibid., 58.

80. MacKinnon shows sympathy with Kierkegaard's implicit critique of Kant's formalism and sees an analogy with Butler's criticisms of Wollaston. *BT*, 121–8. He also argues that 'Catholic thought, in direct opposition to Kant and the whole moralist tradition, ceaselessly affirms, the complexity of the human person, and the necessity of baptizing that whole. Kant, who is often in Mill's mind in *Utilitarianism*, set morality over against psychology, and by so doing inevitably emptied the moral life of any content. As Catholics, we are rightly sceptical

legacy – a largely forgotten figure in moral philosophy today – even if something of a luminary of the eighteenth-century British Anglicanism.[81]

For Butler, the empirical turn did not lead with any inevitability to utilitarianism nor did it necessarily close off the potential moral insights of concrete religious existence. His approach was to adopt a style of moral reasoning that avoided a stark distinction between the realm of ends and the realm of nature as proffered by Kant.[82] Butler developed a conscience-based natural law approach with broad resonances with Kant's notion of moral imperatives, according to MacKinnon, but he also cultivated a very un-Kantian concern for 'the passional side of human nature', evident by the way he 'will suddenly interject an explicit reference to the authority of the religious imagination' when discussing moral propositions.[83] MacKinnon refers to St. Paul's legacy in a similar vein in as far as his apostolic ministry embodied a moral dispensation. Paul is a case of the mixing of an introspective intensity that is common to the modern deontological tradition, with the revolutionary fall-out from an encounter with the risen Christ.[84]

While offering an appreciative reading of the alternative utilitarian tradition emerging in the wake of eighteenth to twentieth-century empiricism and positivism, MacKinnon never places it at the front and centre of his forays into moral philosophy. Kant is judged to have 'achieved a level of intellectual sophistication and subtlety as well as of introspective concentration, which [the utilitarians] lacked'.[85] This is not to say that the two positions are without important overlaps. Both tended to reject the notion that morality requires a metaphysical foundation, God or a universal natural law in order to secure its content.[86] Both are clear that reason (or some other faculty) reveals moral obligations that we have an imperative to follow. Moreover, both are routinely analysed in terms of whether they adopt forms of constructionism or realism. Finally, and negatively, both, at least

---

of categorical imperatives, and affirm against Kant that the imperative – Do – is subordinate to the indicative –Thus is man. For the gospel of God is itself the proclamation that thus and thus is He, and that thus and thus has He done. We must seek so to clarify our concept of man as to exhibit his relation to physical nature, and avoid at all costs the error, that underlies so much modern Protestant theology, and that is surely derived from Kant's substitution of ethics for ontology, that man's essence is revealed when he is admitted to be morally responsible. It is only after that he is exhibited as in his wholeness created by and for God, who is love ever diffusive of itself, that we can begin to define his peculiar responsibilities.' D. M. MacKinnon, 'No Way Back: Some First Principles of Catholic Social Judgment Restated (Book Review)', *Christendom* 9 (December 1939): 294–5.

81. *SET*, 194–202.
82. Ibid., 252.
83. Ibid.
84. Ibid., 257–62.
85. Ibid., 234.
86. Ibid., 234–6.

in the forms that MacKinnon knew them, tend to hamper attentiveness to the manifold complexity of particular lives and can smooth over the texture of tragic moral compromise.

In the instance of Butler and St. Paul, MacKinnon shows the way in which Christian moral approaches may take account of the historical and existential dimensions of experience, together with an acknowledgement of an absolute moral imperative, albeit in the context of a robust claim for human freedom. In other words, it has the potential to reflect elements of utilitarian and Kantian approaches without the reductionism or the formalism that sometimes plagues the work of the more ardent defenders of these traditions. This is not to make the claim that Christianity can somehow provide an easy synthesis of the great divide between utilitarianism and deontology. As pointed out above, MacKinnon is not interested in attempting such reconciliation or trying to vindicate 'Christian morality' against rivals and detractors in any definitive way. For him, Christian moral discourse is as much subject to the purgative critiques of positivist-inspired utilitarian as it is to the Kantian's, even as it retains a stubborn focus explicating the moral implications of the incarnation.

MacKinnon contra modernist theology

One of the reasons to see MacKinnon as a genuinely creative and independent spirit, is that despite his appreciation of Kant's achievement, he aptly avoided the path of liberal modernist theology – arguably the tradition that was channelling 'Kantian religion' in MacKinnon's context.[87] Broadly speaking, this was a diverse collection of approaches that embraced a reductionist view of Jesus, the church and the believer primarily in terms of a *particular kind* of moral possibility.[88] It often arose in antagonism to other modes of knowledge that prioritized the ontological, metaphysical and historical, which had been more central to past expressions of Christian orthodoxy.

According to Bryne, liberal modernist theological trajectories of the post-war period placed 'the ethics of religion before its doctrines and historical myths'.[89] One manifestation is a form of Deism that 'more or less identif[ies] the concept of God with the concept of an eternal moral law in nature', which in turn allows the theologian to posit a form of theism shorn of any super-naturalistic claim to revelation or any crude dependency on the historical contingency of one or more particular religious traditions.[90] In this approach, morality becomes a way to justify references to God, once history and metaphysics have proved unreliable

---

87. See for example MacKinnon, *The Church of God*, 26.
88. David Fergusson, *Community, Liberalism and Christian Ethics* (Cambridge: Cambridge University Press, 1998), 49–51.
89. Byrne, *The Moral Interpretation of Religion*, 1.
90. Ibid., 4.

supports for theism.[91] The result was often forms of non-cognitivism: 'Either religious claims are not propositional at all, having some kind of non-cognitive (non-fact-stating) function in human discourse, or these claims are cognitive only in being descriptive of entities or states in the empirical world.'[92] Even where a realist commitment to theism persisted, it tended to be heavily 'revised': vestiges of antiquated metaphysical baggage were purged relative to the neo-Thomists, and evocations of the 'freedom of God' in revelation were radically depreciated relative to the neo-Orthodox position, for example.[93] At a bare minimum, a generic notion of transcendence was extolled, associated with 'the goal of human striving, [and] the source and supreme embodiment of value. Morality may lead to something outside itself which … occupies religious space, and likewise, reference to transcendence will only be possible in relation to the moral space.'[94]

Theologians who adopted these premises were too often willing victims of what MacKinnon regarded as 'facile Kantianism'.[95] Here, religion subordinated itself to an otherwise independent morality as a kind of survival strategy. Realist theistic ontology informed by the person of Christ and patristic theology was no longer the ground for defining Christian morality's uniqueness, which was now to be remodelled to reflect the sensibilities of enlightened moral self-awareness of individuals within liberal, secular democracies.[96] The new-found commensurability of theology and philosophy could be symbolized in a dubious analogy – or actual confluence – between Kant's categorical imperative and a truncated, anti-metaphysical divine command ethic.[97] Christianity could be deemed reasonable and the continuing role of the quasi-established or established

---

91. Gary J. Dorrien, 'Kantian Concepts, Liberal Theology, and Post-Kantian Idealism', *American Journal of Theology & Philosophy* 33, no. 1 (2012): 5–10.

92. Byrne, *The Moral Interpretation of Religion*, 4.

93. Insole discusses some contemporary exponents of this approach such as John Hick and Gordon Kaufmann with great insight. Insole, *Realist Hope*, 115–47.

94. Byrne, *The Moral Interpretation of Religion*, 6.

95. MacKinnon found such a vice particularly crippling for Anglican theology in the midst of the crisis of the Second World War. MacKinnon, 'Revelation and Social Justice', 139.

96. Insole, *Realist Hope*, 148–59.

97. MacKinnon explicitly rejects this sort of conflation, but such a move is understandable if the liberal has whole-heartedly embraced the non-realist elements of a Kantian-inspired 'rational religion': 'The agnostic temper of [Kant's] first Critique is never lost; yet the God of whom he writes is always the guarantor of men's [sic] acceptance of themselves as standing under the moral law, of which they are themselves the authors. There is never the remotest hint of compromise with the suggestion that this law constrains us categorically because it is the expression of the divine will, or even with the view that religious belief somehow conveys a special insight disclosing dimensions of the moral order withheld from those who are without it.' *SET*, 101.

state churches could be reinforced to the extent that the doctrines believed and the behaviour encouraged accorded with 'rational ethics'. O'Donnovan observes that

> the ethical conception of the truth was the essence of the modern; and this program [i.e. liberal theology] was ex professo 'modernist', taking for granted that the highest and noblest ideals were being grasped and realized in contemporary history.[98]

While MacKinnon saw great promise in Kant's 'moral turn' and the possibility of a theological re-articulation via practical reason, he was critical of the sort of emaciated theology he detected in this sort of liberalism. He resisted the naïve expulsion of the problem of metaphysics and feared that concrete suffering and tragedy may be muted by liberal notions of moral consensus and progress.

For all this, it must be remembered that modernist or liberal theology was a highly varied movement in Britain, which manifested in very different forms throughout MacKinnon's life. Indeed, there were distinctive interwar and post-war expressions, as well as a significant flowering in the 1960s and 1970s marked most famously (or notoriously) by sensationalist non-realist 'death of God' theologies.[99] MacKinnon appears to have been open to its insights *in as far as* it took the Kantian purgation seriously, and was implacably critical where he detected a hollowing-out of Christology. His attitude largely explains, and is explained by, his participation in the Catholic wing of Anglicanism from his student days in Oxford and then consistently to the end of his life.

Post-war British Anglo-Catholicism was diverse and fractious, mainly due to differences over how to respond to liberal and modernist challenges. In general, its character was conservative, shaped by its beginnings as a movement of protest and retrieval. It exhibited an in-built suspicion towards modernizing trends in theology, but its reactionary edge was moderated by *Lux Mundi* and the second generation of reformers. While MacKinnon subscribed to this movement he was also known to chide fellow Anglo-Catholics whenever he perceived this conservatism fostering a wilful ignorance of the serious gains of modern philosophy and political science, or on the other hand, betraying this conservative impulse with an uncritical subscription to modernist intellectual fads.[100] In this way, MacKinnon was something of a serial 'outsider', often showing inordinate sympathy to forces that were hostile to theology (such as Logical Positivism and Marxism) while retaining

---

98. Oliver O'Donovan, *A Conversation Waiting to Begin: The Churches and the Gay Controversy* (London: SCM Press, 2009), 8–9.

99. Stephenson gives a useful and detailed history of this broad movement within the Church of England. Alan Stephenson, *Rise and Decline of English Modernism* (London: SPCK, 1984).

100. This is particularly evident in MacKinnon's often tense relationship with the Christendom Group. Muller, 'True Service', 113–30.

some of his harshest criticism for the theologians and church leaders who were in all respects closer to him in terms of philosophical and religious commitments.

The motivation for MacKinnon's antipathy towards certain types of twentieth-century theological liberalism arose not only from concerns about its adequacy for a sufficiently orthodox and philosophically rigorous account of the faith, but also from the way it failed the moral demands of the historical moment. He saw it as an attempted therapy that failed in its diagnosis and its attempted cure. In observing trends in the early to mid-twentieth-century English ecclesiology, Lawson observed that

> the post-First World War Church of England remained inherently hopeful about the future and theological liberalism dominated across the church's political spectrum, notwithstanding the continued importance of Anglo-Catholicism within the broad Church of England. Yet even the triumph of hopeful liberalism was challenged by domestic and international crises between the wars. By the time the generation of Christian social radicals came to dominate the church hierarchy in the 1940s … their particular brand of incarnation theology and their effort to construct the Kingdom of God … appeared increasingly anachronistic … . The hopefulness of Christian sociology appeared meaningless when faced with both the religiosity of political dictatorship on the continent and the prospect of national annihilation in war. Lower levels of the Church, clergy and laity for example, seemed to take refuge in a quite different, pessimistic theology of redemption which emphasised the otherness of God and the sin of man [sic].[101]

MacKinnon was a theologian who showed solidarity with these so-called lower levels of the Church. His conviction as to the failure of this optimistic interwar theology stayed with him in such a way that made him suspicious of later versions of liberalism. Indeed, to the extent to which he saw any theology rejecting a confrontation with 'the otherness of God and the sin of man [sic]', MacKinnon was suspicious. This may explain why he was more critical of Cosmo Lang as Archbishop of Canterbury than he was of his successor, William Temple.[102] The former seemed too uncritical in his support of government policy in the lead-up to the Second World War and scandalously naïve in believing that the coronation of King George VI was going to spark renewal within the established church. Temple shared the hopes of 'a generation of social radicals', initially embracing nineteenth-century notions of progress in the midst of the post-First World War recovery. As Europe lurched towards war again, however, the doctrine of original sin became the dominant note sounding in his public theology.[103] European society was set in the midst of violent, degenerative forces and Britain was facing a dire existential

---

101. Tom Lawson, *The Church of England and the Holocaust: Christianity, Memory and Nazism* (Woodbridge: Boydell, 2006), 9–10.

102. Muller, 'True Service', 138–9. See also *ET*, 73.

103. Lawson, *The Church of England and the Holocaust*, 9–10.

threat. As such, Temple realized that liberal theologies and sociologies geared towards engineering continuous betterment were 'clanging symbols'. MacKinnon appreciated this sort of realism and he did not want to lose sight of these lessons in the period of optimistic reconstruction following Temple's death and the Allies' victory, particularly as the horrors of the holocaust became known. Where postwar liberal theology produced a reductionist God tied-up with the achievements of human culture or reason, or when it anchored itself in the presumption of the moral superiority of the present, MacKinnon voiced dissent via invocation of the tragic and by insisting that the most important lessons of Kantian morality had not been heeded.

As noted above, Kant was an undergirding influence on modernist and liberal theology, but MacKinnon's divergence from these positions arose – at least in part – from his perceptive reading of Kant. While they may have been more faithful to Kant's legacy in terms of giving form to 'rational religion', MacKinnon was unwilling to grant them custodianship of the legacy in its entirety. According to Kant, religion purged of its most ambitious metaphysical and revelatory claims could be justified in as far as it enabled an intensified focus on duty in respect of the moral law; a law ultimately secured through introspective reason rather than historical revelation.[104] MacKinnon observed that

> Kant is concerned primarily with religion as a separable aspect of human life. He treats it as, in fact, the name of a family of practices including here a number of beliefs, but beliefs regarded essentially as subordinate to the practices which they both inculcate and/or sustain.[105]

Notions familiar to Kant from his pietistic upbringing such as grace, justification, final judgement and the sanctifying work of the Spirit were modified in a thoroughly anthropocentric direction within 'the bounds of reason'. Perhaps it is on this basis that MacKinnon noted that 'it is ... by Kant that the contradiction between the ethical and the religious standpoint seems sometimes to have been most sharply brought out'.[106] For MacKinnon, the enthusiastic take-up of Kantian style of moral religion by certain liberal and modernist streams of theology not only meant the truncation of, or departure from, orthodoxy, but he also thought that aspects of Kantian moral rigour were missing.[107] Whether this is exactly what MacKinnon meant when he criticized 'facile Kantianism' is an open question, but it

---

104. Hare defends the notion that Kant cannot easily be classed as a deist because he retained a notion of revelation 'within the bounds of reason'. He is – according to Hare's analysis of Book 4, Part I of *Religion* – a 'pure rationalist' who may accept 'special revelation but nevertheless does not think its acceptance is without qualification necessary to religion'. Hare, *Moral Gap*, 43.
105. *TT*, 22.
106. *SET*, 235.
107. *TT*, 22.

is a phenomenon also flagged by O'Donovan, who notes that 'if the program of the "primacy of the ethical" is Kantian, it is not the Kant of the *second* critique ... into which [theological] liberalism never really ventured'.[108] The nub of the criticism is that exponents were often too ready to baptise whatever intellectual trends were in vogue, losing sight of the moral realism Kant fostered, with its absolute claims that overwhelmed individual subjective feeling or utilitarian optimism.[109]

MacKinnon followed Kant in seeing practical reason as the locus in which claims to transcendence and metaphysics were likely to re-emerge in a compelling way, yet he parted company with Kant when it came to the latter's exposition of 'rational religion'. This raises the question, Can he have one without the other? That is, can MacKinnon take as much inspiration as he does from Kant in terms of his views on the possibility of metaphysics and the epistemological limitations that beset us without also taking on the form of 'Kant's religion'? Perhaps a negative answer would be justified if MacKinnon had been an uncritical disciple of Kant, but as demonstrated above, this is far from the case. MacKinnon agreed that the ontotheology of old needed to yield to the purgation of realist empiricism, but MacKinnon also insisted that the anthropocentrism of rational religion needed to yield to the purgative claim of revelation-in-history. This left him in a place of difficulty, but the only place he could stand with integrity. The moral concerns that provided the impetus for the continuation of metaphysical language and the possibility for a transcendent referent in philosophy did not provide an unambiguous prolegomenon or foundation for theology. Nor did a focus on morality take away the difficult ontological considerations that a theologian must face to sustain and defend the possibility of a realist notion of God and revelation in history.

For MacKinnon, a focus on moral philosophy helped to identify some points on which philosophy and theology may become more intelligible to each other, but there was no sense in which such a focus provided a ready solution to theology's marginalization or a rationale that somehow lessened the scandal of revelatory particularity. In this respect, we can see the influence of a Barthian trajectory in as far as the Kantian decoupling of theology from classical metaphysics provided the impetus for a very non-Kantian re-articulation of revelatory uniqueness.[110] Kant's

---

108. O'Donovan, *Conversation*, 10.

109. Hare, *Moral Gap*, 48. MacKinnon explored this insight when he writes, 'Coleridge recognises that in his subordination of religion to morality Kant was not pursuing a simple essay in reductionism; rather he was insisting that religious ideas should be used not as a means of confirming men's belief in their individual significance and the validity of their purposes, whether personal or collective, but rather imaginatively to enlarge their perceptions by giving them a vivid sense of that absolute by which their conduct was continually judged, of which indeed as autonomous members of the realm of ends they were in some sense bearers.' D. M. MacKinnon, 'Coleridge and Kant', in *Coleridge's Variety: Bicentennary Studies*, ed. John B. Beer (London: Macmillan, 1974), 199.

110. Fergusson, *Community*, 22–3. See also Timothy Stanley, *Protestant Metaphysics after Karl Barth and Martin Heidegger* (London: SCM, 2010), 105–7.

argument regarding the inability to know God beyond the mere notion of God practically conceived, coupled with a respect for empirical realism, opened the door to a theology that proposed a revelatory act as the radical point of departure for modern theology. Yet, if Barth was the foremost exponent of such a move, it is apparent that MacKinnon went along with him only so far. MacKinnon did recognize and respect the metaphysical dimension of Barth's project,[111] something which accords with his conviction that 'the denial of the possibility of metaphysics … leads inevitably to the repudiation of any sort of religious language whether of immanence or of transcendence'.[112] He notes that Barth's project, 'unlike much that calls itself radical theology', refused to sidestep 'the problem of metaphysics upon christology'.[113] Yet MacKinnon remained too much in Kant's orbit, and perhaps more influenced by the modernists than he would care to admit, to become a full-fledged Barthian. He saw the moral domain 'threading through' and uniting secular and 'revealed' history, relativizing the distinction in a way that required the re-positing of the 'problem of metaphysics' in conversation with the classical tradition and in this way countenancing experiments in analogical discourse that Barth refused.

Moral realism

Moral realism was a commitment that was reinforced for MacKinnon via his interactions with Kant and Barth, and in the final section of this chapter I would like to contextualize this doctrine further, making suggestions as to the sense in which the term may explicate convictions that emerge in MacKinnon's writings.

PM opens with an emphasis on 'an aspect of Plato's Republic' and attention rests on the fact that our linguistic and conceptual resources are regularly stretched to a breaking point as we try to apprehend the world in which we find ourselves. It is in the domain of rich, textured and often perplexing moral dilemma, specifically that of Glaucon and Adeimantus, where such limits are particularly well represented according to MacKinnon.[114] Invoking St. Augustine, he observes that they 'express their aspirations, revealing the restlessness of their hearts till they find rest in the Good'. Nevertheless, MacKinnon goes on to add in parenthesis that the 'restlessness of heart is not by itself evidence that there is a Good in which the restless heart may find rest; a very different therapy may be required'.[115] Indeed, one can inhabit such a dialogue about morality 'without raising the absolutely crucial question whether or not in this sort of discourse we draw nearer to what is the case, whether or not something is being represented in this sort of discourse that is there to be

---

111. *BT*, 60.
112. *SET*, 233.
113. *BT*, 31.
114. *PM*, 22–4.
115. Ibid., 26–7.

represented'.[116] In this way, as soon as MacKinnon raises the possibility of 'resting in the Good' restlessness immediately returns and the sceptical question arises. This particular restlessness is MacKinnon's concern not Plato's; an empirical emphasis in his account of realism leads MacKinnon to insist that its absence in Plato may potentially stymie the philosophical quest of the moralist

> Plato's highly significant quarrel with the tragedians we find the birth of a kind of ethical reflection which deliberately eschews the method of description and re-description and substitutes the quest for an authoritative transcendent norm which at once supplies a standard of judgment and a resting place for the interrogative spirit. More than perhaps we realize we are in bondage to the consequences of that revolution.[117]

In the moral domain, 'thrusting against the limits of language' amounts to immersion in the concrete situation and a continuing dialectic where moral questions are posed but not resolutely answered, or if they are, it may be at the cost of tragic compromise. This need not cause us to give up on the quest, in the same way that the difficulty in applying language to God should not cause the end of theology. With Butler our struggle to articulate what we mean by the word 'God' as the 'source' of the world or a being with whom we have familiarity is a 'deficiency [which] need not disturb us; indeed it has a genuinely therapeutic value, provided we can lay to heart its lessons'.[118] In philosophy, it means that the approaches of positivist realism and classical idealism must be found wanting though neither abandoned entirely.[119] In the domain of moral thought it means holding to the possibility of moral factuality, the strong realism of the 'ought', while accepting tragic inability to perceive or fulfil it in concrete situations and to repress it.

In the mid-twentieth century, Bernard Williams noted that one of the problems with moral discourse was the 'remarkable assurance with which people think they already know what moral questions are about and consequently what can and what cannot be called 'moral'.[120] This was a fault of moralists on all sides, yet it is a temptation to which moral realists have been particularly prone, for they have a tendency to take for granted the fact that they have common sense and intuition on

---

116. *PM*, 26.

117. *BT*, 22. Identifying and addressing this bondage is a cause that MacKinnon associated with Isaiah Berlin, particularly his 1953 lectures on 'Historical Inevitability'. *SET*, 124.

118. *PM*, 53–4.

119. Here we see a parallel with Cavell, who wondered why conceptions of rationality in morals should be biased towards achieving consensus and agreement rather than ongoing purgative dialectic. Stanley Cavell, *The Claim of Reason: Wittgenstein, Skepticism, Morality and Tragedy* (Oxford: Clarendon Press, 1979), 323–5.

120. Cited in S. L. Goldberg, *Agents and Lives: Moral Thinking in Literature* (Cambridge: Cambridge University Press, 1993), xiv.

their side.[121] Critics will point out, however, that one only has to interrogate taken-for-granted notions of 'moral fact', 'intuition' and 'common sense' to discover a nest of conceptual vulnerabilities that the sceptic is only too ready to exploit. In a paper published in 1958, Anscombe argued that all moral 'ought' claims were dependent, whether knowingly or unknowingly, on the presumption of a divine law-giver (and therefore impossible) while urging that ethical discourse could continue intelligibly only as a discipline of philosophical psychology emerged to clarity notions of pleasure, action, virtue and human flourishing.[122]

The possibility of moral realism is a vast topic riven with complexity and intense conjecture, but it is essential to gain sufficient purchase on the notion so that MacKinnon's claims can be contextualized and responsibly critiqued.[123] It is all the more frustrating, therefore, that he never sets out to systematically defend the realist motifs he frequently invokes. The possibility of such a way of speaking reveals itself fleetingly in the midst of attending to the exercise of moral agency in specific contexts – a form of attentiveness that MacKinnon's therapy helps us to practice.

For MacKinnon, and many of his generation, the conviction inherited through the linage of Descartes and Kant was that one of the central problems of philosophy and, by implication, moral philosophy, was the relationship between a subject and the external world. In this regard, Platts (discussing the Anscombe work) makes a telling distinction between two different directions of 'fit' when attempting to give a philosophical account of the connection between mental states and the world:

> Beliefs aim at the true, and their being true is their fitting the world; falsity is a decisive failing in a belief, and false beliefs should be discarded; beliefs should be changed to fit the world, not vice versa. Desires aim at realization, and their realization is the world fitting with them; the fact that the indicative content of

---

121. Geoff Sayre-McCord, 'Moral Realism', http://plato.stanford.edu/archives/sum2011/entries/moral-realism/.

122. In this way, her vision was to associate moral discourse with the realm of desire, and then challenge psychology to come up with objective and empirical accounts of realm of desire so that the legitimacy of moral discourse may be secured. G. E. M. Anscombe, 'Modern Moral Philosophy', *Philosophy* 33, no. 124 (January 1958), 6–7.

123. The discussion in this section is informed by engagements with Sayre-McCord, David Brink, Sabina Lovibond, John E. Hare and Rufus Black, among others, although their detailed perspectives can only be the subject of brief mention here. Brink and Lovibond represent secular philosophical defences of moral realism writing in modes indebted to contemporary analytical moral philosophy. Hare and Black represent engagements with moral realism from within the Christian tradition, with the former attempting to mount an ambitious dialogue between 'the Grisez School', O'Donovan and Hauerwas, and the latter developing a form of Christian moral realism drawing on Kant and divine command theories in the tradition of Scotus and Calvin.

a desire is not realised in the world is not yet a failing in the desire, and not yet any reason to discard the desire; the world, crudely, should be changed to fit the desires, not vice versa.[124]

In their effort to articulate a position on the status of moral claims, the realist tends to give greater weight to the first type of 'fit' and the non-realist the second, although any strict distinction tends to collapse when the actual moral convictions of liberalism, Marxism and Christianity are explored (for instance). In these instances it becomes impossible to entirely separate 'belief' and 'desire', 'is' and 'ought'.

Sayre-McCord argues that moral realists are those who think that evaluative judgements 'should be taken at face value – moral claims do purport to report facts and are true if they get the facts right. Moreover, they hold, at least some moral claims actually are true.' For Sayre-McCord, 'That much is common (and more or less defining) ground of moral realism.'[125] This view does not necessarily come with any fixed idea regarding the content of these truth claims, nor does it presume any standardized metaphysical commitment. DeLapp offers the following, more sophisticated, definition:

> Moral realism [is] the view that moral values exist in a way that is causally and evidentially (though not conceptually) independent from the beliefs of anyone and everyone (including idealized agents) such that evidence and beliefs do not determine or constitute those values, though they may adequately and reliably measure or reflect them.[126]

If God is one such 'idealised agent', and such a claim *is* debatable, then many Christians would not count as moral realists. This, presumably, is the conclusion implied by DeLapp, and one shared by anyone who emerges from consideration of the Euthyphro Dilemma with the conviction that one cannot speak of the goodness of God and the moral excellence of God's commands without independently establishing the meaning of notions such as 'goodness' or 'excellence'.[127] It is a logic that many modern theologians, whether those in the orbit of Augustine and Barth or Aristotle and Aquinas, would reject with references to God's transcendence, human disobedience and human limitation

---

124. He is explicating section two of G. E. M. Anscombe's *Intention*. Mark de Bretton Platts, *Ways of Meaning: An Introduction to a Philosophy of Language* (London: Routledge and Kegan Paul, 1979), 256–7.

125. Sayre-McCord, 'Moral Realism.'

126. Kevin DeLapp, *Moral Realism*, Bloomsbury Ethics (London: Bloomsbury, 2013), 17.

127. In MacKinnon's context, one might point to explorations by Kai Nielsen and Ian Ramsey as articulating the problem. Kai Nielsen, 'Some Remarks on the Independence of Morality from Religion', *Mind* 70, no. 278 (1961): 175–86. And also Ian T. Ramsey, *Christian Ethics and Contemporary Philosophy* (London: SCM, 1966), 140–71.

resulting in the impossibility of realizing fulsome notions of goodness without some prior participation in the non-arbitrary goodness of the Divine.[128] A grossly inadequate generalization, but not one without some truth, is that moral theologians in the orbit of the former tend to be tempted towards a version of divine command voluntarism while the latter are more likely to seek refuge in a natural law of abstract universals. Lovibond has noted that the 'theme of partisanship, or voluntarism, might be regarded as the crux of the non-cognitivist theory of ethics: its "moral", so to speak'.[129] In this vein, while theological voluntarists of an extreme variety may think they are securing a version of moral realism, the deep structure of their proposals has more in common with their non-realist rivals. The presence of the natural law tradition as a moderating check on divine command theories is sign enough that significant constituents of the theological tradition are willing to develop a more nuanced account of God's command.[130] It is such a possibility that led MacKinnon to tentatively identify himself at key moments with the language of 'natural law', while still seeking to learn from Barth's command ethics.

The great challenge to moral realism came with the rejection of all traces of theological and metaphysical grounding for moral claims typically associated with various forms of naturalism, the collapse of 'traditional metaphysics' orchestrated by Kant, Nietzsche's protest against bourgeois Christian morality and analytical philosophy's linguistic and conceptual dismantling of claims relating to objective moral 'facts'.[131] For those committed to 'naturalism' of one kind or another, 'the only facts we should believe in are those countenanced by or at least compatible with, the results of science'.[132] The result is that moral claims are reduced to being mere expressions of individual or collective preference. Those that attract widespread assent are no more than expressions of strong cultural settlement that may have been otherwise. A. J. Ayer's Emotivism, R. M. Hare's Prescriptivism, J. L. Mackie's Error Theory and Allan Gibbard's Norm Expressivism are examples of significant contributors to the non-realist school.[133]

Sayre-McCord goes on to engage with two positions that stand in opposition to moral realism: the first being that of the non-cognitivists and the second the error theorists. Non-cognitivists hold that 'moral claims are not actually in the business of reporting facts, but are rather our way of expressing emotions or of controlling

---

128. DeLapp, *Moral Realism*, 15.

129. Sabina Lovibond, *Realism and Imagination in Ethics* (Oxford: Blackwell, 1983), 22–3.

130. Rufus Black, *Christian Moral Realism: Natural Law, Narrative, Virtue and the Gospel* (Oxford: Oxford University Press, 2000), 46–100.

131. Alasdair C. MacIntyre, *After Virtue: A Study in Moral Theory*, 2nd ed. (London: Duckworth, 1985), 22.

132. Sayre-McCord, 'Moral Realism'.

133. Hare, *God's Call*, 2.

others' behaviour, or, at least, of taking a stand for and against certain things'.[134] Lovibond notes that

> the theory denies that there are any truths about intrinsic values. The concept which is jettisoned by non-cognitive theorists is that of a value which is both objective and intrinsic. Such theorists are quite ready to allow that there can be propositions, in the strict logical sense of the word, about instrumental value: it can perfectly well be a 'fact', on their view, that such and such means are conducive to such and such an end, and hence the means are good, given the end as determined'. [Yet, she continues], ... judgements of intrinsic value are held to be warranted not by the actual obtaining of a certain state of affairs which they declare to obtain, but by some phenomenon which, pending a better use for the word, can be called 'subjective': candidates for this role include desires, reactive attitudes, personal decisions or prescriptions.[135]

Alternatively, error theorists hold 'that moral claims are in the business of reporting facts, but the required facts are not to be found'.[136] J. L. Mackie is a high-profile proponent, whose *Inventing Right and Wrong* was published a year before MacKinnon's retirement, but it reflects elements of the debate in preceding years.[137] He accepted that ordinary 'common-sense' moral judgements involve a claim to objectivity, yet he insisted that this must be met with scepticism even while the language continues to dominate everyday moral judgements. It would seem that there is not much that is substantively different between this approach and non-cognitivism, except that the former holds it necessary to keep the language of moral factuality alive while sceptically redefining its character from the 'inside out', whereas the latter views it as meaningless from the outset.

In any case, differences over the language of moral factuality are only symptoms of a deeper divide; one connected to the distinction Anscombe captured relating to the 'fit' between mental states and the world. A crude but not entirely misleading assertion is that the distinction between 'fact' / 'value' or 'is' / 'ought' forms the nucleus of controversies between and among realist and non-realist moralists. In this vein, Black seeks to capture 'what is widely understood as Hume's contention that it is not logically possible to derive an "ought" from an "is"' and he takes this to mean that

> the starting-point for moral reasoning must be practical reason (the sort that people use to plan action) and not theoretical reason (the type of reason that tests the truth of a proposition by seeking to establish its conformity to some prior reality, for example scientific reason). [Black further asserts, that] ... to

---

134. Sayre-McCord, 'Moral Realism'.
135. Lovibond, *Realism*, 14–17.
136. Sayre-McCord, 'Moral Realism'.
137. J. L. Mackie, *Ethics: Inventing Right and Wrong* (Harmondsworth: Penguin, 1977).

respect this claim is not to say that the nature of reality is unrelated to an ethic of practical reason but rather that reflection upon this relationship cannot be the logical foundation for ethical reasoning.[138]

The implication here is that notions of value and obligation need not be disconnected from a set of theoretical premises or naturalistic observations, yet they cannot be entirely determined ('founded') by these either. The general question implicit here pertains to the relationship between claims to knowledge in the domain of the empirical sciences and those that emerge from moral discourse. The specific question for the moral realist is how to respond to those who see any affirmation of the fact–value distinction as requiring a form of moral non-realism. In relation to the first general question, Brink assists the search for clarity by offering three options:

1. Realism about science and anti-realism about ethics. Placed within this category are 'traditional nihilists, non-cognitivists (e.g. emotivists and prescriptivists), moral skeptics, and relativists'.
2. Realism about science and ethics: 'Although many traditional cognitivists found important dis-analogies and discontinuities between ethics and the sciences, most of them, including the intuitionists (e.g. Richard Price, Thomas Reid, Sidgwick, Moore, Ross, Broad, and H. A. Prichard), believed that ethics does or can possess these marks of objectivity.'
3. A third alternative proves difficult to capture because it involves proponents claiming a 'global subjectivism or antirealism', yet regarding their position as realist or objectivist in redefined terms. According to Brink, 'the idea is that, although ethics cannot fit the common-sense view of scientific objectivity, this establishes nothing interesting about the objectivity of ethics, since science itself does not satisfy the common sense view of scientific objectivity'. I take this position to involve a version of scepticism which undermines the objectivity of the sciences, thus purporting to bring discourses that were formally seen as incapable of producing objective knowledge, such as ethics, onto a 'more even epistemological playing field'.[139]

The option that I will focus on is the second: realism about science *and* ethics. MacKinnon's position is well described by it, even if he finds himself in disagreement with the moral philosophers whom Brink associates with it. It is a position that shares substantial points of commonality with theological approaches that refuse any sort of strict demarcation between fact and value, such as those put forward by Hauerwas, O'Donovan, J. E. Hare and anyone who rejects the logic of the Euthyphro

---

138. Black, *Christian Moral Realism*, 6–7.
139. David O. Brink, *Moral Realism and the Foundations of Ethics* (Cambridge: Cambridge University Press, 1989), 6.

Dilemma in the way mentioned earlier.[140] It was D. Z. Phillips who observed that a common misappropriation of the distinction in the realm of the philosophy of religion was that 'one cannot argue from a descriptive statement about God to the assertion of an obligation to God'.[141] Phillips offers the example of common ways of speaking about a son's obligation to a decrepit father as a means to illustrate the point that the 'distinction between descriptive and evaluative statements in this context is confused and misleading' and he sees this as having analogous import for the way ethics is done in religious communities.[142] In a similar vein, Hauerwas, who like Phillips is indebted to the later Wittgenstein, has insisted that accepting the distinction would be the death of Christian ethics. He argues that 'this alleged separation of "facts" from "values" drives an artificial wedge between our beliefs and our actions, for there is an intimate connection between what a man [sic] believes and what he finds intelligible to approve or disapprove morally'.[143]

Hauerwas seeks to learn from the non-foundationalist, communitarian and linguistically focused sensibilities of the Wittgensteinian trajectory. He would also agree with MacKinnon when he extols Barth for avoiding a substandard theology that continues on 'as if we were enabled to avoid the sharp needle of enquiry concerning how best to represent the one with whom we have to do [i.e. Christ] by suggesting that in the end even as the proper study of mankind is man, so Christian man finds his appropriate study in himself'.[144] Yet avoiding this manifestation of idealistic anthropomorphism in the development of a distinctively Christian moral position has dangers, namely that 'to conceive of human nature or theological beliefs in terms of facts implies a universalism in the first case and, in the second, an epistemological foundationalism'.[145] Barth, MacKinnon and Hauerwas sought to explore this tension albeit with different emphases, avoiding any facile articulation of universalism or foundationalism in their ethical writings, but holding to the possibility that moral facts could and must be apprehended.

In the face of a consolidation of non-realist ethics, British moral philosophy in the twentieth century hosted various attempts to defend the meaningfulness and factuality of moral claims. Perhaps the most notable, given MacKinnon's context, is that of G. E. Moore, and in different ways, Iris Murdoch and John McDowell. MacKinnon sought to avoid the mysteriousness of Moore's moral intuition of the good, which the latter took to be a simple, indefinable, non-natural property

---

140. Black, *Christian Moral Realism*, 115–25, 48–58.

141. D. Z. Phillips, 'God and Ought', in *Christian Ethics and Contemporary Philosophy*, ed. Ian T. Ramsey (London: SCM Press, 1966), 133.

142. Ibid., 135. For criticism see Black, *Christian Moral Realism*, 27–32.

143. Stanley Hauerwas, *Vision and Virtue: Essays in Christian Ethical Reflection* (Notre Dame: University of Notre Dame Press, 1981), 70. Here, Hauerwas was influenced by a one-time student of MacKinnon, Philippa Foot. Black, *Christian Moral Realism*, 33.

144. *BT*, 31.

145. Black, *Christian Moral Realism*, 34.

that delivers us into the realm of objective moral factuality.[146] On this point, Hare observes that 'to say that it is non-natural is to distinguish it [i.e. the moral intuition of goodness] both from natural properties (like producing pleasure) and supernatural ones (like being commanded by God)'.[147] MacKinnon desired a course that honoured the same distinction, yet found Moore wanting.[148] MacKinnon also avoided a qualified reversion to a platonic form of the good such as that advocated by Murdoch; he was too much the Kantian to adopt any realist or quasi-realist Platonism even if the influence of A. E. Taylor could have pushed him in this direction.[149] Instead, he developed the distinction between naturalistic and moral knowledge claims with reference to a unique form of historical and existential practical reason. This gives rise to 'facts' necessarily different from the those verified by the natural sciences, yet not ultimately unrelated to these in terms of a shared commitment to some form of correspondence theory of truth.

The result is a conviction that while it may be impossible to derive the 'ought' from the 'is' in ways that reflect the legacies of Hume and Kant, the strength of this assertion depends on the how narrowly one defines the 'is' or the realm in which we are permitted to speak of 'facts'. If, in the spirit of someone like Levinas, for instance, one admits to this realm the question of the possibility and character of moral personhood from the beginning, as well as the historical, existential and imaginative dimensions of moral existence, then a narrowly conceived fact–value distinction comes under intense strain.[150] There is no way of embracing a quest to apprehend the world without also apprehending ourselves as moral agents whose ascriptions of value and apprehensions of the claim of the 'good' can ever be finally cut loose from particular people with a history and a future.[151] MacKinnon liked to quote Butler's dictum that 'everything is what it is and not another thing', with the implication that the uniqueness of moral facts must be respected and one cannot seek to justify them by jettisoning their particularity through over-determined analogies.[152] It is as if MacKinnon would prefer richer and wider notions of 'empiricism', 'is' and 'fact' than what many positivists would typically allow, giving space for the 'empiricism' of the poet. This was seen as a better way to proceed compared to the alternative routes of securing moral knowledge claims

---

146. G. E. Moore, *Principia Ethica* (Cambridge: University Press, 1903).

147. Hare, *God's Call*, 5.

148. *SET*, 10–14.

149. I am thinking here of MacKinnon's sympathetic reading of Taylor's 'The Right and the Good' and the explicit Platonic dimension to his advocacy of a kind of natural law dimension to Christian ethics which will be noted in the final chapter. A. E. Taylor, 'The Right and the Good', *Mind* 48, no. 191 (1939): 273–301.

150. A point noted with reference to D. Z. Phillips and Hauerwas above. *ET*, 106–12.

151. A point also articulated in: Christian Smith, *Moral, Believing Animals: Human Personhood and Culture* (Oxford: Oxford University Press, 2003).

152. *SET*, 249. Joseph Butler, *Fifteen Sermons Preached at the Rolls Chapel and a Dissertation upon the Nature of Virtue* (London: G. Bell, 1949), 351.

through esoteric, self-authenticating and a-historical sources with the intuitionists or, with the emotivists and error theorists, giving up on the possibility of moral factuality altogether.[153] In this respect, he reflected the influence of moralists in the generation before him, such as Sorley and Taylor, both of whom feature in the next chapter. MacKinnon decries any absolute distinction between fact and value, descriptive and evaluative claims, yet at the same time seems very aware that not making this distinction at all, or making a confused distinction, is no way forward either.[154]

Reference to this point can be found in MacKinnon's later forays into the ethics of nuclear proliferation, where he avows

> the facile invocation of the alleged distinction between fact and value. If in what follows we seem to advance into metaphysical territory, it may be that only by such floundering will we avoid the damaging consequences of saying that such and such a question is question of fact, and such and such a question of value. The need to understand what we are about in this respect is all the greater because in the debates which concern us, there are concepts which slither, and are indeed encouraged to slither by those who use the distinction of fact and value, from the factual to the ethical and back again. ... If I am concerned with abuse of the murky distinction between fact and value, it is because through abuse of that alleged distinction we are prevented among other things from seeing the possible relevance to our whole situation of the concept of temptation.[155]

MacKinnon mentions a form of metaphysical discourse (here undefined) as usefully transcending the distinction, relativizing it and helping observers to prevent the 'slithering' he found so offensive. He resented the way in which proliferation and the doctrine of deterrence had become a 'fact': something that subsumed and pre-empted substantive judgements of value.[156] The very structure of debate prevented serious consideration of the question as to whether the state was an entity that could justifiably require the use of such weapons to protect its interests and ensure its own perpetuation.[157] Indeed, there is a way of speaking about factuality that undermines the presence of human agency and, as MacKinnon insisted, a way of establishing the distinction so that distortions of perspective and motivation remain unexamined. A metaphysic is needed to give expression to

---

153. Such is indicated by his rather loose application of the term 'empirical' in *PM*, 104–13 and also his critiques of De Burgh's philosophy of religion noted by Muller, 'True Service', 107–8.

154. Cf. Cavell, *Claim of Reason*, 323.

155. *TT*, 116–17.

156. Ibid., 117–20. MacKinnon was particularly distressed at the way this 'fact' had been accepted by the church. *BT*, 38.

157. MacKinnon's loyalty to Kant is paramount here, most evidently the vestiges of a notion of the inalienable dignity of human life. *TT*, 121.

the complex dialectic between 'moral facts' and 'facts of nature', and also a moral discipline by which human agency is preserved, contemplative critical distance is achieved and self-delusion held in check.[158] For MacKinnon an enriched empiricism and an unflinching attentiveness to the tragic is the context in which such a metaphysic may be explored.

Conclusion

MacKinnon seemed uneasy with aspects of Wittgenstein's moral scepticism, just as he was with the sort of 'command ethics' that emerged from the Barthian and Augustinian traditions. Likewise, he found fault with the formalism of Kant, the positivism of the utilitarians and the moribund inflexibility of some natural law approaches that he observed in the history of moral theology. For all this, he sought to make the moral realism (which lay at the heart of many versions of these approaches) workable because he found alternatives unconvincing.[159] What MacKinnon *did* like about non-realist and relativist approaches was their therapeutic potential. They tended to emphasize the sort of immersion in the 'concrete particular' that he came to see as vital for any attempt at serious moral discourse. For non-realists and relativists, a disciplined focus on the particular tended to be an integral step on the road to scepticism regarding moral truth claims and fuelled scepticism of language of 'factuality' and the 'absolute'. With Isaiah Berlin, MacKinnon refused to see non-realism as an inevitable outcome of such sceptical reserve.[160]

MacKinnon mounted an exploratory argument that sought to counter non-realist approaches to morality. He sought to demonstrate that an empirical and existential attentiveness to history and culture would reveal moral imperatives, and do so in a way that gives succour to the realist who persists in invoking ascriptions

---

158. MacKinnon's insistence on the distinction between action and event is crucial here: 'Any teacher of moral philosophy is familiar with the necessity of helping the student at the elementary level to distinguish between an action and an event. The Lisbon earthquake of 1 November 1755 was an event; its impact on European thought was tremendous, reflecting in works as different as Kant's three Kritiks and Voltaire's Candide. Men had to live in a world in which such things had happened, and whose claim therefore to be 'the best of all possible worlds' had been impugned. When we are however told that we must 'live with the atomic or hydrogen bomb', what we are being told we must 'live with' is not something that has happened like the Lisbon earthquake or the great storm of January 30, 1953'. D. M. MacKinnon, 'Natural Law', in *Burden*, ed. John C. McDowell (London: T&T Clark, 2011), 125–7.

159. *SET*, 233–76.

160. Isaiah Berlin, *Historical Inevitability*, Auguste Comte Memorial Trust lecture (London: Oxford University Press, 1954), 68–77. *SET*, 124–5.

of moral 'factuality'.[161] MacKinnon perceived intimations of consistency in the form of common questions persisting within the description and re-description of particular moral dilemmas.[162] It is in a focus on these persisting elements, including the reoccurring experiences of 'absolute' moral obligation and an existential dimension that can only be described in terms of the language of 'freedom' and 'tragedy', which keeps a robust moral realism and a related language of metaphysics alive.[163]

This has been a wide-raging chapter that has sought to 'place' MacKinnon's work by approaching it from a number of discrete vantage points. The first aim was to explore the sense in which MacKinnon's method was 'therapeutic'. Secondarily, I sought to explore the Kantian nature of this therapy while moving on to document the ways in which MacKinnon's moral realism moved beyond Kant's formalism and his 'rational religion'. In the next chapter, I will seek to delve deeper into the intellectual influences on MacKinnon in a way that will further help to explain the restiveness and irresolution of his thought.

---

161. The dynamic at work here has been noted by Murray, who invokes 'van Huyssteen's distinction between a *post* foundationalism that acknowledges *both* the contextually rooted nature of all discourse *and* the force of the truth claims that such discourses nevertheless exert and a *non*foundationalism, or *anti*foundationalism, which rejects even the aspiration for truth'. Murray, 'Reason, Truth and Theology', 5.

162. *ET*, 106–12.

163. MacKinnon, 'Moral Freedom'; and D. M. MacKinnon, 'Ethical Intuition', in *Burden*, ed. John C. McDowell (London: T&T Clark, 2011).

Chapter 2

BEYOND KANT AND BACK AGAIN: FURTHER INFLUENCES ON MACKINNON

Introduction

This chapter continues to advance an appreciation of those influences that shaped MacKinnon's moral theology and will be divided into two sections. The first will consider A. E. Sorley and W. R. Taylor as figures of the preceding generation, who took Kant seriously and influenced MacKinnon's formation, particularly as they sought to advance 'moral arguments for God's existence'. The second section will reflect on the analytical turn in British philosophy, to the extent that MacKinnon found in it resources for a purgative therapy that corrected the idealism inherent in the apologetic strategies of Sorley and Taylor.

As noted above, Kant took the irreducible fact of human freedom and the objectivity of moral duty as posing a question that a reductionist, naturalistic worldview could not adequately answer. Sorley and Taylor are both cited by Byrne as standing with him on this point.[1] They do not begin by postulating God as the source of morality (at least not consciously), but rather seek to examine elements of moral experience and then posit God as one possible option to help explain these. Like Kant, they distinguish a rational moral system from an irrational one on the basis that the latter upholds some standard of ethical perfection that can be conceived, that such a standard is integral to the coherence of moral philosophy generally, and also that it could credibly be met. For all of them, moral 'ought' implies 'can'.[2] Resolution of the tensions created by this account of moral 'rationality' is addressed in each case by integrating theism into the argument. Theism becomes a guarantee that there will be some correspondence between virtue and happiness; between the life we experience and the moral order apprehended by practical reason. Regarding this argumentative strategy, Byrne makes the following observation:

> The notion that to be complete a morally good life must be part of a satisfied life lies at the heart of the traditions of thinking about morality inherited from Greek philosophy. … The moral life has to be seen as the constitutive means to attaining the human good. The idea of the good includes: the moral perfection of

---

1. Byrne, *The Moral Interpretation of Religion*, 22–3.
2. Godlove, *Kant and the Meaning of Religion*, 2–3. And *PM*, 58.

the individual, the advancement of good over evil in the world's history and the fulfilment of human wellbeing. The natural order taken as it stands runs counter to, or is at best indifferent to this deep teleology. ... So morality is pointless unless the given, experienced order is part of a larger order of justice which will fulfil the deep teleology of morality. The notion of God provides the best (that is, most intelligible, most reasonable) anchor for belief in this all-encompassing, hidden moral order.[3]

Both Taylor and Sorley have the distinction of seeing moral discourse as giving rise to the need for transcendental concepts, but more still, a notion of a personal God in something approaching a conventionally realist sense. While they might be placed on various points along a post-Kantian theological trajectory, they differed from Kant in finding far greater potential for conventional apologetics arising from within this tradition.

A. E. Taylor

In *Faith of Moralist* Taylor writes in a way that resonates with what would become MacKinnon's own interrogative, sometimes tortured, style:

> It may be, as von Hügel held it is, that the costingness of a faith which will sacrifice neither history nor metaphysics, the torment of mind, if you like to call it so, by which faith is won, or held fast, is itself evidence of its worth.[4]

We may take this as advance notice that Taylor did not see his project as having made life easy for the theist, yet he certainly hoped that his arguments added weight to its intellectual credibility. Charles Virtue describes the way Taylor's early allegiance to non-realist and constructivist forms of morality gave way to a comprehensive embrace of a thoroughgoing form of moral objectivism.[5] He further notes that

> Taylor's philosophic pilgrimage led from his early rationalistic agnosticism, through the gradual analysis of rationality, to the acceptance of an a priori element in experience, and through a steadily deepening insight into the nature and implications of purposiveness to his final Christian-Platonic philosophy in which human purposiveness is held to be a phase of the value-reality of a

---

3. Byrne, *The Moral Interpretation of Religion*, 38–9.
4. A. E. Taylor, *The Faith of a Moralist: Gifford Lectures Delivered in the University of St Andrews, 1926-1928, Natural Theology and the Positive Religions*, 2 vols., vol. 2 (London: Macmillan, 1930), 42.
5. Charles F. Sawhill Virtue, 'The Axiological Theism of A. E. Taylor', *Philosophy* 27, no. 101 (1952): 110.

temporal order having its roots in an eternal order which is determined by an eternal being.[6]

In his intellectual biography of MacKinnon, Muller makes the case that Taylor had a significant impact on MacKinnon's life at a critical juncture of intellectual and professional formation. MacKinnon spent a year as assistant to Taylor at the University of Edinburgh working in the field of moral philosophy; a subject that focused on the ethics of Mill, Bentham, Hume, Kant, Butler, Plato and Aristotle.[7] Taylor was the foremost interpreter of Plato in Britain at the time, having published a well-received commentary on the *Timaeus*. He was also 'at home dealing with the moral philosophy of Kant or Butler, and the metaphysics of Aquinas or Bradley'.[8] Add to this his impressive grasp of modern literature and trends in the natural sciences, together with his continuing commitment to Christianity, and it is easy to understand why MacKinnon would have looked to him as someone who modelled a breath of conversation partners with a level of sophistication worth emulating.

It is possible to identify at least three related points on which MacKinnon followed his early mentor. First, the suspicion that idealism, whether articulated by Hegel or the later British idealists, no longer provided a convincing metaphysical proposal, nor did it take account of historical evil and the existential condition of the 'ordinary' estranged subjects of modernity with sufficient seriousness.[9] Secondly, MacKinnon joined Taylor in continuing to find the language of metaphysics helpful. This mode of speech was not invoked to defend a pre-critical project, or lofty attempts to unifying knowledge under a single concept, but a means by which the moral imperative, the limits of language in the face of the 'ultimate' and the perennial tussle of realism and idealism, may play a role in a way that supplemented the insights of the natural sciences, not competing with or 'completing' them. Thirdly, like Taylor in the broad Kantian trajectory, MacKinnon perceived the moral domain as one from which questions continued to arise that may encourage the philosopher to turn to theological resources. In sum, Muller notes that

> in Taylor MacKinnon found a philosopher who shared his own dual concern to make sense of his faith and defend its intellectual cogency in a post-idealist context without compromising either orthodox Christian belief or the demands of reason in the way that the modernists did.[10]

---

6. Ibid., 113.
7. Muller, 'True Service', 88.
8. Ibid., 108.
9. MacKinnon: 'I well remember Taylor saying to me: "You know, MacKinnon, Kant is a very great moralist indeed. The Hegelian criticism of him is largely irrelevant. Hegel was a man without a conscience and could never understand anyone who took the moral struggle as seriously as Kant did"'. MacKinnon, 'Kant's Agnosticism', 27.
10. Muller, 'True Service', 110.

MacKinnon began his year as Taylor's assistant following his immersion in the world of the Oxford positivists. To the extent that he was unconvinced by the adequacy of the philosophical atomism and metaphysical minimalism (or outright purgation) being proposed, Taylor would have been a welcome source of inspiration. To the extent that MacKinnon heeded the seriousness of the attack on the very possibility of intelligible theological speech acts, Taylor's apologetic efforts would have struck MacKinnon as overconfident. What we have in Taylor's later work is something of a meeting between philosophy of religion and natural theology. The claim is that any significant degree of 'moral seriousness' will allow objective imperatives grounded in moral realism, as well as supporting metaphysical construction, notions of self-transcendence, reference to the tragic, and a realist notion of God as the capstone.

In this section, I will survey some of Taylor's later publications, focusing on those that contain themes which overlap with MacKinnon's work.

First is Taylor's encyclopaedia entry 'Theism', which attracted effusive praise from MacKinnon.[11] With impressive erudition he charted major philosophical justifications for theism from selected figures in the Western canon from the classical to modern periods.[12] Then there was *Vindication of Religion* in *Essays Catholic and Critical*, which placed Taylor as a key contributor to a work that informed a generation of Anglo-Catholics in the Church of England in the lead-up to the Second World War.[13] In this way Taylor played a formative role in the ecclesiastical milieu in which MacKinnon moved, although this chapter showcases MacKinnon's divergences from his mentor just as it does their shared convictions. MacKinnon also read and appreciated Taylor's Gifford Lectures published in 1930s under the title *The Faith of a Moralist*.[14] At the heart of the first volume of the lectures is the claim that moral life creates the conditions where notions of God become necessary for coherence and consistency.[15] Finally there is Taylor's brief monograph *Does God Exist?* published in 1945.[16]

Commenting on Taylor, MacKinnon notes his early affinity with the Hegelian F. H. Bradley at Oxford, yet a break with this tradition was clear as early as his first publication *The Problem of Conduct* (1901). Here, Taylor 'maintains that ethics

---

11. Ibid.

12. A. E. Taylor, 'Theism', in *Encyclopædia of Religion and Ethics*, ed. James Hastings, John A. Selbie and Louis H. Gray (Edinburgh: T&T Clark, 1908).

13. A. E. Taylor, 'The Vindication of Religion', in *Essays Catholic & Critical*, ed. Edward Gordon Selwyn (London: Society for Promoting Christian Knowledge, 1929), 29–82.

14. Muller, 'True Service', 111.

15. A. E. Taylor, *The Faith of a Moralist: Gifford Lectures Delivered in the University of St Andrews, 1926-1928, The Theological Implications of Morality*, 2 vols., vol. 1 (London: Macmillan, 1930).

16. A. E. Taylor, *Does God Exist?* (London: Macmillan, 1945).

2. Beyond Kant and Back Again: Further Influences on MacKinnon

is independent of metaphysics and its study can only take an empirical form'.[17] The influences which drew Taylor away from his earlier idealist commitments include his contact with Samuel Alexander's realist epistemology and the latter encouraging Taylor to read the work of Austrian physicist and philosopher Ernst Mach. Taylor's reading of Galileo, Leibniz and Descartes were also important in solidifying this move according to MacKinnon.[18] Additionally, one might imagine that there is no easy way to speak of 'Spirit' bringing coherence and progressive integration of a historical dialectic while hearing accounts of the Battle of the Somme. Taylor argues that

> among all the creatures, many of whom are comic enough, man is alone in being tragic. His life at the very best is a tragi-comedy; at the worst it is stark tragedy. And naturally enough this is so; for, if man has only the 'environment' which is common to him with the beasts of the field, his whole life is no more than a perpetual attempt to find a rational solution of an equation all whose roots are surds.[19]

For both Taylor and MacKinnon, the idealist drive towards the sublation of particulars within a programme of monist metaphysics comes under the intense scrutiny of empirical history and is found wanting. For MacKinnon, the theist may risk faith as long as it submits to continuous empirical-realist therapy and abandons fantasies that it can secure itself. To some degree this scepticism was a response to Taylor's more assertive rationalist defence of traditional apologetics.

Vindication sets out a three-pronged defence against scepticism, with Taylor noting irreducible questions arising from nature, moral reflection and religious experience that, at least to his mind, cannot be sufficiently answered within these domains alone, yet call for answers nonetheless. He offers a perfunctory restatement of arguments for God's existence from the Aristotelian-Thomist tradition drawing on notions of causation and infinite regress in order to furnish a cosmological argument for theism. *Theism* is more ambitious as Taylor expanded his line of attack, attempting a rebuttal of criticisms that Kant and Russell made against arguments for God's existence. Provocatively, Taylor challenged any claim that Kant had definitively refuted the ontological argument and, because he accepted Kant's judgement that the ontological argument was the root of other attempted proofs, he sought to revive arguments from design or teleology as well. As part of the latter case, he considered the impact of evolutionary biology on

---

17. D. M. MacKinnon and Mark J. Schofield, 'Taylor, Alfred Edward (1869-1945), Philosopher', in *Oxford Dictionary of National Biography* (Oxford: Oxford University Press). https://doi.org/10.1093/ref:odnb/36426.
18. Ibid.
19. Taylor, 'The Vindication of Religion', 60.

moral philosophy, as well as a defence of the unique epistemological status of religious experience in conversation with insights from Rudolph Otto.[20]

It is the moral argument where the force of the argument lies, however. It 'suggests God more directly and much less obscurely' than the other arguments.[21] This is a position that Taylor develops briefly in *Vindication*, in *Theism*, in *Does God Exist?* and then most expansively in his Gifford Lectures (1926–28) *The Faith of a Moralist*. While MacKinnon was impressed by the breadth and style of Taylor's *Theism,* he was unconvinced by his critiques of Kant and Russell, and together with them, he was committed to disciplining logical and metaphysical claims through a rigorous agnosticism born of a focus on empirical limits. Yet MacKinnon remained loyal to his mentor in carrying on a conviction that empirical history and moral experience demand a bolder metaphysical articulation beyond that allowed by Kant and first-generation analytical philosophers.

All this should not mask the fact that there is much in Taylor's approach to morality that mirrored Kant. He argued, for example, that there is an irreducible feature of moral life which is captured by the term 'duty'.[22] Duties cannot be turned aside or rejected without the rejection of the whole moral order, which is Taylor's way of arguing that forms of relativism, non-realism and nihilism are tantamount to the dissolution of moral discourse in any meaningful sense. These are duties 'to which I must need sacrifice everything else, must be something which cannot even be appraised in the terms of a secular arithmetic, something incommensurable with the "welfare" of Church or State or even of the whole human race'.[23] Taylor goes on to claim that

> whoever says "ought", meaning "ought", is in the act bearing witness to the supernatural and supra-temporal as the destined home of man. There are some acts that should or should not be done regardless of the goods or lack of goods … for the reason of the greater good.[24]

Here, perhaps, is a vindication of Anscombe's observation noted in Chapter 1 regarding the mutuality between certain ideas pertaining to moral obligation and supernaturalism. The objectivity of the 'ought' is held to be self-evident and resultantly Taylor may be guilty of a Cartesian slight-of-hand, placing too much weight on *his own* sense of the natural light of reason operative within him and his cultural milieu.[25] Any sound moral thinker will apparently come to a point

---

20. Taylor, 'Theism', 261–86.
21. Taylor, 'The Vindication of Religion', 59.
22. Taylor, *Faith of a Moralist*, 157–9.
23. Taylor, 'The Vindication of Religion', 61.
24. Ibid., 62.
25. One only has to read Stevenson demystifying language of 'ought' to find Taylor's assertion question-begging. Charles L. Stevenson, *Ethics and Language* (New Haven, CT: Yale University Press, 1944), 17–18.

where an absolute principle is discerned in any given situation, meaning one not explicable in terms of advantage, or in purely naturalistic terms. This entails a strong appropriation of Kant's distinction between the realm of nature and the realm of ends and also a strong teleology whereby the 'ought' serves progress towards the good. For Taylor, the tensions involved here are the mark of the philosopher who takes the moral task 'seriously'. Speaking of Plato and Kant in this respect, he notes that they 'insisted most vigorously on what the secularly-minded call, by way of depreciation, the "dualism" of "this world" and the "other world", or in Kantian language, of "man as (natural) phenomenon" and "man as (supernatural) reality"'.[26] To deny the reality of this antithesis is to eviscerate morality. Indeed, in regard to positing a dualism at the heart of moral anthropology, Taylor affirms that

> Kant seems to be unquestionably right as far as this. Even where there is nothing else to suggest to us that we are denizens at once of a natural and temporal and of a supernatural and eternal world, the revelation of our own inner division against ourselves afforded by conscience, duly mediated, is enough to bear the strain.[27]

The next step from here is to posit the need for an eternal dimension to moral discourse; an update of Kant's discussion of the 'immortality of the soul'. The invocation of an ideal which ought to inspire and regulate all our conduct includes the possibility of its real attainability by us, yet its unattainability inexorably leads to a conclusion that our final destiny must lie in the non-temporal.[28] Taylor claims that 'if the fruition of all secular good fails to attain this ideal we may reasonably infer that the ultimate good of man is non-secular and eternal and that the facts of our moral being point to the Christian conception of the transformation and completion of nature by "grace"'.[29] The nature of the 'reason' justifying this point remains opaque and its implicit universality contentious.

C. F. Virtue contends that

> the Gifford Lectures, 1926-27 and 1927-28, gave Professor Taylor the stimulus and the opportunity to work out a 'natural theology' for the Christian faith he so devoutly held. He spoke as a moralist, 'who took morality seriously' and generalized his moral theory into an objective axiology with metaphysical implications. ... [The argument put forward] is similar to A.N. Whitehead's objectivistic relativism, but more explicit in its distinction between being and value and in its characterization of value. It is in sharp contrast to R.B. Perry's interest-centred neo-realism, which is naturalistic and ultimately subjectivistic,

---

26. Taylor, 'The Vindication of Religion', 60.
27. Ibid., 63.
28. Ibid., 65.
29. Taylor, *Faith of a Moralist*, xi.

and is in outright opposition to D.W. Prall's and D.H. Parker's naturalist subjectivistic relativism.[30]

Taylor used the final lectures to explore the implications of his notions of value and eternity. Both are held to be beyond naturalistic explanation and both are seen to be indispensable to the coherence of human claims to knowledge in the historical and moral spheres. The result is what Virtue calls an 'axiological argument for theism'. At the conclusion of the argument we find Cartesian echoes and intimations of the ontological argument:

> The nature of temporal value experience is such as to be explicable only upon the assumption that it is grounded in a non-temporal perfect Being, the most real of beings, the absolute and primary source of actuality, and the most perfect of beings, so good that none better can be conceived.[31]

Whereas Kant's God provided a means whereby the two incommensurable domains of nature and ends might find eventual integration, Taylor explores the themes of time and value to show that the dualism can never be conceived as incommensurable in the first place. Indeed, Taylor saw Kant as a progenitor of a particularly extreme manifestation of the fact/value distinction and criticized him for it:

> We may trace [the distinction] back, in the first instance, historically, to Kant's first Critique, where the purpose of the smashing assault on speculative theology, and, indeed, of the whole Dialectic of Pure Reason, is to divorce value completely from fact by denying that the 'ideals' of speculative reason have any contact whatever with genuine knowledge.[32]

What Taylor attempted was a Kantian approach to morality while opting for (what he saw as) a weaker dualism between the realm of nature-fact and that of end-value. With Kant he claims that theological implications of morality would not arise if 'ethics is concerned exclusively with values, and fact and value are *ultimately* disconnected'.[33] Yet against Kant he claims that the integration of the two is always and everywhere part of 'nature's factuality' rather than awaiting integration by a regulative supernatural agent at some faraway point. This is the basis on which Taylor can see rather un-Kantian synergies between the argument for God's existence from morality and those from nature and experience; all are part of a realist apprehension of an integrated fact–value reality which cannot fully

---

30. Virtue, 'The Axiological Theism of A. E. Taylor', 113.
31. Ibid., 122.
32. Taylor, *Faith of a Moralist*, 33. Italics added.
33. Ibid., xi. Italics added.

explain or justify itself without an external referent. A more definitely realist God becomes necessary for Taylor relative to Kant's proposal.

In commenting on the moral approaches of Taylor and Kant respectively, Virtue notes that

> both theories rest upon faith in the veridicality of moral insight; but for Taylor, moral judgements are not merely objective, in the sense of humanly universal, but are realistic. Moreover, Taylor's profound sense of the deepening of the genuine moral consciousness, and its increasingly tragic cost is nowhere matched in the high-minded, but somehow pedantic, moralism of Kant.[34]

Describing a movement beyond Kant in this respect touches on the heart of what MacKinnon learnt from Taylor. Indeed, mention of the tragic immediately makes one mindful of MacKinnon, for whom the category was an important component of the therapy he enjoins. Yet it is also on the question of tragedy, and more specifically on the related question of evil, where MacKinnon moved beyond Taylor. For instance, when Taylor says that 'it is possible to do better than to abstain from complaints or to cultivate pride; it is possible … to make acceptance of the worst fortune has to bestow a means to the development of a sweetness, patience, and serene joyousness which are to be learned nowhere but in the school of sharp suffering,'[35] MacKinnon would in all likelihood sound a note of caution, if not dissent. MacKinnon's attentiveness to accounts of the crucifixion and also to the Marxist critique of religion made him sceptical of any claim pertaining to the positive benefits of suffering as a 'veil of soul making'. Indeed, he was suspicious of any easy integration of suffering into an account of developing personhood, or as a necessary step on the way to the full realization of the greatest good.[36] His comments on the person of Judas make this more than clear.[37]

The broad similarities between Taylor and MacKinnon are captured well by Muller when he argues that the former etched out a 'third way' in-between the idealists and the logical positivists. This was

> a kind of modern reworking of the Augustinian-Thomist tradition – tentative, unsystematic, open to dialogue with its detractors, but based upon a firm conviction that a serious investigation of human action would not only vindicate the intelligibility of faith, but also reveal that it was only by acknowledging the given that lay behind our moral and intellectual striving that the meaningfulness of that striving could be guaranteed.[38]

---

34. Virtue, 'The Axiological Theism of A. E. Taylor', 119.
35. Taylor, *Faith of a Moralist*, 154.
36. *BT*, 90–1.
37. As discussed by Anthony Cane, *The Place of Judas Iscariot in Christology* (Aldershot: Ashgate, 2005), 70–86.
38. Muller, 'True Service', 111.

Despite sharing a similar post-Kantian trajectory, MacKinnon refused Taylor's move from morality to any firm theistic apologetic. This is true even in light of the qualifications Taylor makes and his admission that theism is only one possible way to 'ground' rationality, history, morality and the purposiveness of the world generally, even if it is the best answer in his view. MacKinnon doubted whether Taylor had seriously apprehended the challenge of ethical naturalism and offered a far more minimalist conclusion.[39] There could be no 'vindication' of faith, except whatever vindication could be discerned in the crucifixion and resurrection of Jesus. MacKinnon shared Taylor's attempt to enhance the realism and objectivity of the Kantian 'ought' by proposing a more integrated field of fact and value, yet preferred to remain in the orbit of Kant's agnosticism.

W. R. Sorley

Like MacKinnon, Sorley was tempted towards ordination as a young man, but this option was passed over when a life of full-time academic research and teaching beckoned.[40] Again like MacKinnon, Sorley held the post of Professor of Moral Philosophy at Aberdeen early in his career, only to move to Cambridge thereafter. The former would make a permanent shift to Divinity, whereas Sorley remained in a chair of moral philosophy at Cambridge until his retirement in 1933. Tennant notes that

> [Sorely] was initially influenced by the idealism of T.H. Green and Bradley ... but he became increasingly critical of philosophical idealism, which he regarded as unable to account for the existence of evil. For example, he criticised idealists for describing an individual's moral activity as the reproduction of an eternal reality even though selfish interests so often prevailed over the common good. He found deeply unsatisfactory attempts by all non-theistic theories to explain the struggle between good and evil.[41]

Tennant also describes Sorley's Gifford Lectures *Moral Values and the Idea of God* as his 'chief work ... [that] played an important part in the education of students of philosophical theology'.[42] MacKinnon clearly appreciated it as 'a minor classic' on

---

39. MacKinnon and Schofield, 'Taylor, Alfred Edward (1869-1945), Philosopher'. MacKinnon: 'It seems simply untrue to assert that ethical naturalism has been definitively demolished by the arguments of [A. E.] Taylor and [W. R.] Sorley'. D. M. MacKinnon, 'Religion and Philosophy by W.G. de Burgh [Book Review]', *Laudate* 15 (1937): 225.

40. F. R. Tennant and S. M. den Otter, 'Sorley, William Ritchie (1855-1935), Philosopher', in *Oxford Dictionary of National Biography* (Oxford: Oxford University Press), e-book https://doi.org/10.1093/ref:odnb/36197.

41. Ibid.

42. He does not quantify or qualify this claim further. Ibid.

the theme of 'an ethically grounded and orientated theism'.[43] Indeed, he sees it as a representative work of unique clarity: 'If the modern analytical philosopher wishes to "get inside" the ethical theist's outlook, he could well be referred to Sorley's work.'[44] At its heart is an affirmation of Lotze's dictum, following Kant, that 'the true beginning of metaphysics lies in ethics'.[45] Indeed, like several of the works authored by Taylor mentioned above, *Moral Values* made a connection between the continuing intelligibility of metaphysics, together with talk of God, and the persistence of moral discourse of a certain realist character. The constellation of ideas leading up to an overtly theistic appeal includes a phenomenology of moral experience and reflections on the possibility of self-conscious apprehension of personhood, as well as the perception of value and purposiveness in history. All contribute to a claim regarding the inadequacy of naturalistic reductionism in the moral domain.

Anticipating debates that continue unabated, Sorley accepted evolutionary naturalism as the best explanation for the emergence of life, yet claimed that it was 'unable either to set up a comprehensive ideal for life, or to yield any principle for distinguishing between good and evil conduct'.[46] The fields of history and biography are held as irreducible to the natural sciences because of the particular way they apprehend the contingency of their respective subjects. According to Long, 'It is the individual that is the focus of [Sorley's] research: the life of a particular human being or the life of a nation.'[47] Most importantly, it is in the latter domain where individuals are apprehended as persons; bearers of value who routinely make judgements of value in their apprehension of reality.[48] Yet, universals and regulatory law-like theories will emerge from this domain just as they do in science: 'The [value] judgement … always involves both something assumed as existing and a universal by means of which it is approved or disapproved.'[49] Moral knowledge arises in history and among persons; it resists naturalistic reduction, yet constituent claims are (apparently) factual and law-like

43. D. M. MacKinnon, 'A Note on Sorley as a Philosopher', in *A History of British Philosophy to 1900*, ed. W. R. Sorley (Cambridge: Cambridge University Press, 1965), xvii.

44. Ibid.

45. Eugene Thomas Long, 'The Gifford Lectures and the Scottish Personal Idealists', *The Review of Metaphysics* 49, no. 2 (1995): 384.

46. Sorley, *Moral Values*, 31.

47. Long, 'The Gifford Lectures and the Scottish Personal Idealists', 386.

48. Sorley: 'Ethics is distinguished from the natural sciences by the fact that its propositions are value-propositions and not causal propositions: it predicates value, not causation; and it is further distinguished from mathematics and abstract science generally because its main propositions are not concerned with the logical implication of concepts. It does not predicate causation, and its propositions are therefore unlike those of natural science'. Sorley, *Moral Values*, 85.

49. Ibid., 87.

in a way analogous to those of the sciences.[50] Indeed, value judgements constitute crucial data for apprehending reality and cannot be relegated to a 'second order' form of knowledge:

> The goodness of something is recognized in a concrete situation and the moral judgement is in the first instance a perceptive judgment in Aristotle's sense of the term. Ethical science is based on these perceptive judgements just as natural science is based on sense perception. The data of ethics then are the particular judgements of good or evil passed in certain concrete situations.[51]

Sorley also claimed that

> the validity [of ethical values] could not be verified in external phenomena; they cannot be established by observation of the course of nature. They hold good for persons only: and their peculiarity consists in the fact their validity is not in any way dependent upon their being manifested in the character or conduct of persons, or even on their being recognised in the thoughts of persons. We acknowledge the good and its objective claim upon us even when we are conscious that our will has not yielded to the claim; and we admit that its validity existed before we recognised it.[52]

Sorley (like Taylor) continued to see a useful purpose for employing the classic distinctions between 'is' and 'ought', 'fact' and 'value', yet he also blurred the boundary with his particular brand of personalist idealism, which attempted to account for a notion of a metaphysical whole that avoided pluralism on one hand and the monism of Absolute Idealism on the other. The idealistic temper of Sorley's proposal shines through as he eventually came to argue the *sublation* of 'is' into 'ought'.[53] With the evolutionary emergence of human beings as self-aware agents cognisant of moral value comes the conviction that the recognition of the good and the apprehension of duty is a realist, objective component of reality which is as much part of 'nature' as any other 'fact' apprehended about the world by the senses. Sorley claimed that 'the moral universe has a different principle from that which science describes for the actual universe, though it is only in the actual universe that the moral universe seeks and can find its realisation'.[54] In this respect, MacKinnon noted that Sorley balanced an 'idealism of freedom' with

---

50. In this way, he prefigured figures such as J. Soskice, A. Peacocke and W. van Huyssteen who have sought to build far more sophisticated accounts of theological rationality in conversation with the empirical sciences. Andrew Moore, *Realism and Christian Faith: God, Grammar, and Meaning* (Cambridge: Cambridge University Press, 2003), 43–8.
51. Sorley, *Moral Values*, 285.
52. Ibid., 355.
53. Ibid., 183–9.
54. Ibid., 151.

the constraint implicit in the common-sense view that the 'world is in no sense a construct of our understanding'. He goes on to observe that

> Sorley's philosophical master is Kant; indeed his whole work may be construed as an elaboration of Kant's bifurcation of the 'realm of ends' and the 'realm of nature'. If the 'realm of ends' is sovereign, the sovereignty is something to be won and achieved, not taken for granted, let alone affirmed as already actual. Sorley follows Kant in his resolute separation of the so-called 'realm of ends', the domain of moral value, from the natural world; but he rejects the instrument Kant used for effecting this separation in his doctrine of the subjectivity of space and time.[55]

A 'resolute' separation is not absolute incommensurability; resolution can be hoped for and worked towards. Yet relative to Kant, it may be that Sorely had a far more 'immanent' sense of the overlap of the two 'closed and self-consistent systems', which then needed God or 'purposiveness' as a point of connectivity.[56] For this reason, he ended up proposing a God that was far more immanent than Kant's. Sorley argued that moral values

> are manifested in selves and persons; and persons live in and interact with the world of nature. The causal system may be considered by itself; but the abstraction is made for the purposes of science, and is in this respect arbitrary: it is only one aspect of the world. And moral values ... are another aspect of reality, dominating or claiming to dominate the lives of persons. We must regard the two systems, therefore, not as the orders of two entirely different worlds, but rather as different aspects of the same reality.[57]

The question animating Sorley's argument is whether the world expresses a moral meaning. As human beings are an aspect of the world and *they* express moral meaning, he takes the answer to be affirmative. Here Sorley's idealistic leanings shine forth: there is a clear reaction against any empiricist temptation to operate with a model of the transcendent 'self' accounting for the world's features all the while remaining blind to the irreducible moral personhood of the one doing the

---

55. MacKinnon, 'A Note on Sorley as a Philosopher', xviii.
56. Sorley, *Moral Values*, 336.
57. Ibid., 339–40. Earlier in the work he tries to provide reasons for challenging any absolute distinction between domains: 'The reason which justifies us in applying moral ideas in interpreting the world is similar to that which justifies us in understanding it as an orderly and causal system. Moral ideas are not a system of concepts without relation to existence. They apply directly to conscious agents, and are realised in the lives of those conscious agents – lives which are immersed in a material environment and thus connected with the whole physical universe. Morality, therefore is connected with the whole physical universe, the problem is to show the nature of this connection.' Sorley, *Moral Values*, 292.

perceiving.[58] The perceiving 'self' in all its historical and psychological complexity needs to be included in any account of reality, as Hegel insisted.

Furthermore, for Sorley, in as far as this discussion contains reference to the partial good it implies the absolute good as well. He asserted the Platonic-sounding idea of the Supreme Good, the notion of a universal law, and the categorical imperative.[59] This led him to see a certain anthropocentric teleology at work in nature: a 'world process' developing in such a way that certain values are becoming manifest and certain moral ends are revealing themselves as the regulating determinants of value judgements, the goal of life and the purpose of history. In this vein, Sorley claimed that 'the objective moral value is valid independently of me and my will, and yet is something which satisfies my purpose and completes my nature'.[60]

In all of this, Sorley sought to avoid what he saw as the unhelpful developments of 'traditional intuitionism' and Kantian formalism. According to Sorley, both held that 'moral judgement is an application of the general principle that goodness belongs only to will in so far as it is determined by the conception of a law which admits of use as a universal principle'.[61] Whereas intuitionism posited notions of goodness and its correlates, such as happiness, perfection, justice and so on, as being resistant to naturalistic reductionism, it also tended to reject theistic or rational bases for such subjects. Thus, in the end, it could only secure these conceptions by reference to particular experiential phenomena, or even less adequately, it posited these notions as free-floating 'foundations' irreducibly and immediately present within human consciousness.[62] The question as to how to prevent a collapse into facile subjectivism remained open. Kantian formalism sought to remove subjectivity from the apprehension of moral obligation altogether, reducing 'the

---

58. In this respect, MacKinnon argues that 'Sorley is no absolutist, yet he shares with the idealist tradition the conviction that men [sic] enjoy privileged access to their inner lives. Thus in his argument it is to the deliverances of introspection that he continually appeals. We have as human beings a unique insight into the business of being human that no sophistry of philosophical construction can take from us.' MacKinnon, 'A Note on Sorley as a Philosopher', xviii.

59. Sorley, *Moral Values*, 89.

60. Ibid., 388.

61. Ibid., 90.

62. Brink notes that 'intuitionists such as Sidgwick, Moore, Broad, and Ross ... conceived of the foundations of ethics broadly, as including a wide range of metaethical and normative issues ... . Most intuitionists accepted three metaethical claims: a realist or cognitivist commitment to the existence of moral facts and moral truths whose existence and nature are independent of our moral thinking, a foundationalist epistemology according to which our moral knowledge is based ultimately on self-evident moral truths, and a radically nonreductive metaphysics of moral facts and properties, known as nonnaturalism, according to which moral facts and properties are metaphysically independent of, for example, natural facts and properties and so are sui generis.' Brink, *Moral Realism*, 3.

principle of morality to the formal proposition that the good will alone is good or that goodness ought to be realised or willed' in a way that was disconnected from the concrete location of moral actors'.[63] Sorley rejected these alternatives and this is his main legacy upon MacKinnon.

What Sorley attempted to posit was a conception of the good which was universal and objective in a Kantian sense, yet also more self-consciously embedded and responsive to concrete experience in the vein of the intuitionists. He said that 'the universal of morality is contained in particulars and at first concealed by them; and the moralist's problem is to elucidate the universal by reason of which these particular cases are appropriate subjects for the moral judgement'.[64] For Sorley, the starting point is concrete moral judgements with all their contextual limitations and fallibility, and the claim is made that in working through the conditions that make such a claim intelligible one will be driven to the language of universals and the language of realist, objective moral claims.

Naturally, such claims are vulnerable to the sort of attacks that the likes of Mackie and the non-realists before him would make. Even so, there is no sense that Sorley was blind to the huge array of contradictory judgements of good and evil that can be easily documented in every sphere of human discourse; it just didn't lead him to see non-realism as the inevitable conclusion to be drawn. What he did perceive was a common receptivity to the good as a fixed point around which all these judgements could be incorporated into a rational system. As noted, Sorley's insistence was that the exercise of sound rationality here will demand the positing of an absolute Good, and also the realization that moral judgements are made in a way that is analogous to more primary judgements arising from sense perception. As such, these judgements must be open to the law of non-contradiction and also to the test of consistency; that what is right for one to do in a certain circumstance must be right for anyone else if they were in exactly the same circumstance.[65] Reasoning about moral judgements will produce pattern and convergence. It will reveal more and more the sense in which to say 'this is good' is to imbue 'this' with a judgement of a 'determinate kind' with a 'universal element'.[66] Reflecting on Sorley's proposal, MacKinnon noted,

> There is in his work a clear awareness that metaphysical construction, of the sort which he undertakes, has in it a visionary or imaginative element. The philosopher commits himself to his *idèe maîtrise* almost by an act of faith and thence, in a movement of thought which surely deserves to be described as an essay in 'faith seeking understanding', he interprets the totality of what is under its inspiration.[67]

63. Sorley, *Moral Values*, 90.
64. Ibid., 91.
65. Ibid., 94.
66. Ibid., 99.
67. MacKinnon, 'A Note on Sorley as a Philosopher', xviii.

MacKinnon has identified something critical here: Sorley's confident metaphysics of self-evident moral value is in fact an expression of faith. For all its attractiveness in bringing a degree of clarity and stability to the notion of moral order, the analogy between sense perception and the exercise moral judgement is question-begging. Sorley implicitly concedes this as he calls upon theism to further secure his commitment to moral realism. He noted that 'analysis sunders a thing into its elements; synthesis puts these elements together again; synopsis views the thing as a whole'.[68] What the natural and the moral sciences do in their respective domains is provide analysis and synthesis, yet Sorley is convinced that human intellect requires a synopsis; 'something more and something less than synthesis ... [the contemplation of] a whole of which the parts may not be distinct'.[69] Sorley is well aware that 'philosophers are divided on the question of whether this synoptic view is to be recognised as a valid attitude of thought' and that it is 'often ignored and sometimes definitely rejected'.[70] Yet Plato, Spinoza, Kant, Hegel and Coleridge gave him cause to persist. In the end, Sorley concluded his Gifford Lectures by attempting a robust defence of classical theism as being more effective than pluralism and monism in terms of available options for synoptic ways of thinking that could sustain the moral order. In a summary of his own argument Sorley notes that it is

> not that the order of nature and the moral order agree in their manifestations. On the contrary, it started from the fact that there are values which have no actual existence in the world, that the moral law is often broken, that the moral ideal is something unrealised. The argument was that the natural order might be shown to be adapted to the moral order, but only upon two conditions: first, if nature were interpreted as a purposive system, and secondly, if it were recognised that morality required for its realisation the free activity of individual persons.[71]

It is in posing such 'conditions' that the cracks in the edifice become obvious. All this leads to Sorley's claim that the only way the good can have any reality analogous to the reality of the world we know and experience is if it exists in a supreme mind.[72] To adopt theism as a synoptic view of the world is necessary if we are to make sense of ourselves in a purposive universe within which we access objective or absolute moral values and it is also necessary in order that people might 'confront evil via their own free choices, with the assurance that an omniscient, omnipotent and omnibenevolent agency will bring those choices to fruition'.[73] The chief problem with all this has already been identified: Sorley's misplaced confidence in moving

---

68. Sorley, *Moral Values*, 252.
69. Ibid.
70. Ibid.
71. Ibid., 392.
72. Ibid., 351.
73. Byrne, 'Moral Arguments for the Existence of God'.

from a reception of a moral imperative by means of a faculty analogous to sense experience, to positing a realist moral ontology undergirded by an absolute moral agent. The links binding each move of the argument are far more tenuous than Sorley imagined. Commenting on 'transcendental arguments from truth to God', that is, arguments which claim that 'God is the necessary condition for our beliefs about truth and objectivity', Moore observes that

> we need God to exist in order to ground our view of truth, but ... all we [are given is] (widely contested) arguments for God's putative existence. Without knowing that these are true we cannot know that God exists, but we cannot know that God exists without knowing that the arguments are true. The argument from truth to God requires that we can know that the arguments are true, but this begs the question and so render the argument viciously circular because it assumes its conclusion as a premise.[74]

Perhaps it is for this reason that the argument achieved only limited impact. Long notes that

> within a few years after Pringle-Pattison and Sorley delivered their Gifford Lectures the movement which they helped initiate had almost entirely receded into history. And this, coupled with the strong blasts of dogmatic theology blowing down from Switzerland, appeared by mid-century to have put the whole idea of philosophical theology in doubt.[75]

MacKinnon remained committed to many of the concerns of his predecessor's forays into philosophical theology, yet he shared the disillusion identified by Long, especially as his theology came under the influence of Barth and later, Balthasar. Additionally, there is no evidence that he ever presumed that arguments from morality (or any notion of 'objective' truth) could be relied upon to provide any direct path to theism. MacKinnon learnt much from Taylor and Sorley and he came to share their conviction that God becomes the subject of a question articulated in light of our perception of freedom and the experience of evil. Yet, under the influence of the neo-Orthodox movement, this becomes inseparable from an ontology of 'Christological realism' and further still, his exposure to

---

74. Moore's purpose is to oppose more recent 'transcendental arguments from truth to God' from B. Hebblethwaite and I. Markham, but I think the critique applies to Sorley and Taylor too. Moore, *Realism*, 15.

75. Long, 'The Gifford Lectures and the Scottish Personal Idealists', 395. C.D Broad is similarly critical, placing Sorley far behind Sidgwick and Moore in terms of impact on the 'mainstream' of Cambridge philosophy'. A.C. Ewing, 'Recent Developments in British Ethical Thought', in *British Philosophy in the Mid-century: A Cambridge Symposium*, ed. C. A. Mace (London: Allen and Unwin, 1957), 50.

philosophers of the analytical turn encouraged MacKinnon back into the orbit of Kant's agnosticism.

To be sure, MacKinnon *did* admire the legacy of Kant's categorical imperative in these thinkers. It is something that he takes with him as he eventually sought to articulate a rather messy moral position with reference to a dynamic understanding of the natural law tradition and a form of intuitionism. It led him to cite concrete examples in history and literature where the moral 'ought' is experienced as 'absolute' yet for all that prone to tragic misapprehension.[76] Indeed, reflection on historical and literary tragedy led MacKinnon to write about a 'surd' element which must find expression in any truly realist apprehension of history; a kind of interrogation of experience and a form of language that demands a move beyond naturalism and scientism to pose the question of transcendence.[77] What MacKinnon embraced in light of all this was not so much a moral apologetic but a moral theodicy in which the Christian claim becomes, in Niebuhr's phrase, an 'impossible possibility'. This is a path which can only be travelled by means of a kenotic self-abandonment and without any ultimate guarantee of vindication or the kind of hopeful resolution of the sort that Kant maintained (at least in *Religion*) as the key reason for embracing theism.

The analytical awakening

If Taylor and Sorley represent one pole of influence on MacKinnon, then the other must be the analytical turn in philosophy, dominant throughout his years as a student and tutor at Oxford. Swinburne provides a sweeping view of the relevant philosophical landscape:

> 'Analytic philosophy' is the somewhat misleading name given to the kind of philosophy practiced today in most of the universities of the Anglo-American world. This stream of philosophy started off in the Oxford of the 1950s; it saw the task of philosophy as analysis, clarifying the meaning of important words, and showing how they get that meaning; and this was done by studying in what circumstances it was appropriate in ordinary language to use the words. The philosopher investigated when it was right to say that something 'caused' something else, or someone 'knows' something. Metaphysics was deemed a 'meaningless' activity.[78]

---

76. I will examine this further in the final chapter.
77. *PM*, 125–35.
78. Richard Swinburne, 'The Value and Christian Roots of Analytical Philosophy of Religion', in *Faith and Philosophical Analysis: The Impact of Analytical Philosophy on the Philosophy of Religion*, ed. Harriet A. Harris and Christopher J. Insole (Aldershot, Hants; Burlington, VT: Ashgate, 2005), 8–35.

2. Beyond Kant and Back Again: Further Influences on MacKinnon 63

According to Christopher Insole's broader definition of the phenomenon, three phases can be identified in the emergence of Analytical Philosophy.[79] The first is the empiricism of Locke, Berkeley and Hume. The second is the logical positivism of Ayer and the early Wittgenstein and the logical atomism of Moore and Russell. And third is the 'post-positivist analytical period', characterized by a cautious re-engagement with formally rejected modes of metaphysics, and in some cases, heavily qualified openness to notions of transcendence. In respect to this third phase, Fergus Kerr identifies the later Wittgenstein as a figure who left wider spaces for uses of religious language, which signalled a softening of hostility to religion maintained by early advocates of the analytical turn.[80] This kind of openness coincided with a renewed confidence in the programmes of explicitly theistic analytical philosophers. In this vein, Swinburne speaks of a 'metaphysical turn' of the 1970s, which then 'gave philosophy of religion the more obvious task of expounding religious claims, clearly and coherently certainly, but with their natural metaphysical sense, investigating whether they were true, and/or whether we are justified in believing in them'.[81]

Despite the ground-shifting importance of the first phase of analytical philosophy as described by Insole, my focus is the second and third because the former had a direct and formative impact on MacKinnon, and the latter entailed commitments reflected in his project. The second phase coincided with a crucial period in his own intellectual formation as an undergraduate at Oxford in the 1930s.[82] The fact that MacKinnon was still writing about Ayer's 1934 attack on metaphysics in the 1990s suggests that the questions raised by this period remained with him until the final years of his life.[83]

In his intellectual biography of MacKinnon, Muller reports that in his early days at Oxford, Isaiah Berlin took him to a lecture by John Wisdom on the philosophy of Moore and Wittgenstein.[84] This lecture was one of a number of engagements with key figures of the analytical turn in Britain which was to prove decisive in MacKinnon's conviction that British Idealism was a spent force and that positivism represented a breakthrough intellectual achievement that would shape the agenda of philosophy and theology from that moment forward. While MacKinnon was an admirer of the achievements of the positivists, his engagement was never uncritical.

---

79. Christopher Insole, 'Political Liberalism, Analytical Philosophy of Religion and the Forgetting of History', in *Faith and Philosophical Analysis: The Impact of Analytical Philosophy on the Philosophy of Religion*, ed. Harriet A. Harris and Christopher J. Insole (Aldershot, Hants; Burlington, VT: Ashgate, 2005), 164.

80. Fergus Kerr, *Theology after Wittgenstein*, 2nd ed. (Oxford: Basil Blackwell, 1997), 145–50.

81. Swinburne, 'The Value and Christian Roots of Analytical Philosophy of Religion'.

82. Muller, 'True Service', 30–8.

83. MacKinnon, 'Ayer's Attack'.

84. Muller, 'True Service', 35–8.

MacKinnon's relationship to Insole's so-called third post-positivist period of analytical philosophy is worthy of mention too. In this regard, a further distinction between two very different types of analytical philosophy emerging in the wake of the second movement should be made, perhaps justifying reference to a third *and* fourth movement. This division was intimated above, but it should be made more explicit. The third accounts for those analytical philosophers who felt growing dissatisfaction with Vienna Circle-inspired logical positivism and a subsequent expansion of the possibilities as to the sorts of linguistic phenomenon that could be deemed meaningful. Figures that would prove important for MacKinnon in this regard are the later Wittgenstein, John Wisdom, Antony Flew and Karl Popper. More immediately in MacKinnon's context were Basil Mitchell, Austin Farrer and others within the circle of scholars at Oxford who began to meet shortly after the end of the Second World War and labelled themselves 'the metaphysicals'.[85] They focused on efforts to clarify notions of reason, revelation and morality in ways that provided direct responses to the positivists without accepting uncritically their ontological and epistemological agenda. Exchanges with figures such as John Wisdom and Antony Flew were extremely important for MacKinnon in as far as both stood firmly within the analytical tradition and yet, contra Ayer and (to some extent) Russell, found the notion of God worth discussing.

The fourth movement refers to the later appropriation of analytical tools into the philosophy of religion in more robust, confident and explicitly apologetic ways, such as that observed in the Swinburne's early work (as well as Plantinga and Wolterstorff in the United States). MacKinnon's sympathies were with the third and, it is safe to presume, not so much with the fourth. The lasting impact of his immersion in the philosophy of the second period as well as his explicit aversion of self-styled 'apologetic' projects became too dominant in this regard. One might suspect that MacKinnon found (or would find) such efforts limited in their persuasive power, to the extent that their methodologies tended to display a misplaced confidence in the possibility of systemizing theological statements and attempts to render scriptural texts philosophically plausible in a way that artificially reduced their scandal, irreducible uniqueness, literary imaginativeness and moral challenge.[86]

---

85. A representative sample of their work can be found in: Basil Mitchell, *Faith and Logic: Oxford Essays in Philosophical Theology* (London: Allen and Unwin, 1957).

86. For this reason, I suspect that MacKinnon may have – had he lived long enough – been more sympathetic with more recent figures such as Oliver Crisp and perhaps the later work of Swinburne in the 1990s and early twenty-first century, in as far as they embody a development sometimes labelled 'analytical theology'. Crisp, for example, takes the analytical approach more deeply within the traditional domain of dogmatic theology. By this I mean to say that he de-emphasizes, indeed avoids, the apologetic tone and seeks to employ some of the tools of analytical philosophy to explicate and clarify particular theological doctrines in a way that those within the Christian tradition may find coherent and illuminating. Oliver Crisp, *God Incarnate: Explorations in Christology* (London: T&T

MacKinnon was interested in the way the language of metaphysics had the habit of re-emerging chastened yet reinvigorated in the wake of those philosophical periods from which it had been forcibly purged.[87] The same was the case for notions of transcendence. Even if MacKinnon did intimate that Kant either misunderstood or underestimated what some of the metaphysical projects he had rejected were trying to achieve in their own contexts, there was no going back: Kant's purgation had changed everything.[88] In the same way notions of transcendence, at least for Christian theologians, would have to be more apophatic and more deeply cruciform than they had been under the influence of idealism. The sheer stubbornness and longevity of the metaphysical impulse and notions of transcendence is a sign for MacKinnon that an immersion in empirical history itself demands recourse to such language even if it must be subject to continued purgation and re-articulation.

The rejection of idealism in Britain

The analytical turn in British philosophy occurred in the wake of late-nineteenth-century British idealism and gained further momentum after the First World War, providing the sort of bold intellectual purgation and renewal called for by that historical moment. It was a movement that valued clarity and rigour, viewing philosophy as the handmaid of the empirical sciences and theology as an obfuscating enemy.[89] To different degrees, its adherents absorbed positions associated with the linguistic turn and logical positivism/atomism. Together they proved to be a potent intellectual force. The former focused on the way philosophical problems could be identified and potentially solved if the uses

---

Clark, 2009). That MacKinnon may have been sympathetic is suggested by the fact that similar tendencies are occasionally detectable in his own work. Connor, *Kenotic Trajectory*, 215. Reading MacKinnon's essay 'Does faith create its own objects?' provides an example. In this case, he references J.M. Creed's use of the logical distinction between synthetic and analytic statements about Jesus, judging the former to involve claims about his divinity, and the latter to pertain to aspects of his historical existence. By doing so, Creed 'gave hostages to logic' in as far as his analytical distinction created a situation in which what was being said about Jesus could not be reduced to expressions of subjective aesthetic judgement, but was rather grounded in a question of factuality that demanded historical judgements. Despite the faults MacKinnon identifies with Creed's approach, this 'initial insistence that we use methods of logical analysis to determine precisely what is involved in predicating divinity of Jesus remains significant' – or at least it was to MacKinnon in 1990. D. M. MacKinnon, 'Does Faith Create Its Own Objects?', in *Burden*, ed. John C. McDowell (London: T&T Clark, 2011), 209–22.

87. *PM*, 1–16.
88. *TT*, 31–40.
89. Frederick C. Copleston, *Contemporary Philosophy: Studies of Logical Positivism and Existentialism* (London: Burns & Oates, 1956), 26–38.

of language and its limitations were brought into focus. The latter advanced an epistemology focused on restrictive standards of verification and received impetus from the members of the Vienna Circle. Speaking of verificationism, MacKinnon observed,

> In the 1930s, the term *fact* became, in philosophical discussion, a synonym for that which verifies, confirms, or falsifies a hypothesis; the word, indeed became a label for the deliverance of observation in so far as such deliverance established or invalidated claims concerning what was the case. If, in the previous phases of this discussion, the term had had primarily ontological import, in this second phase the emphasis was epistemological.[90]

For MacKinnon, a telling expression of this latter movement came in the form of Moritz Schlick's hope 'that one day there would be no more books on philosophy but all books would be written philosophically'.[91] MacKinnon adds that for the philosophers of the linguistic turn, it was desired that

> the day of the speculative treatise would yield to that of the scientific exposition in which the expositor knew how to give precise case-value to the terms he was using, and not allow the unfamiliarity of the territory he was mapping to beguile him into supposing that he was opening the doors on to a mysterious ultimate.[92]

For the remainder of this section, I will provide an impressionistic overview of the projects of Russell, Moore, Ayer and the early Wittgenstein; key figures of MacKinnon's *Sitz im Leben*. The first two found the language of metaphysics helpful when explicating the role of analytic statements pertaining to logic and mathematics (when they wished, they could 'play the part of a metaphysician' as Copleston noted), whereas the latter two were closer to the Vienna Circle philosophers in their conviction that all such language was counter-productive. All except Moore contributed to a climate of non-realism in moral discourse.

Bertrand Russell was a convinced realist when it came to the philosophy of science, meaning that like Moore he held to the doctrine that the 'facts' about some external object are completely independent of our perception of it.[93] His commitment to realism developed over a series of stages – three according to Bostock – which includes the famous crisis brought about by Wittgenstein's

---

90. *PM*, 33–4.

91. MacKinnon, 'Does Faith Create its Own Objects?', 212.

92. Ibid., 210. As noted above, among the second period analytics, truth claims about God were ruled not so much untrue, but impossible and meaningless. That is, propositions such as 'God exists' were seen to fail rules pertaining to the meaningful use of language.

93. Bertrand Russell, 'On Verification: The Presidential Address', *Proceedings of the Aristotelian Society* 38 (1937): 6–8.

criticisms.[94] The key, however, was a deepening allegiance to atomism: a doctrine that attempted to steer a course between the idealism of philosophers such as F. H. Bradley and what Kerr describes as the evolutionism of individuals such as Nietzsche, Bergson and the American pragmatists.[95] In this vein, Russell identifies a core element of his project as follows:

> The logic which I shall advocate is atomistic, as opposed to the monistic logic of the people who more or less follow Hegel. When I say that my logic is atomistic, I mean that I share the common-sense belief that there are many separate things; I do not regard the apparent multiplicity of the world as consisting merely in phases and unreal divisions of a single indivisible reality.[96]

Mander's magisterial account of British Idealism examines the complexity and diversity of that movement that Russell was reacting against. He claims that idealists tended to hold a view that language expressed greater truthfulness as it moved from descriptions of single particulars to more and more general concepts that subsumed many related particulars.[97] In this vein, Warnock notes that Bradley

> regarded the unitary nature of reality as both the most important and the least dubitable part of his whole metaphysical account of the universe; and he meant his statement that reality was one to carry the implication, among others, that anything less than unity, such as a distinction between a person and the object of his thought, is necessarily unreal or illusory. To aim, therefore, at identifying oneself, whether with the object of one's thought or with the world in which one is living and acting, is to do no more than to aim to remove illusion, and to exist in reality. In this context self-realisation [the goal of moral striving] means … not only satisfying oneself, but actually making oneself exist. It means making oneself real instead of illusory.[98]

Russell was convinced that the fallacy driving the emergence of idealist metaphysics could be uncovered by considering common sentences. For instance, he argued that monists like Hegel, Spinoza and Bradley held as a matter of dogma that every proposition pertaining to an external object could potentially involve a fact with a

---

94. David Bostock, *Russell's Logical Atomism* (Oxford: Oxford University Press, 2012), 201–10.
95. *TAW*, 61.
96. Bertrand Russell, *Logic and Knowledge, Essays 1901-1950*, ed.Robert Charles March (London: Routledge), cited in Ibid.
97. W. J. Mander, *British Idealism: A History* (Oxford; New York: Oxford University Press, 2011), 6–7. See also Mary Warnock, *Ethics since 1900*, 2nd ed. (London: Oxford University Press, 1966), 5–6.
98. Warnock, *Ethics since 1900*, 6.

corresponding description of a quality that belongs to it.[99] That is, 'any proposition can be put into a form in which it has a subject and a predicate united by a copula', that is, a joining verb.[100] For Russell, idealists held that this structure pointed to the fact that the two parts of the sentence are related, and in being so related must share a common attribute which 'transcends' them. Typically, they start using metaphysical terms to describe the common 'third thing'; the singularity that unites the two. As they follow this logic to its inexorable limits, they give into a temptation to articulate a singular substance or an all-embracing 'Absolute'. Yet, if these sentences were analysed according to his system of mathematically inspired atomistic logic, the impulse towards monist metaphysical projects would be circumvented altogether.[101] Reliable knowledge comes from seeing things in their simplest terms, with the wider web of relationships blanked out as far as possible for the task of definition and analysis. In this way, the axiom of internal relations beloved of the idealists was rejected and MacKinnon found this move a compelling one.[102] Cell argues that for Russell

> the world ... was pictured as having a form corresponding to the 'truth function' or 'extensional' form of mathematical logic, since this logic provided the model in terms of which the atomists conceived the nature of our everyday and scientific propositions. ... The kind of world pictured is, consequently, one in which no simple entity stands in any necessary relation to any other. ... Against Idealism, the atomist believed [in a] picture of the world as an aggregate of separable things, quality and relations.[103]

For Russell, as was the case for Moore, a type of metaphysics *is* needed but it was of a radically different sort to that proposed by the idealists.[104] Russell uses

---

99. Bertrand Russell, *History of Western Philosophy*, 2nd ed. (London: Routledge, 1991), 662–4.

100. Edward Cell, *Language, Existence and God: Interpretations of Moore, Russell, Ayer, Wittgenstein, Wisdom, Oxford Philosophy, and Tillich* (Nashville, TN: Abingdon Press, 1971), 59.

101. Bostock, *Russell's Logical Atomism*, Ch 12, e-book.

102. According to Muller, Moore was the bigger influence on MacKinnon's approach to the logic of 'internal relations'. Muller, 'True Service', 44–50. This is borne out in D. M. MacKinnon, 'Aristotle's Conception of Substance', in *New Essays on Plato and Aristotle*, ed. Renford Bambrough (London: Routledge, 1965), 99–112.

103. Cell further clarifies, 'To refer to mathematical logic as 'extensional' means that the truth or falsity of any one simple proposition bears no necessary relation to the truth or falsity of any other.' Cell, *Language, Existence and God*, 58.

104. Bostock, *Russell's Logical Atomism*, 202–52. Cell states what was being offered with 'this sort of analysis was openly metaphysical. Under the leadership of Wittgenstein, the atomists formulated a theory that the simple sense-data propositions "pictured" the facts they expressed – a kind of one-to-one correspondence in which the subject of the

metaphysical language not to refer to any real object within or 'beyond' the external world, but to name the content of analytic judgements pertaining to the logical conditions necessary if we are to trust that our language captures the truth of the external world. Famously, Russell held that a kind of logic derived from demonstrable mathematical proofs provided the content for this type of metaphysics; a very different conclusion to that of Kant.[105] At the heart of this logic was the claim that every complex mathematical statement could be broken down into a strictly limited number of basic mathematical statements. Further still, what was revealed in Russell's mathematical logic was not only true for that particular domain, but for all other types of knowledge as well. The logical truths uncovered by mathematical reasoning were universal.[106]

For the atomist metaphysician, the purpose of philosophy was not found in proposing facts about the world for that was the domain of the natural and social sciences. Philosophy provided a methodology for breaking down any proposition about the world into its most simple constituent parts so that it could most economically capture the truth of the object it sought to describe. Mander states that between Russell and the idealists

> the point at issue ... was not whether we were in direct contact with reality ... but what was the correct account of its nature; whether it was something to be found by application of thought to sense, or something to be found by scraping away the distortions of thought from sense.[107]

As a result of Russell's purgation, three forms of statement were possible: (1) analytic statements which expressed logical forms derived from mathematical principles; (2) statements verifiable in some way by sense experience, and (3) statements that were meaningless.[108] Statements about God and universal

---

proposition simply named or pointed to a simple substance, and the predicate named a simple quality or relation. This simple form of proposition was preferred metaphysically, because it alone showed the form that world really had. If language is conceived by the analogy of a map, there is, allegedly, a kind of photographic map, a map that is somehow drawn without using any particular method of projection. In this way philosophy serves the purpose of enabling us to see more clearly the nature of knowledge about the world.' Cell, *Language, Existence and God*, 57.

105. Ibid.

106. Cell: 'The atomists reasoned that since all these [complex mathematical] forms are reducible to a few basic forms then all statements of our language – or at least all significant rational statements – must be reducible to statements having these basic forms.' Cell, *Language, Existence and God*, 57.

107. Mander, *British Idealism: A History*, 397.

108. Elizabeth Burns, 'Transforming Metaphysics? Revisioning Christianity in the Light of Analytical Philosophy', in *Faith and Philosophical Analysis: The Impact of Analytical Philosophy on the Philosophy of Religion*, ed. Harriet Harris and Christopher Insole

moral truths were relegated to this latter category; observations about practical moral convictions find a place in the second, although Russell joins his student Ayer in denying that there is anything like falsifiable ethical *knowledge*. Schultz notes that

> excepting a relatively brief period (roughly 1894–1913) when he became a Hegelian under McTaggert's influence, a Platonic realist, and then an adherent of Moore's view ... Russell cleaved to the Humean belief in reason as the slave of the passions – 'outside human desire there is no moral standard', nor any action for that matter.[109]

Pigden adds that he 'combined an emotivist analysis of "good" and "bad" with a consequentialist/relativist reading of "ought" and "right"'.[110] Russell maintained a long-running dialogue with G. E. Moore, accepting his critique of naturalism but rejecting his notion of the 'good'.[111] Moore's philosophical notoriety began in 1903 with a paper entitled 'The Refutation of Idealism' and, like MacKinnon, Bishop Butler's aphorism that 'everything is what it is and not another thing' was evoked as a shorthand indication of this commitment.[112] Idealism was seen as collapsing analytic and synthetic; the structures of perception and the world itself, and this form of realism sought to preserve the independence, objectivity and integrity of the known object over and against the knower. MacKinnon credited Moore as having a definitive impact on his thought:

> Moore made it possible for me to be a realist; his laborious arguments concerning the status and nature of objects of perception made it clear that, whatever perceiving was, it was a finding rather than a fashioning. Further, truth was not to be identified with an internally coherent whole of judgements; it resided in the correspondence of proposition and fact. Thinking had a reference beyond

---

(Aldershot, Hants; Burlington, VT: Ashgate, 2005), 46–9. See also Mitchell, *Faith and Logic: Oxford Essays in Philosophical Theology*, 3.

109. Bart Schultz, 'Bertrand Russell in Ethics and Politics', *Ethics* 102, no. 3 (1992): 597. Citing Russell's *Why I am not a Christian*, Pigden notes that Russell's dominant view from 1913 was a form of emotivism, and hence of non-cognitivism. There were, however, two significant 'wobbles'. In 1922 he proposed a version of the error theory, anticipating J. L. Mackie by over twenty years. And in 1954 in *Human Society in Ethics and Politics*, he endeavoured to inject a little objectivity into ethics by developing a form of naturalism, [later] ...reverting to the emotivism of 1935.' Charles Pigden, 'Russell's Moral Philosophy', in *The Stanford Encyclopedia of Philosophy*, ed. Zalta Edward (2014). https://plato.stanford.edu/entries/russell-moral/.

110. Pigden, 'Russell's Moral Philosophy'.

111. Tom Baldwin, 'George Edward Moore', in *Stanford Encyclopedia of Philosophy*, ed. Edward Zalta (2010). https://plato.stanford.edu/entries/moore/.

112. Cell, *Language, Existence and God*, 27.

itself; even if it was hard to speak of any sort of 'sufficient reason' in things, yet things were somehow there to come to terms with. They might lack any sort of connectedness; it might even be possible to speak of being per se as intelligible. Yet for the logical atomist, there were things with which men were coming to terms; the world was not simply an expression of their immanent rationality, but something given.[113]

Working from these convictions, Moore's approach to the task of philosophy was to raise all the questions he could pertaining to the precise meaning and reasons for believing particular statements of fact, confident that clarity could be achieved through his method of analysis and definition.[114] Like Russell and Ayer, he worked on the basis of a sharp distinction between analytic and synthetic statements.[115] In as far as Moore transposed this distinction into the linguistic realm, his analysis of statements took place by means of the task of articulating definitions, in which a distinction was made between concepts that could not be broken down into further component parts and those that could. Cell observes that for Moore, 'a definition can be given only of complex things, and is possible logically only if there are non-complex elements – the "parts" to be enumerated'.[116] Thus, in the process of definition the philosopher will identify the different properties and qualities of concepts and their relationships and what will emerge is a distinction between complex and non-complex concepts. There are clear limits to definition here, in that non-complex words cannot be defined; their meaning is discerned in looking at the way they are habitually applied in concrete settings of language use.[117]

It would be false to see a form of linguistic reductionism as *the* defining feature of Moore's approach. Unlike some of the positivists who followed, Moore employed a metaphysical register in as far as he maintained that the meaning of a complex concept may be clarified in an articulation of its components parts, yet it is not entirely reducible to those component parts. That Moore's epistemology demanded something rather more nuanced than a simple exercise in linguistic reductionism or a rejection of metaphysics *tout court* and this is carried over to his ethical thought.[118] Turning to *Principia Ethica*, Moore asks,

---

113. *BT*, 63.
114. Cell, *Language, Existence and God*, 27.
115. Charles Parsons, 'The Transcendental Aesthetic', in *The Cambridge Companion to Kant*, ed. Paul Guyer (Cambridge: Cambridge University Press, 1999), 74–6.
116. Cell, *Language, Existence and God*, 33.
117. Baldwin, 'George Edward Moore'.
118. In her analysis of Moore, Coliva states that one of the key characteristics of his common-sense approach was to 'oppose those who, in doing philosophy, deny the existence, or the possibility of knowing that there are physical objects, the self with its own mental states, other minds, space and time. A philosopher of common sense holds that all these theses are not only paradoxical, but altogether *false*. For, if they were true, it would then be

What, then, is to be understood by metaphysical? I use the term ... in opposition to natural. I call those philosophers pre-eminently metaphysical who have recognised most clearly that not everything which *is* is a natural object. Metaphysicians have, therefore, the great merit of insisting that our knowledge is not confined to the things which we can touch and see and feel. They have always been much occupied, not only with that other class of natural objects which consists in mental facts, but also with the class of objects or properties of objects, which certainly do not exist in time, are not therefore parts of Nature, and which, in fact, do not *exist* at all. To this class, as I have said, belongs what we mean by the adjective good. It is not *goodness*, but only the things or qualities which are good, which can exist in time – can have duration, and begin and cease to exist – can be objects of *perception*.[119]

Moore commits to a metaphysical notion of the good yet finds both 'naturalists' and 'metaphysicians' guilty of the naturalistic fallacy. Both seek to 'explain the type of ethical truths by supposing it identical with the type of scientific law'.[120] 'The metaphysicians think that there is some absolute necessity in the laws, derivable from the nature of the universe, while the naturalists do not', yet both share the error of holding that the good is something to be analysed or defined in terms of something non-ethical.[121] For Moore, linguistic analysis is a means to an end; when applied to the term 'good' it purges mistakes in definition yet it also reveals a distinctively ethical truth.[122] Not so with Ayer.

Ayer saw himself following Russell in the broad sweep of the analytical tradition, but he wanted an even more rigorous form of reductionism, rejecting Moore's notion of the good out-of-hand, calling it 'absolutism'.[123] MacKinnon noted that it was Russell's 'more technical work on the foundation of mathematics

---

impossible, in his view, to formulate all the propositions we commonly use in everyday life, that are either about an external world, or about one's own and other's bodies and minds, or about space and time.' Annalisa Coliva, *Moore and Wittgenstein: Scepticism, Certainty, and Common Sense*, History of analytic philosophy (Houndmills, Basingstoke, Hampshire; New York: Palgrave Macmillan, 2010), 13.

119. Moore, *Principia Ethica*, 161.
120. Ibid., 124.
121. Ibid., 124–5. Warnock doubts that Moore is being entirely fair to the ethical traditions of Kant, Spinoza and Hegel. Warnock, *Ethics since 1900*, 32.
122. Warnock, *Ethics since 1900*, 63.
123. Ibid., 58. In his paper entitled 'Demonstration of the impossibility of metaphysics', Ayer states that his purpose is to 'prove that any attempt to describe the nature or even to assert the existence of something lying beyond the reach of empirical observation must consist in the enunciation of pseudo-propositions, a pseudo-proposition being a series of words that may seem to have the structure of a sentence but it is in fact meaningless. I call this a demonstration of the impossibility of metaphysics because I define a metaphysical enquiry as an enquiry into the nature of the reality underlying or transcending the

2. Beyond Kant and Back Again: Further Influences on MacKinnon

that Ayer employed to give greater rigour and plausibility to Mill's conception of material things as constellations of "permanent possibilities of sensation".[124] Rejecting Russell's atomist metaphysic under the influence of the Vienna Circle, Ayer adopted the typology mentioned above, which stipulated three types of possible statement for capturing 'facts'. The notion of 'God' as a nameable object was declared meaningless. He then set down a criterion for what might count as a truthful sentence:

> In every case where we have a series of words which seems to be a good grammatical sentence, and we wish to discover whether it really makes sense i.e. whether it expresses a genuine proposition – we must consider what are the circumstances in which the proposition apparently expressed would be called true or false: what difference in the world its truth or falsity would entail.[125]

For Ayer, a truthful sentence is one where the conditions for the determination of its truth or falsity can be clearly stated with the tools of the 'special sciences'. All other sentences are at best fodder for psychological analysis or aesthetic expression. It is the case that some non-empirically verifiable statements in the realm of morality, religion and aesthetics may be more or less expressive and useful than others, but nevertheless, they cannot be considered true or false in any meaningful sense. The poet, according to Ayer realizes this, but the metaphysician and the theologian only succeed in 'produc[ing] plain nonsense in the attempt to give straightforward information'.[126] A person who says that God exists is merely describing a private experience rather than naming any object.[127] In this way, Ayer is making strong truth claims about the inability of certain modes of discourse to produce truth claims, as Ewing notes,

> That ethical judgements are not objectively true [for Ayer] is a judgement that itself claims objective truth and theoretical, not practical justification. It is vindicated, if at all, by the standards of truth, and not by rhetoric or congruity with one's emotional needs, and to its truth practical utility is irrelevant.[128]

Ayer saw himself as having submitted to the purgation of Kant's *Critique of Pure Reason*.[129] At the same time, he was heavily influenced by the critiques of

---

phenomena which the special sciences are content to study.' A. J. Ayer, 'Demonstration of the Impossibility of Metaphysics', *Mind*, no. 171 (1934): 336.
    124. MacKinnon, 'Ayer's Attack', 52.
    125. Ayer, 'Demonstration of the Impossibility of Metaphysics', 338.
    126. A. J. Ayer, 'The Genesis of Metaphysics', *Analysis*, no. 4 (1934): 4.
    127. Ayer, 'Verification and Experience', *Proceedings of the Aristotelian Society* 37, no. 1 (1936): 151.
    128. Ewing, 'Recent Developments in British Ethical Thought', 65–6.
    129. Muller, 'True Service', 51–3. MacKinnon argued that Ayer 'was much nearer to Kant than he realized in as much as the notion of verifiability in principle came in practice

Kant which emerged from the Vienna Circle such as Moritz Schlick, in as far as the latter rejected Kant's notion of the synthetic *a priori* and any residue of realist metaphysics thought to be embedded therein (especially in his moral philosophy).[130] This formed the basis on which the early Wittgenstein and Ayer would distance themselves from the metaphysical dimensions of Moore and Russell. What was manifest here was a transition by which the positivist project of reductionism was moving from a focus on ontology to a focus on epistemology. Referring to Russell, MacKinnon noted that

> [The 'reductionist' method] sought to reduce the number of independent entities involved in the description of the world by defining through a very subtle method of definition, the relatively unfamiliar in favour of the familiar. 'Reductionism' so conceived was an ontological program concerned to give an inventory of the irreducible elements of the world; its earliest form was that of logical atomism. ... But with logical positivism 'reductionism' was virtually re-defined as an epistemological program, aimed at completing the work of Ernest Mach in formulating a descriptive, radically empiricist conception of science, seeking to eliminate as metaphysical non-sense from scientific theories, any assumption of the unobservable.[131]

The last major figure of the positivist 'second' period of analytical philosophy is the early Wittgenstein.[132] With the *Tractatus*, 'logical atomism reached its fullest and most rigorous expression'.[133] Indeed, Wittgenstein took the linguistic turn to a new level, breaking down the analytic-synthetic distinction that formally separated the logical conditions that make language possible from actual language usage.[134] Cell observes that for Wittgenstein, 'a proposition expressed or pictures a fact, and what is expressed by a proposition cannot be the subject of a proposition'

---

very near to Kant's 'experience in general'. Even so, it 'cannot be denied that Kant had a far greater sympathy with the goals the transcendent metaphysician sought to attain'. MacKinnon, 'Ayer's Attack', 51.

130. 'Ayer's Attack', 51. MacKinnon goes on to comment: 'Where however Ayer's fundamental quarrel with Kant lay only becomes clear when close attention is paid to their divergence of the understanding of necessary truth. If they enjoyed a general measure of agreement in their attitudes to transcendent metaphysics, unlike Kant, Ayer had no room for the transcendentally a priori: this even though in Kant's understanding of our knowledge of the external world, a strong vein of phenomenalism is discernible, and it is well known how much of his energies Ayer devoted in his early years to testing the phenomenalist programme to destruction, eager if he could by its means rid our commerce with the world around us of any temptation towards admitting that which was unobservable in principle.'

131. MacKinnon, 'Ayer's Attack', 53–4.

132. *TAW*, 61–70.

133. Cell, *Language, Existence and God*, 117.

134. *TAW*, 62–4.

and also that 'there are no facts about facts for a proposition to picture'.[135] At this point, Wittgenstein was engaged in a project riven with paradox, whereby he was concerned to make all sorts of propositions about language use, but with these constituting a kind of scaffolding which one must mount, only to push away once one begins to use language correctly.[136] In other words, the philosopher must engage in a lot of strictly meaningless statements – statements that do not represent empirical facts in the world – so that meaningful statements can be identified and put into use.[137] Only statements about particular states of affairs in the physical world can meet this criterion; a position that makes moral theorizing redundant, yet turns the whole task of describing the way people use language into a *type* of ethical reflection. I will return to MacKinnon's interaction with Wittgenstein's legacy in Chapter 5.

Options for the theologian in light of the analytical turn

What were the options for theists in light of the rise of hostile forms of analytic philosophy in their midst? In the wake of the apparent inability to name God meaningfully, non-cognitive, non-realist approaches to God such as that of Don Cupitt and D. Z. Phillips followed.[138] Rejecting 'traditional' theism, they nevertheless saw religion as providing a context for moral formation, communal belonging and life-enhancing aesthetics. Another trajectory would follow Tillich in effectively ignoring the positivists, drawing on Heidegger's notion of being and the wider existentialist trajectory to refigure notions of theism and revelation. Yet another option was to place oneself within the Barthian trajectory, asserting the independence of the Christian notion of God from the metaphysics of 'onto-theology' and thus claiming its immunity from the latter's decline.[139] One last option was mentioned above in terms of a 'fourth period' of the analytical turn, which really amounted to a neo-Calvinist effort to revive apologetic philosophical theology from the margins of the analytical tradition.

The influence of the hostile second period of analytical philosophy drove MacKinnon to embrace (at least) two conclusions. The first was noted in Chapter

---

135. Cell, *Language, Existence and God*, 117.
136. Cora Diamond, 'Throwing Away the Ladder', *Philosophy* 63, no. 243 (1988): 20–6.
137. Cell, *Language, Existence and God*, 117.
138. D.Z. Phillips rejects the categorization on Wittgensteinian grounds, but Cupitt embraces it. MacKinnon criticized the former on the issue: 'For all his indebtedness to Wittgenstein, Wisdom is alert, in ways in which some writers, for example Mr D.Z. Phillips in his recent, very interesting book, The Concept of Prayer, manifestly are not, to the crucial importance for the philosopher or reckoning with what does and with what does not exist.' *BT*, 223. I have found Moore's reflection on 'Realism and the Christian Faith after Wittgenstein' most helpful in what follows. Moore, *Realism*, 73–92.
139. *BT*, 220.

1: while theology can never do without the resources and critiques of philosophy, it involves a distinctive philosophical position of its own and must not allow itself to be entirely absorbed into an alternative programme, or be tempted by the illusion that such a move could provide a methodology or content to secure its ultimate coherence.[140] At the same time, theologians should also be aware of an equally dangerous temptation to ignore the resources and provocations of philosophy, seeking refuge in revelatory positivism or ecclesiastical fundamentalism.[141]

Another significant influence wrought by the second period analytical philosophers on MacKinnon was a strengthening of the apophatic commitment that had already been gleaned from Kant. The analytical turn further marginalized theology within the academy, yet it also provided therapeutic tools for avoiding theological excess and promoting the clarity of theological language.[142] MacKinnon accepted the thrust of the positivist's rejection of idealism and appreciated the purgative potential of atheism.[143] He wrote that 'somehow, although this atheism (i.e. of the positivists) challenged and unsettled me, it seemed a more honest and somehow less corrupting a thing than the monistic insistence on, for instance, the rational necessity of evil to the articulation of the good'.[144] He added that 'it may be that this seriousness will take the form of saying that, in the last resort, atheism may be less hardly reconcilable with faith than certain sorts of idealism, even if that atheism is a dialectical moment, for some at least, in the argument of faith'.[145]

It seems that MacKinnon's exposure to early analytic philosophy confirmed what had already been set in train with his receptivity to Kant's agnosticism. At the same time, it had not entirely closed the route to a Kantian-inspired opportunity for a theological restatement, buoyed by the perennial questions that the moral dimension of human experience seemed to provoke. MacKinnon found positivist critiques of idealism convincing, yet he also worried that their deployment of the criterion of verifiability and reductionist approaches to language led to impoverished accounts of such phenomena as paradox, metaphor and analogy, along with a marginalization of aesthetic, moral and religious discourse that, in

---

140. MacKinnon, 'Kant's Agnosticism', 35–40. Moore has also noted this. Moore, *Realism*, 131–2.

141. This is why MacKinnon steered clear of Charles Gore's Anglo-Catholic appropriation of ecclesiologies that spoke of 'continuing incarnation' in a way that lacked critical edge and risked triumphalism. Connor, *Kenotic Trajectory*, 91–5.

142. D. M. MacKinnon, *Philosophy and the Burden of Theological Honesty: A Donald MacKinnon Reader*, ed. John C. McDowell (London: T & T Clark, 2011), 5–8.

143. With the positivists he held that 'the world is something that stands over and against the thinking, perceiving subject; it is something with which we must come to terms, not something that can be absorbed within the free play of our intellect. It is something given.' Muller, 'True Service', 45–50.

144. *BT*, 63.

145. Ibid., 65.

the end, undermined realism.[146] He is convinced that if these phenomena are taken seriously, meaning 'on their own terms' or, in trope favoured by MacKinnon, according to their peculiar 'system of projection' then a metaphysical impulse will tentatively re-emerge and await articulation.[147]

A direct engagement with the limitations of positivism is evident in MacKinnon's 1990 lecture pertaining to Ayer's attack on metaphysics, to which I referred above. It is also evident in his much earlier contribution to a series of presentations at the Aristotelian Society entitled 'Verification', something to which Russell, Ayer, Berlin and Wisdom also contributed. In the 1990 lecture, it is clear that MacKinnon can find much to praise in Ayer's legacy. He states that 'it is in the area of logical necessity that the work which Ayer presented the world in his Logic, Truth and Language in 1936 made its most important contribution'.[148] Although he found his execution of the principle too narrow, MacKinnon was sympathetic to Ayer's attempt to limit the sorts of sentences that can be said to refer to facts by 'specify[ing] the circumstances which would confirm or discredit the proposition in question'.[149] This sensibility was appropriated by MacKinnon and is most evident in his insistence on maintaining historical factuality at the basis of Christological claims in opposition to the subjectivizing trends of British modernist theology.[150]

As noted above, Ayer was adamant that the metaphysical project, whether in its classical form or in its revised Kantian form was doomed, and MacKinnon showed sympathy to the extent that the 'metaphysical impulse seeks to come to rest in that which cannot be rejected or modified, in that which is suffused with its own self-sufficiency in that which is ontologically self-authenticating'.[151] There is no doubt for MacKinnon that such ways of speaking can lead to intellectual stagnation and obstinacy in the face of new empirical or logical developments. This was not only the case when it came to the religiously committed. MacKinnon also notes the way in which Ayer was mindful that empiricists of the preceding generation, such as Cook Wilson, had become resistant to developments in non-Euclidean geometry because of a misplaced metaphysical commitment.[152]

MacKinnon saw Ayer as providing a welcome therapy, yet a critical response was called for. Indeed, he wondered whether Ayer really understood 'the impulses that tempted men of genius into such elaborate essays in non-sense'.[153] Ayer suffered from empiricism's tendency to imprison at the same time as it liberated; a tendency noted in reference to MacKinnon's reflections on J. S. Mill's biography in Chapter 1. Yet MacKinnon also referred to figures such as Collingwood, Popper

---

146. Ibid., 238.
147. *ET*, 70–89.
148. MacKinnon, 'Ayer's Attack', 58.
149. Ibid., 49.
150. *BT*, 66–71.
151. MacKinnon, 'Ayer's Attack', 53.
152. Ibid., 53–5.
153. Ibid., 49.

and Braithwaite in as far as their philosophical forays seem to undermine the adequacy of Ayer's approach. Concerning Collingwood, MacKinnon invoked his explorations as to the nature and problems of historical study, suggesting that had Ayer engaged with them fully, he might have realized the need for an expansion of the sort of linguistic phenomenon he was willing to admit as truth-bearing.[154] In the same way, Popper was invoked to the extent that his criticism of the principle of verification entailed dramatic divergence from the legacy of the Vienna Circle. The dependence of the scientific method on a capacity to put forward initially unverifiable, creative and speculative hypotheses suggests that the approach so admired by Ayer requires more latitude to better account for the meaningfulness of speculative and imaginative language forms. In a similar vein, MacKinnon mentions Braithwaite's appreciation literature's capacity to capture facts and convey truths in ways that sometimes surpass that managed by philosophers.

The heart of the problem that MacKinnon identified is the adequacy of the moral thought emerging from the analytical 'stable', where utilitarianism often emerged from emotivist convictions, to supply a workable practical philosophy.[155] Cavell captures this point in a discussion of Sidgwick, whose project was something of a precedent to the sort of moral philosophy that was to gain ascendency in the wake of the analytical turn:

> Sidgwick says that '[his] treatment of the subject is, in a sense, more practical than that of many moralists, since …[he is] occupied from the first to the last in considering how conclusions are to be rationally reached in the familiar matter of our common daily life and practice' (p. vi), but he goes on to caution us, in a way which is very sympathetic to contemporary 'analytical' writers in the subject, as follows: 'My immediate object – to invert Aristotle's phrase – is not Practice but Knowledge. I have thought that the predominance in the minds of moralists of a desire to edify has impeded the real progress of ethical science: and that this would be benefitted by an application to it of the same disinterested curiosity to which we chiefly owe to the great discoveries of physics.'[156]

---

154. In a tribute to MacKinnon, Steiner speaks of his 'historicism', which 'made him a distant heir to Dilthey, but an immediate heir of Collingwood. Thus one of the ways into Donald's spirit is to rethink and restudy his writings on Collingwood, and especially – at the crucial importance of understanding Collingwood's vision of history' Steiner, 'Tribute to Donald MacKinnon', 3. A. E. Taylor also informs MacKinnon's discomfort with Ayer's project. MacKinnon cites Taylor's article 'The Right and the Good' in which the latter cites several historical scenarios to furnish a critique of the emotivist position. *SET*, 243–4.

155. In this respect, MacKinnon participated in a more general disenchantment in Oxford among some students of the 'second period', described aptly by Warnock. Warnock, *Ethics since 1900*, 84–99. A damning – if unsubstantiated – assessment of the moral and political implications of positivism from MacKinnon appears in one of his many book reviews: MacKinnon, 'Religion and Philosophy by W.G. de Burgh [Book Review]', 228–9.

156. Cavell, *Claim of Reason*, 251.

There was a commitment to immersion in concrete particularity, but in a way that excluded the particularity of the moralist: 'Disinterested curiosity' looks outward to external phenomena, but never 'turns within' as the philosophical therapist demands. Russell certainly escaped the full force of this charge by his personal and passionate forays into contemporary ethical problems, and one can only presume that MacKinnon's lack of engagement with these writings came down to a 'Kantian inoculation' against any recourse to emotivism. It was Ayer's simple utilitarianism, however, which seemed to venture nothing bolder than prosaic prescriptions for increases of human satisfaction, which captured like nothing else the limits of the analytical turn as a source of illumination for moral philosophy. Where Ayer 'failed most signally was in his allowing a proper place for the subject to whom that last word [i.e. of empirical fact] had to be spoken. He failed to see that the sort of intellectual self-criticism he practices himself as well as advocated belonged to the biography of a lively, suffering, human being.'[157] There is an intuition here shared by Basil Mitchell and Mary Warnock, who articulated dissent against the pretensions of the narrowed scope of such utilitarianism, as well as that of post-Kantian deontology for analogous reasons. Both approaches needed to be supplementation by 'thicker descriptions'. Mitchell notes,

> To look properly at evil and human suffering is almost insuperably difficult, but there is, however, something in the serious attempt to look compassionately at human things which automatically suggests that 'there is more than this'. This 'there is more than this', if it is not to be corrupted by some sort of quasi-theological finality, must remain a very tiny spark of insight, something with, as it were, a metaphysical position, but no metaphysical form. But it seems to me that the spark is real, and that great art is evidence of its reality.[158]

MacKinnon perceived that the sort of utilitarian ethics arising in tandem with the analytical turn had become tainted by a reductionism that resulted in an all too 'thin' account of the moral actor, as well as an oversimplification which bracketed out elements of the complex historical and cultural web in which moral problems arose. In this vein, MacKinnon was fond of repeating Butler's aphorism that the great virtue of the utilitarian, benevolence, 'is the whole of virtue *only* within the limits set by the claims of justice and veracity'.[159] He went on to argue that

> the utilitarian who says that benevolence is the whole of virtue, is ironing out the actual complexity of human nature in the interest of a principle for which he claims an almost metaphysical universality and necessity; while the

---

157. MacKinnon, 'Ayer's Attack', 61.
158. Basil Mitchell, *Morality Religious and Secular: The Dilemma of The Traditional Conscience*, Gifford Lectures (University of Glasgow): 1974–1975 (Oxford, Clarendon Press, 1980), 67.
159. MacKinnon, 'Kant's Influence on British Theology', 348.

metaphysician is distracted from the familiar effort to follow conscience by his conviction that the place of morality in the scheme of things must first be shown him. If the utilitarian argues for the sovereignty over our inherently complex nature of a principle of benevolence which is too narrow for that nature's manifold diversity, the metaphysically minded moralist is too inclined to flee from the acknowledgement of that nature's claims upon him as something which supplies its own justification.[160]

Together with Pritchard, MacKinnon saw within positivist-inspired utilitarianism the spectre of a serious 'impoverishment' and intuitionism as supplying a potential counterweight.[161] I will return to these dimensions of MacKinnon's moral thought in the final chapter. For now, the focus must shift to Christology, for it is here where MacKinnon sought to apply the insights he had gained from Kant, Taylor and Sorley, and the purgative challenge of the analytical turn.

---

160. MacKinnon, 'Ethical Intuition', 105.

161. *SET*, 2–11. MacKinnon discusses the intuitionism of Ross and Pritchard while making some creative conceptual links with Berlin and Butler. MacKinnon, 'Ethical Intuition', 99–115.

Chapter 3

MACKINNON'S MORAL CHRISTOLOGY

Introduction

The aim of the previous chapter was to document the key intellectual forces that left a lasting impression on MacKinnon: the theistic, morally focused, constructive and apologetic approaches of Taylor and Sorley were placed alongside the purgative and iconoclastic voices of early analytic philosophy. MacKinnon found lessons for the borderlands theologian in both and set them up in something of a dialectical relationship. I now want to continue the exploration by shifting focus to MacKinnon's Christological writings, in the knowledge that the questions posed and the resources offered by these key dialogue partners were decisive.

MacKinnon once wrote, 'Christology … is the name of something that sets in motion, and keeps in restless activity, the whole work of the characteristically Christian theologian.'[1] He goes on to admit that he shares with 'the philosopher' distaste at the way a preoccupation with the question of faith can

> infect disinterestedness with the *parti pris* attitudes of apologetics. Yet [he continues] it is the case that while increasingly both this self-knowledge and a deepening distrust of the ecclesiastical *Apparat* lead me to be mistrustful of a very great deal I have enjoyed, yes enjoyed, in the world of the Christian religion and be aware that I must surely come equally to distrust a great deal more, the domination of the *mysterium Christi* deepens its almost obsessive sovereignty over my mind.

In this chapter I will outline key features of MacKinnon's understanding of the significance of the person of Jesus through three interwoven dimensions.

First is the way he saw any account of the meaning of Jesus's death and resurrection as opening the perennial dilemma pertaining to the unity of the human and divine in Jesus, as well as the relatively modern question of the relationship between the 'Jesus of history' and the 'Christ of faith'. The typical locus for the discussion of these tensions is the doctrine of the Trinity, and this is no different in MacKinnon's case.

1. *BT*, 56.

Second is the way in which MacKinnon's Christology relates to his wider philosophical commitments. His insistence on a form of philosophical and theological realism will be most pertinent.[2]

Third, I will focus on the way in which MacKinnon's Christology interacts with his therapeutic project generally and his forays into moral philosophy more specifically. Important here will be MacKinnon's approach to such themes as divine freedom, soteriology and theodicy as important categories for the explication of the incarnation. Divine freedom involves consideration of motive, action and personhood of God, specifically in terms of a 'kenotic trajectory' within the immanent Trinity and also within the historic journey of Christ from Galilee to Jerusalem. Soteriology involves questions pertaining to the relationship between the work of Christ and humanity's righteousness or lack thereof, while theodicy involves the justification of God's righteousness in the midst of the waste and tragedy of history. That all are implicitly or explicitly enmeshed in notions of the *good* and are thus quintessentially *moral* ways of speaking is not lost on MacKinnon. Christology becomes another way of exploring his overall commitment to moral realism, and yet he differentiated himself from others who took a similar line around the same time, by pairing a focus on the 'moral' content of revelation with a renewed affirmation of the notion of 'substance'.

In explicating these three points, it will become obvious that MacKinnon did not offer a fully worked-through doctrine of the incarnation, but rather a series of critical engagements which may provide useful prolegomena to, or purgation of, such projects. Again, the method is primarily therapeutic. This is something Surin noted when he wrote that

> MacKinnon does not have anything amounting to an elaborate and comprehensive 'doctrine' of the Incarnation. Rather he provides the reader with a series of clues which point to those features that would have to be present in any account faithful to the Gospel narratives and the Christological traditions of the Church. But no attempt is made to press these clues into any kind of systematic framework.[3]

It will also be apparent that he was a mediating figure, working in-between a range of different theological options that became prominent throughout the mid-twentieth century while not fully subscribing to any one of them.

For instance, MacKinnon was comfortable enough with the continuing legacy of nineteenth-century historical critical study of the New Testament to acknowledge the unavoidability of a distinction between the 'Christ of faith'

---

2. Kenneth Surin, 'Some Aspects of the "Grammar" of "Incarnation" and "Kenosis": Reflections Prompted by the Writings of Donald MacKinnon', in *Christ, Ethics and Tragedy: Essays in Honour of Donald MacKinnon*, ed. Kenneth Surin (Cambridge: Cambridge University Press, 1989), 95.

3. Ibid., 93.

and the 'Jesus of history'.[4] Simultaneously, MacKinnon admired early and mid-twentieth-century voices such as P. T. Forsyth, E. C. Hoskyns and J. Moltmann respectively, who, despite the significant differences in the context and content of their work, made the point that one 'side' cannot be fully expressed without the other. They opposed approaches that opted for either rationalistic-historical or subjectivist reductionism. Relatedly, and along with theological liberals and modernists of various types, he was comfortable to apply the notion of 'myth' to the New Testament and creeds. It was a way of making space for an imaginative idiom that ranged beyond minimalist notions of factuality as recognized in so much of the British post-Enlightenment intellectual milieu.[5] Unlike many within the (broadly conceived) modernist movement within the twentieth-century British theology, however, he was unwilling to see mythological language as automatically undermining a serious historical sensibility.[6] Neither did he accept the argument associated with Kierkegaard and Bultmann alike that the empirical historicity of the person of Jesus could or should be downgraded to something less than an indispensable warrant for faith.[7] It is not acceptable to replace the role of historical realism with notions of *kerugma* or to see the New Testament as a series of largely

---

4. *TT*, 145–55.

5. MacKinnon spoke of incarnational theology as 'infected with mythology', which is to say that it is 'a product of an obstinate, hardly dissoluble marriage of the metaphysical and the concretely descriptive'. *BT*, 115. He discussed the notion of Jesus's 'descent' from heaven as 'myth'. Brian Hebblethwaite, *The Incarnation: Collected Essays in Christology* (Cambridge: Cambridge University Press, 1987), 138. MacKinnon also wrote of the doctrine of the incarnation as drawing on a 'crudely mythological idiom, [yet continues to insist that] it suggests not only an event in time but a movement in space. In the so-called 'Nicene Creed' the daunting obscurity of the homoousion is followed by [a] statement that is even more dauntingly mythological, suggestive indeed of the *deus ex machina*, resonant with the theological emphasis so eloquently trounced by the late Professor C.E. Raven, which treats the created universe as no more than the stage-set for the drama of redemption: "Who for us men and for our salvation came down from heaven". Certainly we did not need Rudolf Bultmann to stress the brash, vulgar crudity of the images, or to remind us that such confession is only unforced on the lips of men and women living in a pre-Copernican world. Yet is not such language indispensable in that without it the underlying conviction which arguably the Chalcedonian definition seeks clumsily enough to demythologise would go unformulated?.' Additionally, MacKinnon noted that ontological idioms are an inevitable companion to 'true myth': 'Such explanation is not intended to absorb, and render superfluous, the more haunting and appealing idiom of myth, but to complement and discipline it.' *TT*, 175–6. Cf. D. M. MacKinnon, 'Reflections on Donald Baillie's Treatment of the Atonement', in *Christ, Church and Society: Essays on John Baillie and Donald Baillie*, ed. David Fergusson (Edinburgh: T&T Clark, 1993), 116.

6. *BT*, 97–100.

7. Ibid., 121–8. And D. M. MacKinnon, 'History and Eschatology', *Journal of Theological Studies* 9 (1958): 205–8.

fictional theological or mythical forms which nonetheless 'speak' to the existential conditions of the modern individual in ways that, in themselves, warrant the continued existence of the Church.[8]

For MacKinnon, adopting a rigorously historical approach to the person of Jesus can open up greater avenues for appreciating his theological and existential significance, while *at the same time* allowing weight to be given to the sheer cultural distance between the eras of authorship and contemporary reception in addition to the sheer difficulty of recovering historical facts and shared meanings over such a span.[9] Thus, against movements of liberal theology associated with the influence of figures such as Bultmann, or those contemporaneous with MacKinnon such as Macquarrie or the contributors to Hick's '*Myth of God Incarnate*' collection, MacKinnon sided with what could be broadly described as a Barthian trajectory, fuelled by contemporaneous trends in New Testament studies that had moved beyond the either/or debate between the rationalist-historical and the kerygmatic approaches.[10] In the Barthian trajectory, an uncompromising revelatory idiom is adopted to preserve the possibility of a realist Christology, characterized by an encounter with a particular fact-event and an absolute claim objectively conceived, that nonetheless demands purgation of every notion of 'objectivity'. The content of Christology is in no way derived from or dependent upon subjective intellectual or intuitive faculties, nor is it necessarily limited *a priori* by the philosophical presuppositions underpinning 'mainstream' empirical historiography.[11]

While MacKinnon would go on to speak in very different tones about the problem of metaphysics, he did take Barth, against Bultmann, as having emerged as 'a most powerful champion of the classical Catholic Christology, with its ontological apparatus of substance, essence, nature, etc.', accepting these

---

8. MacKinnon's stinging review of Macquarrie's work on existentialism is pertinent here. D. M. MacKinnon, 'Studies in Christian Existentialism (Book Review)', *Journal of Theological Studies*, no. xviiii (1967): 294–5.

9. G. W. H. Lampe, D. M. MacKinnon, and W. E. Purcell, *The Resurrection: A Dialogue Arising from Broadcasts by G.W.H. Lampe and D.M. MacKinnon* (London: Mowbray, 1966), 78.

10. Bishop Connop Thirlwall helpfully, I think, characterized the liberal Protestant doctrine of the incarnation: '[Christ's] human person might be invested with ideal attributes, independent of its historical reality, but equally suited to the purpose of an example; if indeed a mode of influence which was adapted to the nonage of the world, was any longer needed or useful in the present period of its education. But that which, in such a system, He cannot be, is a Teacher of superhuman authority. His sayings may retain their value, so far as they commend themselves to the reason and conscience of the readers; but that they are His, cannot exempt them from contradiction, or give them decisive weight in controversy.' Thirlwall, cited in Stephen Sykes and Derek Holmes, *New Studies in Theology* (London: Duckworth, 1980), 3. A direct response to Hick's *Myth* can be found in *TT*, 137–44.

11. Connor, *Kenotic Trajectory*, 138.

'traditional formulations when properly understood'.[12] Unlike some of his fellow Anglo-Catholics, however, he was far more interested in discerning the possibility of a renewed metaphysics chastened by the therapy offered by the positivists and Wittgenstein, rather than by reference to neo-Thomism.[13] Even so, according to MacKinnon, forms of modern theology that attempt to understand the unity of Jesus and God in terms of ontologies of personhood, categories of action or morality alone will inevitably reach an impasse that requires the reintroduction of something like a metaphysics of substance.[14] In MacKinnon's case this plays out in a greater openness to the ontological insights of Aristotle and G. E. Moore rather than any recantation of his early and well-documented break with monistic idealist metaphysics.[15] It also occurs with a great sensitivity to the ways in which the kenotic pattern of the incarnation may fundamentally change Christian ontologies in contrast to their secular counterparts.

Much of what has been outlined so far calls for greater clarification and substantiation, yet the point of this introductory section has been to emphasize that Christology was at the heart of MacKinnon's theological enterprise, and that he went about constructing his approach with characteristic creativity, independence, fragmentariness, open-endedness and moral intensity.[16]

MacKinnon on incarnation and revelation

According to his most recent (and to date most exhaustive) biographer, MacKinnon's engagement with Christology began in earnest as part of his

---

12. D. M. MacKinnon, 'Barth's Epistle to the Romans (Book Review)', *Theology* 65, no. 499 (1962): 6. And D. M. MacKinnon, '"Substance" in Christology: A Cross-bench View', in *Burden*, ed. John C. McDowell (London: T&T Clark, 2011), 237–54.

13. I am thinking here of Austin Farrer, MacKinnon's one-time tutor at Oxford and also figures such as Eric Lionel Mascall.

14. MacKinnon, '"Substance" in Christology: A Cross-bench View', 244–5.

15. Muller: 'MacKinnon may have learnt a fundamental ontology from Moore, but it is an ontology that he spends his philosophical career trying to describe. Far from being a definitive answer to a problem, it is the site of continual description and re-description, of hesitancy and exploration. This undoubtedly owes something to the empiricism MacKinnon learns form Moore. It also derives from the ambiguous relationship between the philosophical realism of Moore and MacKinnon's faith. If the absolute idealist doctrine of internal relations posited a world closed in upon itself, the logical atomism of Moore and Russell seemed, to the young MacKinnon, to leave room for the Christian belief in transcendence, even if its demolition of the ontological argument meant that this belief required re-working.' Muller, 'True Service', 46.

16. D. M. MacKinnon, *Objections to Christian Belief* (London: Constable, 1963), 20. See also Connor, *Kenotic Trajectory*, 155–68.

undergraduate education at Oxford in the 1930s.[17] After completing three years of philosophy steeped in the work of Moore, Russell and the logical positivists, MacKinnon took what was considered to be a counter-intuitive step by remaining at Oxford to complete a fourth year in theology.[18] The influences that would prove most decisive in this period appear to be, broadly speaking, twofold. The first was MacKinnon's introduction to a dialectical theology emerging in Germany at this time, particularly as it was mediated via Austin Farrer's SCM study group which met to discuss the work of Emil Brunner. Here, MacKinnon was exposed to the Barth and Brunner debate, as well as the thought of Bultmann and Gerhard Kittel.[19] The second was the New Testament scholarship of Lightfoot.

Farrer's engagement with these trends in Germany was respectful yet critical, and this probably had an impact on the young MacKinnon.[20] While one might presume that MacKinnon's robust engagement with the emerging field of logical positivism would have ensured that he was instinctively cautious about a form of continental theology that was popularly believed to be epistemologically insular and self-referential, it is clear that the uncompromising rigour of its realist incarnational theology struck a deep cord.[21] Specifically, what remained decisive for MacKinnon was the claim common to this school pertaining to the irreducible uniqueness of the Christ event.

For the dialectical theologians the uniqueness of the incarnation, a divine revelation-as-event, rendered the methodologies of empirical history and the natural sciences of limited help for the task of verifying the truth value of theological language.[22] They tended to advance the argument that the epistemological norms pertaining to the knowledge of God's revelatory acts must be governed by the same

---

17. Ibid., 35–53.

18. Yet, in MacKinnon's case it was understandable, given his commitment to Anglo-Catholicism and his early desire to seek ordination in the Church of England. Ibid., 57.

19. Muller observes that 'Farrer's seminar on Brunner probably marked MacKinnon's introduction to the new theological landscape that had opened up on the continent as a result of a crisis within liberal theology that occurred around the time of the First World War'. Ibid., 61.

20. As much as Farrer might have gone against the parochial interwar prejudice towards German theology, he was nonetheless influenced by a general anxiety common to theological circles at Oxford regarding the 'excess' of German theology and more pejoratively, its tendency towards 'irrationalism'. Ibid., 39–40. Farrer's own theological work was much more receptive to forms of thomistic analogical thinking in vogue in French Catholic thought.

21. MacKinnon: 'There is in Barth's thought a note of positive. He is always the champion of the concrete against, for instance, the abstract or the merely possible. In his discussion of the meaning of predestination, he will have nothing to do with any theorizing which averts attention from Christ'. *BT*, 68.

22. MacKinnon discusses problems relating to the employment of notions of 'uniqueness' in theology in *TT*, 168–9.

apophatic restraint pertaining to knowledge of God 'in-himself'. Thus, talk of 'God as a human being' or suchlike did not render Jesus an object whose meaning could be exhausted, or 'factuality' verified, on the same or straightforwardly analogous terms as the regular epistemological norms applied within the realms of nature, psychology or history.[23]

MacKinnon's relationship to Barth on the question of Christology warrants a more forensic consideration than is possible here.[24] I simply note the importance of figures such as Hoskyns and (to a lesser extent) Farrer, who were prominent in mediating Barth to the British context and who were influential on MacKinnon at a formative stage.[25] Additionally, P. T. Forsyth has been viewed as a precursor of Barthian neo-Orthodoxy in the British context and is a name that reoccurs throughout MacKinnon's Christological writings.[26] A realist claim pertaining to Christological revelation is asserted at the heart of Forsyth's work and forms its guiding methodological principle. Indeed, the status of Jesus as the incarnate one is not regarded as a working hypothesis to be argued for apologetically or established on the basis of some other 'first principle'.[27] Furthermore, Forsyth, more so than Barth, was explicit in drawing out links between Kantian morality and Christology; a move that would prove decisive for MacKinnon, particularly given the latter's emphasis on following Kant in discovering new possibilities for metaphysics in tandem with a relentless commitment to the notion of the morally unconditioned.

Alongside these Protestant figures, forming-up on the horizon of MacKinnon's Christological thought was Balthasar, who, given his magisterial (and sympathetic) engagement with Barth's work, can be seen to have shared a broad post-war trend looking for a way between fundamentalist reaction and modernist reductionism

---

23. Thomas F. Torrance, *Karl Barth, Biblical and Evangelical Theologian* (Edinburgh: T&T Clark, 1990), 80–90.

24. A start was made by Richard Roberts, 'Theological Rhetoric and Moral Passion in Light of MacKinnon's Barth', in *Christ, Ethics and Tragedy: Essays in Honour of Donald MacKinnon*, ed. Kenneth Surin (Cambridge: Cambridge University Press, 1989), 1–14.

25. Specifically, Hoskyns's ground-breaking translation of Barth's *Letter to the Romans* was closely read by MacKinnon on its release, as were the former's books on NT exegesis and theology, including the posthumously published *Crucifixion-Resurrection* and the earlier *The Riddle of the New Testament*. Citing MacKinnon's approach to the NT, his fellow student Christopher Stead observed that he 'followed Sir Edwyn Hoskyns and others who understood the New Testament as enshrining the faith of the earliest Christians rather than a mine of facts to be sifted by historians'. Muller, 'True Service', 53.

26. For a defence of the plausibility of this claim, see John Thompson, 'Was Forsyth Really a Barthian Before Barth?', in *Justice the True and Only Mercy: Essays on the Life and Theology of Peter Taylor Forsyth*, ed. Trevor A. Hart (Edinburgh: T&T Clark, 1995), 237–55.

27. Peter Taylor Forsyth, *The Person and Place of Jesus Christ*, Congregational Union Lecture (London: Congregational Union of England and Wales and Hodder & Stoughton, 1909), 35–60.

that nonetheless retained the person of Jesus at the centre theological concern.[28] Kerr notes that much of the initiative for the early reception of Balthasar in Britain was fuelled by Roman Catholic and Anglican theologian-translators in the aftermath of the War.[29] MacKinnon played a role in this reception, mediating Balthasar to a British audience via several essays that appeared over his career.[30] A claim regarding the uniqueness of Christ lies at the heart of each of these influential figures as do avid defences of the inscrutability of God's transcendence. What they attempted to deliver was a certain degree of internal consistency and coherence to the theological system, yet it came with a subsequent need to ward off the accusations of 'fideism'.[31]

MacKinnon remained convinced with Barth and Forsyth that there was no way in which one could ever hope to 'secure' the revelatory character of Jesus's life by means of the various epistemological norms that had come to characterize modernity. Incarnation demands its own, unique category; for 'everything is what it is and not another thing'. While holding to this insight, MacKinnon was always conscious of the risk that theologians can too easily revel in bold claims to positive knowledge after they have artfully justified, with reference to the nature of God and the uniqueness of revelation, the sidestepping of epistemological canons considered indispensable for self-respecting disciplines that seek empirical rigour and public intellectual accountability.[32] This sensitivity may explain why MacKinnon never became an outright disciple of the dialectical school and yet another reason why his theology took on a rather fragmented, apophatic and

---

28. Hans Urs von Balthasar and Edward T. Oakes, *The Theology of Karl Barth: Exposition and Interpretation*, Communio books (San Francisco, CA: Ignatius Press, 1992). See also Quash, *Theology and the Drama of History*, 28.

29. Fergus Kerr, interview by author, 29 January 2013. MacKinnon's own personal and intellectual interest in Balthasar's contribution to Christology can be seen in his brief introductory essay in the English edition of *Engagement*. Hans Urs von Balthasar, *Engagement with God* (London: SPCK, 1975).

30. For example: D. M. MacKinnon, 'Hans Urs von Balthasar's Christology', in *Burden*, ed. John C. McDowell (London: T&T Clark, 2011), 281–8.

31. Given his influence on MacKinnon it is interesting that Moser cites Forsyth as an exponent of this view. Forsyth's 'fideism' is perhaps evident when he argues that 'the certainty in the religious life is bound up with the autonomy of that life, its uniqueness and its independence of other knowledge. Our natural modes of rational certainty are but points of attachment, or under-agents for the certainty of faith; they are not germs of it, and they are not tests of it. ... Our ultimate authority then, which justifies every other authority in its degree and measure, is the Creator of the New Humanity as such.' P. T. Forsyth quoted in Paul K. Moser, *The Evidence for God: Religious Knowledge Re-examined* (Cambridge: Cambridge University Press, 2010), 88.

32. MacKinnon, 'Does Faith Create Its Own Objects?', 208–22.

self-afflicted mode.[33] Indeed, MacKinnon did not uncritically accept Barth's resounding 'no' to Brunner, involving himself in highly qualified forms of natural theology at least in as far as he perceived the question of transcendence arising from within the contemplation of moral dilemmas in concrete history as relevant to the theologian's task.[34]

MacKinnon's concern to avoid the charge of fideism is further encapsulated in the fact that he paired his conviction regarding the uniqueness of Christ with a conviction that it cannot for this reason be isolated from philosophy. This is evident when he says that 'Christology is like nothing else; it is unique; and yet it overlaps here, there and everywhere; and where philosophy in particular is concerned, the overlap presents inescapable problems'.[35] Indeed, for MacKinnon,

> the admission of the sovereignty of the christology is not, for the philosopher, any sort of escape from his own special problems; still less is it a device whereby he [sic] is able to say that theology has its own place, its statements have their own special logic, and that it is enough for him to point out this uniqueness and to defend it against those who would impinge or criticise it.[36]

As will become clear, MacKinnon affirmed the long tradition of theologians drawing upon philosophical terms to explicate the identity of Jesus and the Father. He was also convinced that the purgative focus on revelatory particularity among the neo-Orthodox was mirrored in a similarly purgative emphasis on empirical particularity championed by the logical positivists.[37] Naturally, the protagonists of either school would have protested that such a connection paled into insignificance

---

33. Part and parcel of an acknowledgement of the sovereignty of Christology was the fact that it would make 'serious theological work a less delicately and closely woven unity than the theologian might desire', but this was to be expected as 'that untidiness was itself an expression of his fidelity to the underlying demands of his enterprise'. *BT*, 58.

34. There are indications that MacKinnon regarded Barth as sending 'confused' messages on the possibility of natural theology. D. M. MacKinnon, 'Biblical Faith and Natural Theology (Book Review)', *Epworth Review* 20, no. 3 (1993): 130. See also P. G. Wignall, 'D. M. MacKinnon: An Introduction to his Early Theological Writings', in *New Studies in Theology 1*, ed. S. Sykes and D. Holmes (London: Duckworth, 1980), 78.

35. *BT*, 61.

36. Ibid., 60. Coakley writes in a similar vein: 'Outright rejection of secular philosophy is as dangerous an alternative as outright submission: there has to be a "more excellent way" than the two false alternatives (fideism versus secularism) that currently feature large in theological culture wars. Ironically, Barth's dogmatics and ordinary language ("analytic") philosophy – perhaps the most important developments in the twentieth century for theology and philosophy, respectively – have together combined in a pincer movement to entrench this false disjunction.' Sarah Coakley, *God, Sexuality and the Self: An Essay 'On the Trinity'* (Cambridge: Cambridge University Press, 2013), 18.

37. *TT*, 168–72.

due to the more primary disagreement as to the intelligibility of theism, but drawing out previously unseen, contentious, yet potentially generative resonances between philosophy and theology was the borderland-dwelling vocation of MacKinnon.[38]

I explored MacKinnon's link with the positivists in Chapter 2 and it is sufficient here to reiterate the fact that MacKinnon was convinced by the arguments Russell and Moore mounted against the doctrine of internal relations, especially in as far as it formed a central part of the idealist projects of Joachim and Bradley. For MacKinnon, the positivists were reviving the Aristotelian tradition of correspondence notions of truth; they were introducing a healthy agnosticism in the wake of an overconfident yet seductive idealism; they were resuming 'accents of the authentic Kant', and above all their focus on the 'particular' against holist abstractions was executed with a logical rigour that should be admired.[39]

If one were to transfer this focus on the particular into the theological realm, one can perhaps see the attraction of the dialectical theologians for MacKinnon. And so, it is with some irony that MacKinnon's interests in the philosophies of noted atheists led him into the arms of Barth, Balthasar, Hoskyns and Forsyth whose epistemological focus on realist particularity manifested in a bold proclamation of the sovereignty of Christology.[40] They, too, suspected the way in which some theologians had been seduced into thinking that the monist metaphysics of the idealists could be a refuge by which orthodox theistic claims could escape the fires of secular modernity.[41] Indeed, if Moore was the greatest initial influence on MacKinnon's growing conviction that idealism was the enemy of the philosophical apprehension of the historical particular, rather than its great expositor, Brunner

---

38. *BT*, 41–6.

39. *ET*, 41. Muller, 'True Service', 41. MacKinnon: 'Both Russell and Moore seemed, in different ways, conclusively to refute any sort of ontological argument; here indeed they seemed to resume the accents of the authentic Kant, the Kant of the Dialectic, and to speak his meaning with an inescapable rigour and clarity. There was no road from essence to existence, from concept to reality; no sleight of hand could make of existence a predicate or attribute. Between truths of reason and truths of fact there was a great gulf fixed; by no a priori reasoning was it possible to establish the nature of what is. To know whether or not something existed, appeal must be made to observation' *BT*, 62.

40. In this vein MacKinnon argued that 'to acknowledge the supremacy of Christology is to confess that finality belongs somehow to that which is particular and contingent, to that which has definite date and place, to that which is described by statements that are not "truths of reason", in more modern language, "necessary propositions". Further, it is to involve the confession of faith inextricably with the deliverances of flickering human perception and observation' *BT*, 58.

41. Wignall: 'The seeming opposites of the first two formative influences [i.e. Barth and Brunner], connected for MacKinnon not least in their mutual attack on idealism. The theology of crisis sharpened this by its attack on liberalism while sharing with neo-Thomism an engagement with the grace and nature problem'. Wignall, 'D. M. MacKinnon: An Introduction to his Early Theological Writings', 80.

fuelled the fire from the theological side. Brunner sought to show the ways in which idealism, with its intense focus on the philosophy of history actually distorted history.

Brunner's dialectical unmasking of what he called the 'idealism' of the followers of Ritschl, Dilthey and Troeltsch in *The Mediator* may have helped MacKinnon to see that methods that might appear to take history seriously are sometimes funded by a metaphysical monism that undermines the Christian belief in the historical actuality of divine revelation.[42]

The impetus for this approach was often placed at the feet of Hegel, with his purported conviction that

> religion properly so-called uses inadequate concepts and this inadequacy of its concepts, compared, that is to say, to the adequacy of the *Begriffe* of philosophy, normally consists in the fact that these concepts are either still too immersed in sense imagery though they may be dialectically inter-related (as in the story of a Father-God giving birth to a Son and sending him to die so that he can then return as Risen Lord or Spirit), or they are concepts all right (such as First Cause, necessary Being) and clear of such immersion, but dialectically undeveloped.[43]

That MacKinnon *did* see the need to explicate the claims of the raw biblical material with philosophical concepts, especially when they seem to pose questions of metaphysics and call for a 'philosophy of history', not only locates him in the tradition of orthodox creedal theology; but also makes us pause before we attribute any crass anti-Hegelianism to him. Yet, while this movement between 'tiers of discourse' may initially seem to mimic some of the Hegelian sentiments just noted, MacKinnon is always keen to differentiate his own recourse to metaphysics as being anti-monist in character. Indeed, as already noted, he perceived in the idealist tradition a devaluation of the integrity of the particular historical moment: the uniqueness, irreversibility and irreducibility of the latter was inevitably compromised as it was all-too-quickly subsumed into the realm of the Notion.[44] Thus, contra the theological champions of idealism (as he understood them), any move to further describe historical particulars with philosophical became a kind

---

42. Muller, 'True Service', 68.

43. James P. Mackey, 'Introduction', in *Religious Imagination*, ed. James P. Mackey (Edinburgh: Edinburgh University Press, 1986), 14. In the same vein Davaney notes, 'Whereas the theorists of the Historical School, such as Humboldt and Ranke, asserted the primacy of individual concrete facts and argued that it is with empirical realities that all understandings of history begin, Hegel prioritized the notion of Absolute Spirit from which alone an interpretation of history emerges.' Sheila Greeve Davaney, *Historicism: The Once and Future Challenge for Theology* (Minneapolis: Fortress Press, 2006), 41.

44. *TT*, 50–66.

of contemplative attentiveness to the conditions of sheer historical particularity.[45] The dialectic remains for MacKinnon: philosophical concepts never sublate historical theology or vice versa. In this vein, MacKinnon preferred Balthasar's Christology to that found in Küng's *Menschwerdung Gottes*.[46]

In addition to opening his theology to the purgative gaze of analytical philosophy, MacKinnon's attitude towards Jesus and history emerged as another way in which he sought to avoid the charge of fideism. After all, no self-respecting fideist would make Christological claims vulnerable to 'flickering human perception and observation' as MacKinnon insisted it should.[47] Broadly speaking, his approach is more akin to what we see emerging in the theologies of Pannenberg and Moltmann rather than that of Barth. In the former, there is greater propensity to see the revealed and eschatological dimensions of Christology as needing to be reconciled, or at least perpetually intertwined with Jesus's location under the commonly recognized categories, limitations and norms of empirical history.[48] This is not to deny the nuanced position achieved by Barth in his commitment to upholding the irreducible particularity of the man Jesus as the incarnate one. It is, however, to reiterate Barth's insistence that the incarnation transformed notions of history from the 'inside out': it presented to the human intellect a genuinely novel type of 'revealed history' in a class of its own.[49] What I mean to do here is to identify MacKinnon with a later reassertion of a more conventional historical realism in theological epistemology.[50] Here, the ontology of the incarnation still points

---

45. MacKinnon: 'To set forth its [i.e. the Word made flesh] secret, the writer needs to use the resources of ontological metaphysics; but the resources are used to deepen insight concerning the life itself, concerning what is there and then then done for human kind'. D. M. MacKinnon, 'Subjective and Objective Conceptions of Atonement', in *Burden*, ed. John C. McDowell (London: T&T Clark, 2011), 292.

46. MacKinnon complimented Küng insofar as he drew on Balthasar to explicate a notion of impassibility grounded in the Trinity. *TT*, 165. And D. M. MacKinnon, 'Some Reflections on Hans Urs von Balthasar's Christology With Special Reference to Theodramatik II/2 and III', in *The Analogy of Beauty: The Theology of Hans Urs von Balthasar*, ed. John Kenneth Riches (Edinburgh: T&T Clark, 1986), 164–74.

47. There is something of a dialectic to keep in mind here, in that MacKinnon will not allow the gospel to be subordinated to mere historicism either: 'To the Christian the meaning of history is not something that emerges from within history as events come and pass but something that is perennially being given in Christ to history'. D. M. MacKinnon, 'Mr Murry on the Free Society (Book Review)', *The Christian News-Letter* 310, no. May (1948): 9–16.

48. While I have not found any evidence that MacKinnon engaged at any depth with Pannenberg, he was complimentary about Moltmann's *Crucified God*. *TT*, 146.

49. Balthasar and Oakes, *The Theology of Karl Barth: Exposition and Interpretation*, 233–47.

50. This is perhaps best captured in Pannenberg's famous essay *Revelation as History* and the collection of essays he gathered around it. Wolfhart Pannenberg, *Revelation as History* (London: Sheed and Ward, 1969).

to utter novelty, but in a way that maintains empirical historical epistemology intact, at least as an ideal and limit, rather than putting revelatory events beyond its searching gaze.[51] Unlike Pannenberg, Moltmann was not as willing to expose Christology to the epistemological norms of empirical historical research, nor did he see the establishment of a separate category of revealed event over and against history as a viable option. He held that

> the modern dilemma lies in the fact that the two sides can no longer be reduced to a common denominator. The choice is made between a *Jesuology*, referring to the earthly Jesus, accessible to historical investigation and capable of human imitation, and christology, referring to the Christ whom faith and the church proclaim.[52]

Moltmann questioned the premises underlying the need for any absolute choice of one to the exclusion of the other. In different ways Moltmann and Pannenberg attempted approaches that mediated between liberal, modernist and liberation theologies from 'below', where the focus began with historical 'facts' and/or concrete moral imperative, and those 'from above', in which the imperative lies with an alien, transcendent intervention which breaks apart every temporal epistemological and ontological norm.[53] They attempted approaches that tried to hold both together albeit shorn of pre-critical naiveté, and in this respect MacKinnon's shares their intuitions.[54]

Despite my focus on Moltmann and Pannenberg, these were not the most decisive figures for MacKinnon's early formation. Indeed, core features of his approach to the question of history and Christological 'factuality' were already set in place within the milieu of British New Testament studies during the interwar period. As Muller testifies, in the context of 1930s Oxford, the influence of source

---

51. MacKinnon admired this in Scott Holland: 'Holland does not learn to speak of the transcendence of God in general terms: for he presents that transcendence as something by which we are apprehended in the Crucified.' *BT*, 117.

52. Jürgen Moltmann, *The Crucified God: The Cross of Christ as the Foundation and Criticism of Christian Theology* (London: SCM Press, 1974), 112.

53. I note Lash's critique of the metaphors of 'above' and 'below' in Christology. He also takes Pannenberg to task for the way he develops a Christology from 'below' in which the empirical history of Jesus warrants claims about his eschatological significance and divine status. The extent to which these comments take into account Pannenberg's Systematic Theology Vol. 3 is unclear. N. Lash, '"Up" and "Down" in Christology', in *New Studies in Theology 1*, ed. Stephen Sykes and Derek Holmes (London: Duckworth, 1980), 33–45.

54. Connor: 'In the New Testament attestation of Jesus' mission, MacKinnon argued, the dramatic and the ontological interpenetrate, rendering otiose the now conventional methodological distinction in Christology "from below upwards" and "from above downwards" – Christ is a dynamic reality that "violates the contrast" … his life is an interpenetration of activity and passivity, humility and authority, receptivity and demand, vulnerability and bold assertion.' Connor, *Kenotic Trajectory*, 138. He is citing *TT*, 179.

criticism was waning, as was confidence that it would be possible to extract from the New Testament unalloyed historical data about Jesus. It was Lightfoot who formed 'the principal influence on MacKinnon during his theological studies'.[55] Lightfoot reacted against liberal German historicism and reasserted that the Gospels provided much more historical justification for Christian claims than was being allowed by members of the Tübingen School.[56] He took up its crucial distinction between myth and history, however, and his introduction of Form Criticism to Oxford provided an alternative to the relative naiveté of Streeter's teaching on the four document hypothesis, which looked to St. Mark's Gospel as a kind of unadulterated biography.[57]

The fact that MacKinnon, almost certainly under the influence of the biblical theology of C. H. Dodd, can later say 'that it is John among the four, who is most deeply, if almost unconsciously, concerned with the factual, with the *Logos sarx genomenos*' speaks volumes about his disposition regarding the question of the New Testament's 'factuality', and how far he had moved away from Streeter.[58] Indeed, the more intensive theological layering crafted by the author of John's

---

55. Muller, 'True Service', 62.

56. Morgan judges this argument as a failure: "This was only one stream in Anglican theology, and it was in the long run a failure. If the historian Lightfoot stands at the head of the procession, one might see Sanday at its heart, Headlam at its rump and Stephen Neill at its tail.' Robert Morgan, 'Non Angli sed Angeli: Some Anglican Reactions to German Gospel Criticism', in *New Studies in Theology*, ed. Stephen Sykes and Derek Holmes (London: Duckworth, 1980), 5.

57. Morgan notes that Lightfoot was keen to defend the veracity of the gospel records: '"Veracity" here means historical accuracy; there is no question of Lightfoot distinguishing between their historical and their theological value. The reason is plain in his phrase "the records of the divine life". If Jesus in his earthly historical reality was God incarnate, historical research could be expected to throw light on the revelation.' Ibid., 6. See also Muller, 'True Service', 63–70.

58. D. M. MacKinnon, 'The Evangelical Imagination', in *Burden*, ed. John C. McDowell (London: T&T Clark, 2011), 190. MacKinnon also seems to show forth something of Scott Holland's influence here, of whom Ramsey said: 'His final and greatest service to theology is in his Lectures on the Fourth Gospel, where he shews that it is not that the synoptists are plain and simple and the Fourth Gospel an enigma, but that the synoptists are a puzzle to which the Fourth Gospel gives the solution.' Michael Ramsey, *From Gore to Temple: The Development of Anglican Theology between Lux Mundi and the Second World War, 1889-1939* (London: Longmans, 1960), 13. Perhaps the most important early influence on this point was Hoskyns's commentary on John's gospel, which MacKinnon reviewed in 1941, speaking of a 'closely knit, brilliant, and frankly exciting analysis of the unity of the Gospel tradition, showing again and again how familiar Synoptic themes are woven into the structure of the Johannine narrative and their significance thereby made inescapably plain'. At the same time, MacKinnon credits Hoskyns for 'not fall[ing] into the easy mistake of supposing that in the Fourth Gospel we achieve a "final synthesis" of New Testament

gospel is taken to be a 'drawing out' of the moral struggle and spiritual depth of history rather than an act of concealment or obscurantism. MacKinnon says,

> The presentation John offers of what to him is the judgement of this world is a masterpiece of tragic irony. It is a narrative that invites historical evaluation by reason of its immanent psychological credibility. We cannot accept it as it stands, as an historical record; but the tragic theological and historical dimensions of these pages so interpenetrate that the two forms of criticism (the literary and historical) must both be enlisted to aid the distinctively religious perception, which finds the truth of what human beings ultimately are, not simply revealed but brought into being by the fact that Jesus leaves the place of judgement carrying his cross himself ... and by his death, finishing the work given by his Father and establishing forgiveness and mercy as the *telos* of the whole affair.[59]

Lightfoot's Form Criticism highlighted the fact that in the New Testament, historical facts and their theological interpretation could be distinguished, but both would suffer irreparable damage if separated. This is a view that would be further developed with Redaction Criticism, in which the agency of the authors and compilers, together with their theological convictions, came to the front and centre of the reception of their writings.[60] Where MacKinnon followed his teacher was his scepticism of the liberal Protestant project and an acknowledgement of the potential for imaginative extrapolations to add rather than detract from historical realism. Where he differed and fell in line with the Barthian trajectory was in a rejection of the optimism that revelatory claims may somehow be *secured* by an apologetic based on the results of a historical critical study of the gospels.[61]

---

theology'. D. M. MacKinnon, '"The Fourth Gospel" (Book Review)', *The Oxford Magazine* 59, no. May (1941): 268–9.

59. MacKinnon, 'The Evangelical Imagination', 198.

60. MacKinnon: 'We must read and re-read what is before us. The tools provided by typological exegesis, and by "redaction-criticism" are alike indispensable. The letter (for all the ugliness of the name) embodies a standing protest against a view of the Gospels which in the name of an entirely laudable concern with their factual basis, risks in the end reducing Matthew and Luke to scissors-and-paste compilations, turning aside from the theological density of Mark, and finding in the fourth Gospel something ultimately intractable.' Ibid., 191.

61. Morgan's observation vindicates MacKinnon's move out of Lightfoot's orbit: 'The result of adopting a basically rationalistic method for the modern historical analysis of the gospels was to decide the matter in principle in the direction signalled by Reimarus, Strauss and Baur, and against Lightfoot and his successors. It would always seem more probable, when judged by ordinary historical canons of probability, that the material in the gospels which conflicted with ordinary human experience and corresponded to the early church's belief, was the product of that belief rather than its cause. Only if the gospels were read in

To get a sense as to the arguments MacKinnon would offer in response to the nest of problems related to faith and historicism, one could start at his essay 'Does Faith Create its Own Objects?'[62] This is perhaps MacKinnon at his most restive. He refused to see faith as an escape from the discipline of history, yet he reminded his readers that historical certainty, even if it were possible, could not replace faith or ultimately secure it against scepticism. It is the very history of the man Jesus, steeped in Jewish self-understanding, which gives rise to a theological problem that needed explication in terms of a theological imagination and mythological ascription.[63] Even if greater and greater degrees of historical certainty were achieved, MacKinnon was convinced that faith remains a 'problem and a mystery. Faith is something which goes before historical reconstruction, and is something which even conditions its most radical exercise, relating it to its own intense and searching discipline.'[64]

MacKinnon occasionally spoke about this distinction as one between the 'perceptual' and the 'historical'.[65] When noting the ways in which Kant gives the theologian some clues as to the proper discipline of the imagination, he asked,

> Are there lessons to be learnt by the Christian theologian for whom faith has a perceptual basis? I say: perceptual rather than historical, recalling that the author of the first Johannine epistle ... [who] speaks in his first sentence of that which 'we have heard, we have seen with our eyes, and our hands have handled of the word of life' (1 Jn. 1.1). If Paul found it necessary to remind the Corinthians that they no longer see Christ 'after the flesh', this reminder is warranted by the fact that once he was so seen. It is, of course, the fourth Evangelist who with dazzling intricacy, emphasizes and then seems to depreciate, the perceptual basis of the disciples' faith.[66]

Kant famously argued that sensory information without understanding is blind and, analogously, MacKinnon believed that without accounting for interpretive meaning-making on the part of participants and witnesses, one is left with an incomplete account of historical 'factuality'. A great influence on MacKinnon's refusal of certain forms of reductionist historical empiricism was R. T. Collingwood and I also suspect the earlier influence of Jacques Maritain.[67] In reflecting on St. Thomas's doctrine of analogy in the realm of politics, Maritain

---

the light of the church's dogmatic presuppositions would the alternative appear credible.' Morgan, 'Non Angli sed Angeli', 7.

62. MacKinnon, 'Does Faith Create Its Own Objects?', 209–20.
63. *BT*, 78.
64. Ibid., 79.
65. D. M. MacKinnon, 'Intellect and Imagination', in *The Weight of Glory: A Vision and Practice for Christian Faith: The Future of Liberal Theology*, ed. Daniel W. Hardy and P. H. Sedgwick (Edinburgh: T&T Clark, 1991), 30.
66. Ibid.
67. *BT*, 162–74.

urges a move beyond the 'simple empiric cataloguing of factual circumstances' to an apprehension of history that can include 'the bearing of rational judgments of *value* ... [and] the discernment of the form and significance of the intelligible constellations which govern the diverse phases of human history'.[68] On occasion MacKinnon made pejorative reference to a 'scissors and paste' approach to history, which is almost certainly an allusion to the same phrase used by Collingwood in *The Idea of History*.[69] The mistake here

> was that it (unconsciously) interpreted the verbal evidence of the past as though it were the testimony of contemporaries, and was insufficiently reflective about the preconceptions that it brought to the study of the past.[70]

The 'scissors and paste' approach seemed to draw on the empiricist's assumption that immediate sensory perception is the purest form of knowledge, and that the perception of witnesses can be conveyed unalloyed into the present. Further, to the extent that historical claims lie beyond the possibility of this epistemological guarantee, they must be subject to reductionist purgation. On this theme Graham notes that 'if we want to know what happened in the past, empiricism implies, we must scour the recorded observations of those who were around then, clip the testimony of these contemporaries, and paste it together into a continuous narrative of how the past was'.[71] MacKinnon recognizes the indispensability of the historian who pieces together isolated atoms of eye-witness data into a verifiable 'whole', but he is not willing to see this as an absolute limit of historical truth claims. Most of all he is concerned that such approaches reduce the focus to 'events' to the exclusion of 'actions'. That is, they tend to provide a truncated account of the moral struggles and compromises of history that must be the focus for the philosopher and theologian.[72]

---

68. Jacques Maritain, *True Humanism*, Fourth edition (London: Centenary Press, 1946), 132–3.

69. MacKinnon observes that 'recent work in the field of *Redaktionsgeschichte* has stressed the extent to which the four gospels, very far from being "scissors and paste" compilations, embody carefully distinct presentations of the teaching ministry and work of Jesus, ordered in accordance with serious theological presuppositions, differing in important respects from one evangelist to another, and issuing in highly individual, if significantly complementary handling of traditional material, material which is sometimes common to more than one of the four writers, but which is also preserved for posterity in the writing of one, and not another.' *ET*, 171.

70. Gordon Graham, *Evil and Christian Ethics*, New studies in Christian ethics (Cambridge: Cambridge University Press, 2001), 48.

71. Ibid., 49.

72. D'Oro observes that 'scissors-and-paste historians take themselves to be explaining actions, but in so far as they apply the inductive method to the study of human deeds they explain them not in the manner suited to the category of action but to the manner suited

MacKinnon on atonement

The wariness MacKinnon shows towards Bultmann and Macquarrie is also directed towards Dennis Nineham's work from the late 1970s, in which the latter claimed that there was no longer any possibility of grounding atonement theology in the historical particularity of the man Jesus.[73] MacKinnon warned that moves in this direction risked 'facile depreciation'.[74] In order to offer a response to Bonhoeffer's question: 'Who is Christ for us today?', MacKinnon argued that the response to modernity's challenge to Christianity is to delve more and more deeply into the sheer particularity of his life and death as recounted in the gospel accounts as well as the particularity of contemporary events.[75]

MacKinnon did not spend much time in any of his writings entering acrimonious debates regarding the theories that most faithfully capture a New Testament theology of atonement.[76] This is not to discount the fact that he could turn his characteristically acerbic criticism on theologians that sought to absolutize one of the common metaphors, or who turned the whole tenor of the doctrine into the workings of a deus ex machina.[77] His response to such alienating and abstracting tendencies was to drive the focus back on the messy, unsystematic particularity of Christ's life.[78] The approach arises from a conviction that 'pursuing conceptual clarity comes at the cost of smoothing down reality's jagged contours'.[79] However, this reaction against 'idealism' is no simple move 'back to the Bible' or 'back to the historical Jesus' over and against the doctrinal inheritance of the church.[80]

---

to the category of event. The explanations provided by scissors-and-paste historians are pseudo-historical because whilst they may be studying human deeds their methodology commits them to the existence of only one category of things: events'. Giuseppina D'Oro, 'The Myth of Collingwood's Historicism', *Inquiry* 53, no. 6 (2010): 639.

73. John Hick, *The Myth of God Incarnate* (London: SCM Press, 1977), 167–84.
74. MacKinnon, 'Reflections on Donald Baillie's Treatment of the Atonement', 120.
75. Ibid., 118.
76. MacKinnon, 'Subjective and Objective Conceptions of Atonement', 189–99.
77. Ibid. MacKinnon's criticism of the misuse and over use of sacrificial victory motifs is also discussed by Connor. Connor, *Kenotic Trajectory*, 152.
78. When he looks to Jesus on the cross as reported by the gospels, MacKinnon sees 'one who has entered the darkness of human condemnation' and to take this seriously means that 'abstract theorizing and preaching concerning the final destiny of men which averts from the manner in which the very foundations of their destiny are laid, namely in the ministry, death and resurrection of Jesus, is worse than sterile'. *BT*, 68.
79. Giles Waller, 'Freedom, Fate and Sin in Donald MacKinnon's Use of Tragedy', in *Christian Theology and Tragedy: Theologians, Tragic Literature, and Tragic Theory*, ed. T. Kevin Taylor and Giles Waller (Farnham: Ashgate, 2011), 62.
80. This is a tendency that can be cited in several MacKinnon's contemporaries across the theological spectrum and one that he rejects. For example, both P. T. Forsyth and Archbishop Temple attracted MacKinnon's admiration, but from time to time they

What MacKinnon sought was a therapeutic corrective, but in advancing this he did not see any reason why respect for historical particularity should entail jettisoning speculative doctrinal and metaphysical expression of classical orthodoxy. In a way reminiscent of correlational theological methodologies, it is our very immersion in the historical particularity of Jesus that raises questions only kinds of metaphysical and theological reasoning can hope to adequately explicate.[81] MacKinnon wanted to avoid an unfruitful subordination of Christology to theology; an illness to which he saw Barth applying some much-needed shock therapy.[82] He also saw this wider trend being transposed into the more specific domain of soteriology with comparable deleterious effects. MacKinnon identified a symptom of this wherever the language of redemption came to dominate that of atonement.[83] He asserted that

> the tradition which has linked the concept of redemption to that of atonement, however revolting many of the forms it has assumed in its history, bears witness to a continuing awareness that any presentation of the work of Christ merits rejection as morally trivial, if it does not touch the deepest contradictions of human life, those contradictions which writers of tragedy have not hesitated to recognize, and to recognize without the distorting consolation of belief in a happy ending.[84]

expressed a far greater suspicion of the early church's adoption of classical metaphysics in its Christological formularies. For example Forsyth argued that 'the formula of the union of two natures in one person is essentially a metaphysical formula, and the formula of a Hellenic metaphysics, and it is more or less archaic for the modern mind'. Forsyth, *Person and Place*, 229. MacKinnon: 'It will not be forgotten that a very great orthodox theologian, Peter Taylor Forsyth, shared to the full the Ritschlian rejection of what he called 'Chalcedonism'. MacKinnon, '"Substance" in Christology: A Cross-bench View', 248. On Temple, see *TT*, 172–3.

81. MacKinnon: 'To set forth its [i.e. the Word made flesh] secret, the writer needs to use the resources of ontological metaphysics; but the resources are used to deepen insight concerning the life itself, concerning what is there and there done for humankind'. MacKinnon, 'Subjective and Objective Conceptions of Atonement', 292.

82. *BT*, 66.

83. MacKinnon: 'Where the theologian is concerned, we have to reckon with a readiness to-day to drop (without conscious acknowledgement) the conception of atonement, and to suggest that we content ourselves with that of redemption, the latter's associations with the institution of slavery in the Graeco-Roman world ignored, and likewise its frankly mythological undertones (the suggestion of actually existent alien powers to whom men and women are in bondage) duly demythologised.' The distinction between atonement and redemption is attributed to 'Harbage', but no further details are given. MacKinnon, 'Subjective and Objective Conceptions of Atonement', 290.

84. Ibid., 291.

What MacKinnon seems to be attacking was trends in soteriology that could be characterized as either exemplaristic or 'abstract-declarative'. That is, approaches that (broadly speaking) reduce the saving work of Christ to a kind of moral enlightenment and his person to an object of positive mimesis, or that which speaks of salvation only in terms of an objective transformation in the conscious will of divine or human agents, particularly where the ascription of guilt by the former to the latter is terminated with reference to a kind of quasi-legal transaction.[85] This is redemption without atonement according to MacKinnon: the cross purged of horror, confusion, ambiguity and failure, without which all talk of reconciliation is rendered meaningless. Soteriology must involve an intense focus on the way in which the cross and resurrection constitute events in which the seemingly irreconcilable forces of justice and mercy, evil and love, determinism and free will are brought together at a particular, irreducible moment in time.[86] We see MacKinnon's concern in the following criticism of Wisdom:

> One could wish that in this difficult, but searching essay, he had gone on to point out the extent to which, for instance, in the theology of the fourth Gospel, the judgment which he claims men seek is accomplished in the Passion of Christ; in the great scene of *Ecce Homo* the world is judged by the Son of Man condemned, and forced, in his supreme hour, to wear the robes of mock royalty. It is Christ's objectively achieved atonement which, in the Christian vision, suffuses human actions with their truth by giving them their context in his endurance, by allowing them to find their firm foundation in his overcoming of the gulf between the claims of pity, and the claims of justice, of pity for others and justice towards others, or pity towards ourselves and justice towards ourselves.[87]

This is a soteriology that places an intense historical and ethical focus at the centre. It is not a 'conceptual' reconciliation alone, but something achieved first and foremost within the holistically apprehended existence of a particular person. A sign that we are willing to discipline our Christology by attending to such particularity is openness on the part of the theologian to seeing in these events the characteristic marks of tragedy.[88]

---

85. D. M. MacKinnon, 'Some Reflection on Secular Diakonia', in *Burden*, ed. John C. McDowell (London: T&T Clark, 2011), 68.

86. Speaking about the drawing together of such irreconcilables in John's Gospel, MacKinnon perceives the possibility of 'a kind of a phenomenology of the atonement'. MacKinnon, 'The Evangelical Imagination', 198.

87. D. M. MacKinnon, 'John Wisdom's Paradox and Discovery', *Church Quarterly Review* 168, no. 366 (1967): 73.

88. MacKinnon: 'It is a manifest weakness of much traditional christology that it has evacuated the mystery of God's self-incarnation of so much that must take time, that must be endowed with the most pervasive forms of human experience, its successiveness, its fragmentariness, above all its ineluctable choices, fraught equally inevitably with tragic

MacKinnon's use of the literary designation of tragedy is a controversial and counter-intuitive way of reasserting a historical realist dimension to Christology.[89] It is a move that warrants detailed examination in its own right and I have made an attempt in the proceeding chapter.[90] Reference to the tragic provided MacKinnon ways of plumbing the depths of the historical complexity of the personalities and events of the passion that language of 'sin' could no longer achieve alone. One cannot help but think that Forsyth was an influence here, especially in light of this view:

> In life's daily affairs it may be wisdom not to take things tragically. But they have to be taken tragically if we are to have moral realism at all. … The world as a world has to be tragically taken.[91]

MacKinnon took this insight to heart and this gives rise to a searing burdensomeness in sections of his writing:

> The coming of Christ in the earliest Gospel is portrayed as tragic, and catastrophic. It is not the emergence on the plane of history of one who perfects

consequence.' MacKinnon, 'The Evangelical Imagination', 196. Janz offers an expert summary of what is at stake for MacKinnon here: 'When the cross is abstracted from the empirical history of Jesus, that is, when the tragic is not attended to, it becomes essentially a symbol; and then by its very nature *as* a symbol – even though it is indeed here a powerful symbol of redemption and hope – the cross becomes fundamentally the focus of a supreme kind of resolution. But the hope it then proclaims, if the sheer intractability of the empirical history of God-with-us on the cross is forgotten, is no longer the hope of genuine reconciliation (which must remain the response precisely to utter and intractable *non-resolution* if we are speaking about *genuine* reconciliation in the biblical sense), but only the hope of an ultimate kind of holism. And the integrity of transcendence in the Paschal event, its finality of non-resolution, is lost. It has become a finality of resolution'. Janz, *God, the Mind's Desire*, 177–8.

89. Discussions with Steiner enabled MacKinnon 'to explore the problem of evil theologically, without recourse to traditional theodicies; to re-describe a Christology where Christ was both of one substance with the Father and fully human in his historical appearance; and to present contemporary moral ambivalence without conceding to moral relativism'. G. Ward, 'Tragedy as Subclause: George Steiner's Dialogue with Donald MacKinnon', *Heythrop Journal* 34, no. 3 (1993): 285. MacKinnon's forays in to 'holocaust theologies', such as that of Ulrich Simon, were also significant. *ET*, 9. Cf. Ulrich E. Simon, *A Theology of Auschwitz* (London: SPCK, 1978), 108.

90. David Ford and Giles Waller have made helpful contributions. David Ford, 'Tragedy and Atonement', in *Christ, Ethics and Tragedy: Essays in Honour of Donald MacKinnon*, ed. Kenneth Surin (Cambridge: Cambridge University Press, 1989), 117–29. See also Waller, 'Freedom, Fate and Sin in Donald MacKinnion's Use of Tragedy', 101–18.

91. Peter Taylor Forsyth, *Positive Preaching and Modern Mind* (London: Hodder and Stoughton, 1907), 234.

its process, but rather the sudden, abrupt appearance of one who rejects the very assumption of its movement. Man's [sic] tragedy is a religious tragedy. He has sought security at the cost of his nature. Christ removes that security from him, and shows him the abyss. He presents man with the Will of the Father of which he from all Eternity is the fulfilment. 'There is a Calvary above which was the mother of it all.' He is despised, rejected, crucified. He passes ineluctably to nothingness, and therein is his Father glorified. His life is a question, a riddle; as Barth says – There is no human possibility of which he did not rid himself and therein is he recognized as the Christ.[92]

If a kind of intense realist discipline led MacKinnon to interrogate all atonement theology by means of the concrete circumstances of Jesus's mission, that is, 'from below', it is the domain of soteriology where it is possible to locate a qualified Christology from 'above'. By this I refer to the fact that it is in soteriology where the absolute 'givenness' of Christ is first apprehended; indeed, here is the impetus by which the question of Jesus's divinity arises.[93] Following Forsyth, MacKinnon held to the conviction that a theology of the incarnation is first and foremost not understood as beginning with reflection on the ontological status of Christ: the titles bestowed upon him by his disciples and the gospel writers, or the union of human and divine natures in a merely abstract sense.[94] Thus when I speak of

---

92. MacKinnon, 'Revelation and Social Justice', 147. It is important to note that MacKinnon is aware that import of the tragic motif can become a problem; it is a therapeutic aid towards realism that is always subject to the risk of providing a fake consolation: 'We are all of us familiar with those who, in the name of what is sometimes called "the tragic sense of life", speak lightly of pain, as if it were an inevitable ingredient of a properly human existence. We need not accept Dr Popper's interpretation of Hegel in order to welcome his polemic against the sort of quasi-mystical determinism which would treat the difference between what is, and what is of good report, as ultimately illusion.' *BT*, 156.

93. MacKinnon: 'The aspect of theology, that is of course most closely akin to metaphysical anthropology, is the study of the mystery of grace. It is a fact, familiar to the student, that the doctrine of grace is sheerly incomprehensible apart from the general doctrine of the work of Christ – conventionally called soteriology. What I want to suggest to you is that, if metaphysical anthropology, or that branch of cosmology, which is concerned with man's origin and destiny, is to be saved from the presumption and Titanism that the Barthians infallibly detect in almost all theologizing it can only be so saved by being offset by a stern soteriology. With the late Dr P. T. Forsyth I am increasingly convinced that, if we are wise, we will derive our Christology from our soteriology and not vice versa. It is through the scandal of his work that the Messianic secret is disclosed to his Church which must forever bear it.' MacKinnon, 'Revelation and Social Justice', 159.

94. This is not to say that the ontological significance of the titles is to be continually ignored in favour of a kind of 'functionalism', as Connor notes, '[MacKinnon] questioned the claim that the New Testament christological titles were to be construed functionally rather than ontologically, finding in this tendency to focus on the role or roles which

a Christology from 'above' it is not referencing any attempt by MacKinnon to take a 'God's eye view';[95] it is rather to give priority to the received 'fact' of divine reconciliation. The scandal is not, at least in the first instance, *that* God became man in some abstract sense, but that in the concrete reality of Jesus's life there is a coming-together of guilt and grace, mercy and justice, holiness and sin, the relative and absolute, that stretches language and human conceptuality beyond its limits. It is in being apprehended by this act of wrenching division followed by reconciliation in the historical biography of Jesus that the church was driven to consider the divine identification with humanity and the nature of Jesus's personhood in relation to the Trinity.[96] For MacKinnon, consideration of 'moral soteriology' must precede that of Christological ontology, just as much as it is also, in the end, found to be dependent on it.

MacKinnon was adamant that the significance of Jesus's life could not be reduced to terms of moral exhortation and mimesis alone (i.e. the exemplarist approach), yet nevertheless it *was* to be understood first and foremost in moral terms.[97] Once again, the Kantian-inspired Christology of P. T. Forsyth provided something of a precursor in as far as he asserted that

> the modern moralisation of religion ... prescribes a new manner of inquiry on such a central subject as the person of Christ. It plants us anew on the standpoint of the Bible, where all human ethic is pointed, transfigured and reissued in Christ's new creation of the moral soul.[98]

Forsyth also noted that 'this rebirth of the race is not a thing yet to be done, but a thing already done and given into our hands'.[99] In this context, he also highlighted the 'once and for all' objective, revelatory and reconciling event of the cross and resurrection of Jesus that we noted in MacKinnon's approach above. The affirmation of atonement as a revealed 'fact' leads Forsyth to ask the question:

> How must we think of him who brought it to pass? As the incarnation of natural and arbitrary omnipotence? No, but as one who was potent for everything morally required by the one need of sinful Humanity, and the one demand of Holy Eternal Love.[100]

---

constitute Christ's ministry at the expense of attempts to capture the identity of his person, a limitation which, to MacKinnon's mind, involved a 'philistine and spiritually distorting amputation of our theological reach'. Connor, *Kenotic Trajectory*, 181. Here Connor is citing *TT*, 169–72.

95. Lash, '"Up" and "Down" in Christology', 35.

96. MacKinnon, 'Subjective and Objective Conceptions of Atonement', 288.

97. MacKinnon admits that he can do no other than consider Christology and soteriology from the vantage point of a moral philosopher. *BT*, 96.

98. Forsyth, *Person and Place*, 222.

99. Ibid.

100. Ibid.

In this instance, Forsyth claimed to be articulating a principle that he finds in Melanchthon and at the heart of reformation theology generally, which he thought has been further vindicated in the a philosophical climate informed by Kant.[101] While some reformers sought a purgative rejection of the schoolmen, seeking to prioritize 'concrete' biblical categories over those of abstract metaphysics, it seemed to Forsyth that Kant had opened up the way for both theology and philosophy to mend the rupture and re-establish a more constructive relationship. Thus, morally-freighted categories of holiness, law, sin and grace; of conscience, guilt and forgiveness are returned to the centre of Christology. According to Forsyth, these categories are irreducibly personal and moral.[102]

MacKinnon was deeply influenced by this sensibility.[103] Yet, his loyalty to the idea of the irreducibly moral nature of Christology is qualified and this is no better evidenced than in his insistence that metaphysics cannot be replaced by moral categories in the way Forsyth proposed. Moore's exploration of two 'styles of theology' is pertinent here:

> In very crude terms [one approach] attempts to give clear priority to the liberating authority of God in Christ; the [other] accepts the influence of Kant's moral philosophy, suspects that a theology of a self-revealing God promotes heteronomy, and so places humanity and its experiences as the focus of theological reflection. [Moore then goes on to argue that] … theological realism sits uneasily between the two. It appeals to authoritative traditions of realism in the Christian past as a reason for defending realism in the present and uses authority figures to articulate the defence, yet it is the authoritative experience of these figures, rather than the intrinsic authority of a self-revealing God, to which appeal is made.[104]

Both Forsyth and MacKinnon seem to travel close to the realism so described, at least in terms of their desire to avoid reductionism and heteronomy. The priority given to soteriology does suggest an emphasis on 'authoritative experience', for instance. Yet MacKinnon's insistence that the language of inter-subjectivity and morality can only go so far to explicate the incarnation and inter-trinitarian

---

101. Ibid., 220.
102. Ibid., 230.
103. MacKinnon's comments on St. John's gospel also bear this out: 'What one finds … in John, especially when one sets the Passion-narrative over against the narrative which introduces it, up to the end of his 12th chapter, is a kind of profound moralization of the theme of final judgement. I mean: the sort of treatment which rescues the moral substance of the theme from the apparatus of apocalyptic imagery, by which men try to make their own a part of its finality. The ethical is prized apart from the cosmological; but the very foundations of the moral universe are found in the concreteness of a historical ordeal.' MacKinnon, 'Subjective and Objective Conceptions of Atonement', 298.
104. Moore, *Realism*, 76.

relations before notions such as 'substance' need to be employed, suggests an unwillingness to part with the 'intrinsic authority of a self-revealing God', and a move that distinguishes him from Forsyth. He is very much a defender of the language of creedal orthodoxy.[105]

By way of exploring this aspect of MacKinnon's thought, it is necessary to raise a question that has so far been brushed over. This relates to the way he understands the move from the intense particularity of atonement to additional claims about its universal significance. This is the time in which the theologian must come to a view regarding the relationship between the man Jesus and the eternal Son, the economic and immanent Trinity.[106] Such a question does not arise from the fact of the brutal death of a first-century Jew with a messianic claim alone. Neither does it arise solely from the fact that such a murder was followed by resurrection. For MacKinnon, the resurrection did not constitute a stand-alone proof of Jesus's incarnate status in and of itself, as if the revelatory 'fact' could be secured by the miraculous.[107] The resurrection only raises the question of Jesus's divine status in as far as it was already raised in conjunction with the atoning gift apprehended within his proclamation of the Kingdom and his death. Without the resurrection, the question of the possibility of Jesus's unique relationship with God would have certainly dissolved into meaninglessness, overwhelmed by tragic defeat. Yet with the empty tomb came a renewal of the questions that his life had begun to provoke. Indeed, with the resurrection they reach a new level of criticality, in as far as Jesus's

---

105. The 'Lux Mundi tradition' in British Anglicanism was also an important influence here, as MacKinnon acknowledged, 'It is often said of the Lux Mundi school (indeed its members sometimes described their work so) that they separated the so-called "physical attributes of God (omnipotence, omnipresence, omniscience, etc.) from the "moral" (benevolence, mercy, justice): and their critics blame their Kantian inspiration for this metaphysical philistinism. Certainly Kant's austere moralism was important to them, if only as a corrective to Hegelian elision of ethical distinctions. But their Christology rests on a surer foundation than philosophical confusion. In reality they are challenging just that sort of classification of divine attributes and doing so on Christological grounds. What they are protesting against … is the Church's unconscious *Entmythologisierung* (demythologisation) of its message, of its understanding of being and of God. For what matters in the end is that we should see the power, the wisdom, the presence of God in terms of his love and compassion: something that we could never have so seen apart from the Incarnation.' *BT*, 117.

106. This is what MacKinnon refers to as 'a rigorous analysis of the notion of identification, an analysis carried out in the context of the theology of the Incarnation' MacKinnon, 'Subjective and Objective Conceptions of Atonement', 299.

107. Lampe, MacKinnon and Purcell, *The Resurrection: A Dialogue Arising From Broadcasts by G.W.H. Lampe and D.M. MacKinnon*. Even if it were possible to do the impossible and prove beyond question the resurrection as a fact of empirical history, it would not deliver to the theologian any automatic assurance of Jesus's identity with the Father.

raised existence effects reconciliation between irreconcilables and retrospectively reveals the cross to have been an integral part of this reconciliation.

MacKinnon was fond of quoting Scott Holland's well-known line that 'when he rose, his life rose with him', which could be taken in two senses.[108] The first emphasizes the particularity of the resurrection as an affirmation of Jesus's ministry and a movement beyond tragic downfall.[109] Second, it refers to the whole of Jesus's life being revealed as containing universal significance. MacKinnon argues that 'we see Christ incarnate through his resurrection: and this is because in his glory his work is consummated and made perpetual'.[110] It comes as no surprise that MacKinnon refuses to let talk of reconciliation banish that of tragedy, or the 'universal' override that of 'particular'.[111] Indeed, 'it is paradoxical but true to say that it is only through Easter that we understand Good Friday, and only through Good Friday that the burden of Easter is made plain'.[112] The move from the cross to the Trinity via the resurrection is not 'idealistic'.

For all of MacKinnon's emphasis on the 'historical particular', however, the empiricist temperament is comparatively muted when it comes to the resurrection.[113] In 1962 MacKinnon endorsed Barth's statement that 'the Resurrection is the non-historical relating of the whole historical life of Jesus to its origin in God', and he does this while defending Barth's commitment to the 'historical Jesus' contra Bultmann.[114] Questions remain as to whether MacKinnon is entirely consistent, or whether he sees the cross and resurrection as constituting markedly different types of 'correspondence' in relation to empirical history and the theological imagination. He never gave much focus on the epistemological status of the resurrection appearances in the gospels, for instance. If the only historical

---

108. D. M. MacKinnon, 'The Tomb Was Empty', in *Burden*, ed. John C. McDowell (London: T&T Clark, 2011), 255.

109. Any language of triumph must be heavily qualified. Ward, 'Tragedy as Subclause: George Steiner's Dialogue with Donald MacKinnon', 278.

110. *BT*, 114–15.

111. Again, MacKinnon's insistence on differentiating himself from the idealist forms of theology is clear: 'When the philosopher Hegel saw in the death and resurrection of Christ an expression, in the form of a myth, of the fundamental law of the being of the universe, he was not wrong in seeing a connection between the two but in making Christ subordinate to that law and not seeing how, in his uniqueness, Christ both reveals the true nature of and gives validity to that law.' MacKinnon, 'The Tomb Was Empty', 257–8.

112. Ibid., 256–7.

113. MacKinnon's approach to the resurrection is far less focused on historical particularity when compared to his examination of the trial and death: 'It defies all methods of simple and direct representation', MacKinnon, 'Subjective and Objective Conceptions of Atonement'; MacKinnon, 'The Tomb Was Empty', 293. On this point Steiner notes that '[MacKinnon] had Kierkegaardian doubts about our ability to conceive of a resurrection'. Steiner, 'Tribute to Donald MacKinnon', 2.

114. MacKinnon, 'Barth's Epistle to the Romans (Book Review)', 6–7.

fact we can conceivably access is the empty tomb, and all theological imagination must be grounded and disciplined by such facts (as MacKinnon insists), it does leave open the question of the level of 'realism' MacKinnon is willing to ascribe to the resurrection.[115]

Transition from atonement theology to trinitarian ontology

Putting the apophatic reserve and conceptual vagueness of MacKinnon's resurrection theology to one side, it might be said that the event reveals Jesus to be a man uniquely 'open' to the life and power of God, and in so doing sets before us the 'ontological riddle' of his person.[116] He would not have put it in exactly these terms, however, as speaking of the unique 'openness' of Jesus to the Father is one of a number of Christological idioms cited by MacKinnon as emerging from a temptation to substitute the *homoousion* with more palatable (read less overtly metaphysical) forms.[117] For MacKinnon, any such talk poses the question of ontology rather than replaces it. He was always uncomfortable when metaphysics was banished from explicit theological formulations, convinced that it would continue implicitly, at least when realist notions of God were maintained. In this vein, Connor observes that the dynamic of cross-resurrection presented MacKinnon with a task, which was to set this

> dynamic polarity in its proper relation to the dynamic ontological context of the movement of God to humanity and of humanity to God, that is, in the context determined by the interplay of the 'inhumanization' of the divine and the 'eternalization' of the human.[118]

MacKinnon would concede that there is a kind of epistemological circularity in all this, which goes hand-in-hand with any theology that holds to the scandal of revelatory particularity, yet it is a circularity that he wants to explicate. For MacKinnon, any revelatory epistemology must be developed with reference to at

---

115. MacKinnon: 'Of course this "raising" was something that none could see, none could perceive; it is not an event in time like the burial of Jesus or the visits of mourners to his tomb. But (to speak very crudely) the emptying of the tomb is in some sense such an event, or group of events, as those; that is to say, if the tomb was empty, there must have been a moment in time when the body of Jesus was in the tomb, and a moment afterwards when it was not. And if we say this (and it is the present writer's view that we must), we are in some sense putting ourselves in bondage to the settlement of questions which are questions of historical fact'. *BT*, 76.

116. MacKinnon, 'The Tomb Was Empty.'

117. Schleiermacher was the forerunner here with his notion of Jesus's unique 'God consciousness'.

118. Connor, *Kenotic Trajectory*, 179.

least three domains: the person of Jesus and his sojourn from Galilee to Jerusalem and a back again, the theological interpretation of these facts, and an engagement with the spiritual life and suffering in which a 'refraction of [the] mystery' of the Cross is apprehended. For MacKinnon, all three are dimensions that are interlinked, coming under the 'sign of kenosis'. He adds that 'the final note is of a radical self-abandonment'.[119] In this instance we see what might be called MacKinnon's Kierkegaardian and Barthian side to the fore, in which there is no apprehension of God without transformative and costly personal participation; something which aligns with the therapeutic emphasis outlined in Chapter 1.[120] Knowledge of a 'kenotic God' revealed in Jesus requires an analogous kenosis on the part of the one seeking illumination. In this way, the 'object' of knowledge determines how it is one may come to know it (i.e. through mimesis and participation) and this drives MacKinnon's insistence that it is not just in the realm of epistemology where kenosis plays a role, but also on the level of ontology. For MacKinnon,

> It is clear that if the notion of Kenosis is to have a central place in Christology, that will only be achieved when it is seen as demanding that we extrapolate such concepts as limitation, vulnerability and their like into the framing of our doctrine of God.[121]

In the concept of kenosis MacKinnon finds the potential, not only for our participation in the event of revelation but also for the development of an ontology that might fittingly describe the identity of Jesus with God.[122] The logic seems to be that (a) if the life of Jesus is characterized by a form of self-emptying that is not ultimately self-annihilating but continuous with the fullness of resurrected/eternal life and (b) that Jesus is the revelation of God in history and identified with God in an ontologically significant way, then this pattern forms a reliable 'analogy of attribution' to God's eternal Trinitarian character.[123] Both the life of Jesus and

---

119. *BT*, 80.

120. A position along these lines is developed by Moser, who attempts to articulate a 'personalist' theological epistemology that avoids naturalism and fideism. Moser, *The Evidence for God: Religious Knowledge Re-examined*.

121. MacKinnon, 'Reflections on Donald Baillie's Treatment of the Atonement', 121.

122. MacKinnon was influenced by Bulgakov, 'arguably the greatest Russian Orthodox theologian of the twentieth century and certainly the author of one of the profoundest studies we have of the kenosis of the incarnation'. *ET*, 22.

123. Williams points out the ways in which MacKinnon – for all his similarities with notions of the Trinity developed by Hegel and Moltmann – avoids their 'evasions of the temporal – Hegel by generalizing Good Friday into a necessary moment in the universal dialectic, Moltmann, by weakening the force of the recognition that Jesus's suffering is humanly inflicted, through his concentration on the Cross as the Father's giving-up of the Son, a transaction in a mythical rather than historical space'. Rowan Williams, 'Trinity

the inner life of God can be understood by means of a common kenotic ontology that is shared between them. According to MacKinnon,

> Kenosis is the place where the nature of God's love is seen ... and it the locus where we might find some reconciliation between 'those who insist on divine impassibility as necessarily involved in God's transcendence, and those who, like the late Geoffrey Studdert Kennedy, were moved by their knowledge of the reality of human suffering to deny it'.[124]

As Kirkland has recently noted, the legacy of Henry Scott Holland looms large in MacKinnon's approach here.[125] It helped him to avoid formulating a kenoticism either 'from below', as did those who made historical criticism an absolute test for theological epistemology, or 'from above', as did kenotic theologies proffered by Forsyth among others.[126] In the latter case, 'kenosis is a renunciation from a position of already existing power, albeit moral, and so power itself is not of necessity recast in the kenotic act'.[127] In any case, continuing to affirm the notion placed MacKinnon in tension with contemporaries such as Don Cupitt, Brian Davies and D. M. Baillie. Yet, Surin makes the point that participants in the debate were not always adequately aware of the different meanings that were being attached to the term. He argues that MacKinnon may avoid the charge of incoherence directed at some other kenotic theologies in as far as they understand kenosis to involve a divestment of divine attributes, rather than an act within God that enabled one, by means of a sophisticated notion of analogy, to claim that Jesus's historic kenosis was an expression of and participation in God's eternal nature.[128] To draw on an idiom MacKinnon uses elsewhere there are various 'moves in a game' occurring here, and one must not mistake a single move for the whole game. Developing a prolegomena to Christology, he wrote:

> If ... we allow the mystery of the Incarnation to shed its light upon the formal order of relations of creature to creator, and creator to creature, and if we give

---

and Ontology', in *Christ, Ethics and Tragedy: Essays in Honour of Donald MacKinnon*, ed. Kenneth Surin (Cambridge: Cambridge University Press, 1989), 84.

124. *BT*, 80.

125. Scott Kirkland, 'Part 2 Introduction: "That One Man Should Die for the People": Ecclesiological Fundamentalism, Kenosis and the Tragic', in *Kenotic Ecclesiology; Select Writings of Donald MacKinnon*, ed. J. McDowell, S. Kirkland and A. J. Moyse (Minneapolis, MN: Fortress Press, 2016), 164–5.

126. See Sarah Coakley, 'Kenosis and Subversion: On the Repression of "Vulnerability" in Christian Feminist Writing', in *Powers and Submissions: Spirituality, Philosophy and Gender* (Oxford: Blackwell, 2002), 21–3.

127. Scott Kirkland, 'Part 2 Introduction', 164.

128. Surin, 'Some Aspects of the "Grammar" of "Incarnation" and "Kenosis": Reflections Prompted by the Writings of Donald MacKinnon', 103.

to that mystery the authority it claims, we must reverse any understanding of divine transcendence that sees transcendence as only safeguarded by refusal to admit any sort of self-limitation into the divine, any sort of self-committal in creation that would allow a genuine, if asymmetrical, reciprocity in relations of creation and creator. Of course God must (and the must is of logical necessity) remain invulnerable. One might say that his aseity can be mythologized in terms of an ultimate invulnerability.[129]

Linking the Immanent and Economic Trinity via a language of kenosis gives rise to a tension which the paired language of 'self-limitation' and 'invulnerability' identifies. As kenotic language contributes to this tension, MacKinnon doubts that it can – on its own – adequately capture the unity of divine and human, economic and immanent, which occurred in the incarnation. In this he departs from Forsyth, who claimed that conceiving Jesus's identification with God in the kenotic terms meant that one could achieve a credible notion of the unity of Christ's personhood via a moral notion (kenosis) without recourse to traditional metaphysics:

> The ethical notion of the true unity as the interpenetration of persons by moral action must take the place of the old metaphysics of the union of natures by a *tour de force*. Unity of being need not be denied, but it will be approached and construed on those ethical lines which alone consist with personal relation and explain it.[130]

Such an approach is labelled 'functionalism' by MacKinnon, who took a view closer to that of Oliver Chase Quick, which more or less insisted that a connection or identification of these two movements could not be substantiated without reference to a notion like 'substance' or something equivalent.[131] That is, MacKinnon did not see personal and moral categories, including that of kenosis, as sufficient to articulate a credible integration of the divine and human personhood of Jesus.[132]

---

129. *TT*, 183–4.
130. Forsyth, *Person and Place*, 231.
131. MacKinnon refers to Oscar Cullmann's *The Christology of the New Testament* as an example of a well-argued presentation of a functionalist approach. He argues, however, that it falls short of any adequate explanation of the identity of the Father and Son. MacKinnon, '"Substance" in Christology: A Cross-bench View', 250.
132. The limits of functionalism are evident when Forsyth invokes the analogy of a married couple: 'In marriage the ideal is (however far we may be yet from its general realisation) that two personalities not only united but completely interpenetrating in love, and growing into a dual person. "The two shall be one flesh" – one spiritual personality. This interpenetration is something of which personality alone is capable. Any notion like "a nature" is too physical in its origin and action to rise really above the impenetrability of matter, and the mutual eternality of each such nature. ... The marriage relation is the brief epitome of the social principle of the kingdom of God, of the unity of Christ, and the kind of unity in a Triune God.' Forsyth, *Person and Place*, 230.

He pleads for patience as he seeks to explicate the necessity of maintaining a term like 'substance' in twentieth-century Christology. The aim was not to revive one notion of substance from the past, but to draw on a particular philosophical tradition.[133]

> I say metaphysical *tradition*: for it is important to see the doctrine of substance less as a precisely formulable dogma than as the name of a series of explorations whose very nature oscillates as they develop.[134]

The nature of this oscillation is one that gives attention to both the

> aspects of the world that are at once totally familiar and everyday, and at the same time highly elusive and even mysterious in the paradoxical character that they immediately disclose to more minute inspection.[135]

At risk of gross oversimplification, one can observe that for Aristotle of the *Categories* and *Metaphysics*, an intense focus on the concrete particular gives rise to, and cannot find completion without, notions such as substance, quality and accident.[136] Indeed, MacKinnon seems to think that a strongly analogous dynamic to that which one finds in Aristotle is also at work when one focuses on the gospel writer's reflections on the particularity of Jesus's life and death.[137] 'Realism' in both cases leads to modes of speech that transcend the raw sensory apprehension of objects, yet never fly free of this apprehension. In taking this path, however, he was careful to heed Luther's warning that 'he who wishes to philosophize by using Aristotle without danger to his soul must first become thoroughly foolish in Christ'.[138] Additionally, it is clear that MacKinnon's reading of Kant, Whitehead, Collingwood and Quine shaped his reception of the term:

> Whitehead, whom Collingwood greatly admired, remarked that in the history of metaphysics the modern period was marked by successive attempts to find a

---

133. In this endeavour, he was aided by a close reading of Christopher Stead, *Divine Substance* (Oxford: Clarendon Press, 1977).
134. MacKinnon, '"Substance" in Christology: A Cross-bench View', 238.
135. Ibid., 239.
136. Stead, *Divine Substance*, 55–88. And MacKinnon, 'Aristotle's Conception of Substance', 97–110.
137. Again, it should be remembered that he is not by any means attempting an unalloyed Aristotelian revival: while his explorations often take the 'Aristotelian apparatus as its starting place ... [because] he was justified in fastening attention on these notions [such as thing, individual, form, quality, etc.]', MacKinnon sees 'serious weaknesses' in the way Aristotle understood relations between these notions. MacKinnon, '"Substance" in Christology: A Cross-bench View', 124.
138. Stanley, *Protestant Metaphysics after Karl Barth and Martin Heidegger*, 15.

substitute for substance, the pivotal notion of the classical Aristotelian ontology. Reference was made above to Edward Caird's suggestive comment that with Kant and Hegel subject had usurped this role. Certainly in Kant substance emerges as one of three categories of relation (along with causality and reciprocity), whereby the subject is enabled to establish the kind of permanent background necessary for the apprehension of objective change. It was an indispensable condition of the possibility of objective awareness; but it is established as valid only as such. In other words, its significance lies in the context of the subject's active experience.[139]

According to MacKinnon, the person of Christ confronted the primitive church, as indeed he confronted its twentieth-century successors, with questions which call for notions that attempt to encapsulate the 'indispensable conditions of the possibility of objective awareness'. This is because there is in these notions 'the peculiar ultimacy and the peculiar pervasiveness ... and because ... the person of Christ thrusts upon our attention the question how one identifiable historical individual shall be at once e.g. "one thing" with the Father and yet subordinate to that Father in that the Father is greater than he'.[140] The 'return of substance' is not a simplistic denial of Kant's Copernican revolution; 'substance' is not a metaphysical object but a way of speaking about the conditions that made incarnation and atonement possible, namely the union of the Father and Son.[141] Part of MacKinnon's move here is a critique of what he perceived as a post-Cartesian trend:

> One finds in certain recent and indeed contemporary theological writing explicit reference to arguments contained in modern works both of speculative metaphysics and of analytical philosophy that the notion of event is more fundamental than that of substance, that in fact things in the sense in which living bodies, certain artefacts, human individuals ... are to be regarded as

---

139. D. M. MacKinnon, 'Faith and Reason in the Philosophy of Religion', in *Philosophy, History and Civilization: Interdisciplinary Perspectives on R.G. Collingwood*, ed. David Boucher, James Connelly and Tariq Modood (Cardiff: University of Wales Press, 1995), 89. At one point MacKinnon notes that Quine enabled him to read Aristotle with fresh eyes: 'As soon as we begin to ask ourselves what, if anything, we can make of the question what it is that our thinking ultimately refers to, as soon as we pose Quine's problem of an ultimate conceptual system in more realist terms of the reference of our thought, the character of Aristotelian ontology begins to change, and Aristotle's doctrine of substance emerges less as the account of the essence of things which a bad historical tradition has encouraged us to find in it, than as a way of enabling us to recognise what it is for there to be a world in which distinctions obtain, within which there are many diverse things, yet related in the manner of their being one to another in ways which we can grasp.' MacKinnon, 'Aristotle's Conception of Substance', 111.

140. MacKinnon, '"Substance" in Christology: A Cross-bench View', 245.

141. Ibid., 239.

'logical constructions' out of events, the last being identified with momentary or short-lived occurrences ... what we would in ordinary speech regard as short-lived slices or phases of the history of persistent things.[142]

What MacKinnon goes on to suggest, however crudely at this point, is that the relationship of the notion of a 'thing' (a term which MacKinnon uses in close proximity to language of 'substance') to that of 'event' is not best understood as one in which the former emerges out of the latter, even if it is only in apprehension of the event that the question of substance is raised.[143] Indeed, once the whole context of an event is considered, particularly the actors involved and their particular place in history, MacKinnon comes to the suggestion that the notion of event is actually parasitic on that of 'thing'.[144] Emerging here is what Williams labels as MacKinnon's 'negative metaphysics', and just as recourse to analogy becomes important for negative theology, so it becomes important here. This is evident when MacKinnon notes that

> a metaphysical truth of the kind we are now speaking of does agree with mathematical truth in claiming universality and necessity. Like them it relates to what must be the case, but to what must be the case in a way significantly different from that in which we say of mathematical truths that they must be as they are. Among candidates for the class of such truths we may include the thesis that all that happens belongs to a single time order, that nothing happens without falling along some causal line in terms of which it is explicable, that there are relatively permanent things to which events happen, and that truth itself consists fundamentally in the correspondence of a proposition and a fact.[145]

Kenosis and 'substance' are strongly related for MacKinnon – a reflection of a broader conviction that moral discourse cannot do without metaphysical reference. Rather than acting as a stand-in for metaphysics, a focus on kenotic acts will produce the same impulses and questions that led theologians of old to invoke such terms.[146] And yet, 'habitual routes' by which reference to 'substance' occurred will not provide exact guidance as to how MacKinnon intends its use.

---

142. Ibid., 245–6.
143. Williams contends that a deeper commitment to humanism underlies MacKinnon's argument here: 'The sentient individual is more than a "logical construction out of events" without involving us in speculative fancy about naked individual subjects existing prior to relation and perception.' Williams, 'Trinity and Ontology', 77.
144. MacKinnon, '"Substance" in Christology: A Cross-bench View', 243.
145. *ET*, 102.
146. MacKinnon: 'I would wish to suggest that [the most fundamental task in Christology] ... is one of reconciling the use of the category of substance in the articulation of the Christological problem with the recognition that it is the notion of *kenōsis* which more

The theologian must be on guard lest its invocation leads to an embrace of the illusion that we were being 'enabled to reach something more ultimate in the economy of divine self-disclosure and self-impartation than the person of Jesus Christ crucified and risen'.[147] This becomes clear when MacKinnon refers to Jesus's Gethsemane anguish and speaks of:

> [Jesus's] relation to the Father, the Sonship that is his eternal substance, is now found transcribed into a murky, human obscurity. And through this transcription, the divine puts itself at the mercy of the human as if only so could the limitations of human existence (finitude infected by sin) be converted into an instrument of confession: as if there were depths of the human condition that only the divine could penetrate. ... It is creation and the work of the creator that must be reinterpreted through this experience of the cost and way of redemption.[148]

Here, we see in microcosm the way MacKinnon's soteriology is being worked out via a restless dialectic between 'kenosis' and 'substance', and the way these terms are being continually reshaped as one is seen in light of the other. Criticisms have been made of MacKinnon's invocation of 'substance', but they often fail to capture the tension MacKinnon holds aloft, or they seek alternatives that may bring relief to the tension but sacrifice a commitment to the sort of realism to which he was committed. For instance, Surin draws on Lindbeck to question the return to metaphysics, even in the minimalist form MacKinnon proposes.[149] What is being missed, however, is the way MacKinnon draws the invocation of 'substance' down into the gritty reality of historical kenosis, and also the fact that he saw such a move as essential to moral realism: something that did not concern the likes of Lindbeck in the same way.[150]

Excursus: Alter Christus? *MacKinnon on Lenin*

No treatment of MacKinnon's Christology is complete without commenting on the eccentric way in which he brought Lenin into his reflections. In his 1953 essay *Christian Faith and Communist Faith* and 1978 postscript to an earlier essay *Lenin and Theology*, MacKinnon expressed a conviction that a serious

---

than any other single notion points to the deepest sense of the mystery of the incarnation.' MacKinnon, '"Substance" in Christology: A Cross-bench View', 251.

147. Ibid., 247–9.

148. MacKinnon, 'Reflections on Donald Baillie's Treatment of the Atonement', 117.

149. Surin, 'Some Aspects of the "Grammar" of "Incarnation" and "Kenosis": Reflections Prompted by the Writings of Donald MacKinnon', 102.

150. For a critique of Lindbeck which I suspect would gain a sympathetic hearing from MacKinnon, see Moore, *Realism*, 92–107.

engagement with Marxism and Leninism was crucial for the contemporary theologian.[151] He also perceived that, even in their antagonism towards Christianity, attentiveness to their claims could unearth resources to help the theologian withstand pressure to turn faith into a subjectivist enterprise.[152] Such an enterprise treats 'Christian believing ... as if it could be scrutinized in virtually complete aversion from what is believed', which for MacKinnon is tantamount to de-historicization of Christianity.[153] Attentiveness to recent history and contemporary politics may help prevent the theologian from losing touch with the historicity of Christ, or so it seemed to MacKinnon. It continually refreshed and refocused his attention on the tensions between determinism and freedom, universal imperative and particular adaptation, tragedy and hope, all of which were vital to Christology.

MacKinnon evoked Lenin within an environment where debates were raging over avant-garde declarations of Christian 'atheism' and secularism, revolutionary politics were in vogue on British university campuses, and Marxism still counted as a serious political influence within mainstream academia and politics.[154] On a sympathetic reading, MacKinnon detected the presence of resources that would stimulate the theological imagination and help to maintain focus on articulating the paradoxical heart of the incarnation:

> Where many Christians' understanding of their own faith is concerned, it may be that it is through serious engagement with the claims of Marxist-Leninism, that those vocationally committed to the progress of theology will find their way to a re-creation of the doctrine of Christ's person and work, and of the doctrine of God as Trinity in Unity, that is bound up with it, which neither seeks to ignore the reality of the very difficult intellectual problems that these conceptions raise, nor to admit them only to pretend that a greater theological wisdom would never have allowed the doctrinal development with which they seem inextricably bound up.[155]

---

151. D. M. MacKinnon, *Christian Faith and Communist Faith: A Series of Studies by Members of the Anglican Communion* (London: Macmillan, 1953), 229–41. Also see *ET*, 25.

152. *ET*, 25.

153. Ibid., 27–8.

154. MacKinnon maintained an avid interest in Russian political history. He read the biographies of George Lukacs, David Shub, Louis Fisher and Adam Ulam. He also read Isaac Deutscher's works on Stalin and Trotsky. In 1966 he read J. P. Nettl's two-volume study of Rosa Luxemburg and described it as 'excellent'. Ibid., 12. Add to this list Theodore Dan's 'Menshevik account of the origins of Bolshevism', Donald Treadgold's study of Lenin and his adversaries, Israel Getzler's *Martox: A political biography of a Russian Social Democrat'* and M. Lewin's *Russian Peasants and Soviet Power*. *ET*, 17.

155. Ibid., 25.

In an essay from 1970 Lenin is labelled 'the greatest atheist of the twentieth century' and the 'greatest revolutionary of the twentieth century'.[156] More startlingly, MacKinnon spoke of Lenin in quasi-messianic terms. This raises the question as to whether MacKinnon fell for some of the claims of the propagandistic cult of personality surrounding Lenin in a way that suggests a lapse in his own efforts to maintain 'moral seriousness' and to avoid the worst excesses of idealistic renderings of history. What MacKinnon expected from any prolonged reflection on the life and times of Lenin was not edification, however, but something therapeutic, between purgation and illumination.[157] He acknowledged the perspective of an 'intellectually sophisticated defender of the Leninist enterprise' and their insistence

> that in so far as only through such industrialization can human living standards be raised, human opportunities of life and experience enlarged, provided that the work is set in hand self-consciously it must be regarded as the way humanity must take if it is to assume control of its own destiny.[158]

'Shocking' and 'horrifying' are adjectives used to describe the costs of such a transition and a clear line is drawn from the Bolshevik regime to Stalin's 'unspeakable' outrages against the humane.[159] There is no fawning admiration, just a degree of political realism and perhaps tragic fatalism in the observation that there is no way societies have managed to transition from agrarian feudalism to industrial modernity without amassing huge costs along the way. Rather than make an absolute moral judgement, one can detect in MacKinnon's work a grudging fascination of those visionaries who contemplated the cost of modernity and were willing to push ahead in spite of it, East and West alike. Perhaps it is the kind of respect that Raphael saw at work in the appeal of classical tragedy, where the hero struggles against, but is ultimately defeated by, a much stronger determining agency, and in the end it is some aspect of the hero's virtue in persisting with this hopeless struggle that sets them apart.[160]

MacKinnon expressed a conviction that as a system marked by an acute historical consciousness, Christianity could not avoid serious engagement with one of the most striking epoch-shifting figures of the modernity. Indeed, Lenin posed a particular challenge as he gave the moral theologian no place 'at the table'. In *State and Revolution*, Lenin purportedly argued that Marxism 'contains no shred of ethics from beginning to end' yet speaks of 'the simple and fundamental

---

156. Ibid., 11, 23.
157. Ibid., 11.
158. Ibid., 19.
159. Ibid., 18.
160. D. D. Raphael, *The Paradox of Tragedy*, The Mahlon Powell lectures (Bloomington: Indiana University Press, 1960), 13–36.

rules of every-day social life'.[161] Furthermore, the sort of atheism espoused was not part of some dialectical process on the way to faith; it was not the 'atheism-lite' of the fashionable Christian non-realists.[162] It was a total claim; an intense and thoroughgoing materialism and this is what made it interesting to MacKinnon. What the theologian faces is the 'conscious, deliberate and deeply convinced rejection of the reality of God as a *prius* of informed debate and action concerning the fundamentals of human life and society'.[163]

There were a number of features of Lenin's life and thought that fascinated MacKinnon, but at the forefront was the way issues of causation, freedom and morality came to the fore. MacKinnon observed that

> Marxism is in a very special sense a form of historical determinism: in a very special sense, for the dialectical quality of historical materialism transforms the simplicity of the concept of historical causality with which it operates. [MacKinnon notes that within this view of history are figures such as] Lenin, who in himself existentially (to use a fashionable adverb) reconciled the claims of determinism and freedom.[164]

In his political life, Lenin did what Kant attempted to do in his philosophical system, and indeed, he displayed a particular quality that Kant saw in the figure of Jesus. Here we can find the basis for the limited and controversial analogy that MacKinnon made between Jesus and Lenin. Specifically, some lives are judged as raising questions for the philosopher because of the particular contradictions and paradoxes they hold together, as well as the degree to which their choices interact with events beyond their control to usher significant historical upheaval and cultural redefinition. According to MacKinnon, these are lives that raise the question of the 'absolute' and 'relative' within history.[165] Speaking of Lenin, MacKinnon noted that 'he was a rigorous objectivist, convinced that there were laws of historical development. Yet he was also supremely executant as well as architect of most drastic historical change'.[166] Freedom and determinism are co-located, but so too are theory and practice which achieve a new unity 'in his biography'; indeed, 'the scope of Marxist theory is enhanced by his actual achievement'.[167]

---

161. Eugene Kamenka, *The Ethical Foundations of Marxism*, Second edition (London: Routledge and Kegan Paul, 1972), 3.

162. According to MacKinnon, 'To submit to interrogation by exponents of a most rigorous atheism ... is to say farewell to the more leisurely and gentlemanly styles of apologetic, whose end, Whitehead once said, might be described as "seeking to furnish us with new reasons for continuing to go to church in the old way"'. *ET*, 25.

163. Ibid., 12.
164. Ibid., 15.
165. Ibid., 55–69.
166. Ibid., 15.
167. Ibid.

At this point, some question-begging parallels emerge between MacKinnon's analysis of Lenin's significance and Christology. For instance, MacKinnon spoke of 'apologists' who look upon the violence and upheaval unleashed in the wake of the October Revolution and argue that

> tragedy is of the very substance of human history, and that at least such a man as Lenin showed himself willing not to suffer blindly as the play-thing of an inevitable destiny, but rather to pay the price, if necessary, of the guilt incurred, that seemed demanded, if humankind, and in the first instance the war-weary people of Russia … were to be brought some way towards the promised land.[168]

The theological overtones are explicit, and there is a definite allusion to Christ who 'journeyed to a far off country', necessarily following the path set out for him in suffering obedience, but doing so by a free choice. MacKinnon took the analogy even further, speaking of the 'incarnational' nature of Marxist-Leninism. Thus, while acknowledging the 'dark side' of Lenin's resolute revolutionary dedication, MacKinnon argued that he

> presents the student of his life with a classical realization of the unity of theory and practice, a realization whose fruits abide in the present. In his life and work the Marxist idea of social transformation became terrifyingly incarnate, and we live in the shadow of the impact of that incarnation; for the weight of that incarnation lies abundantly over the world of the bitter Sino-Soviet dispute. Dare we find here a parable of the fundamental Christian reality, the incarnation of the Word of God; the kenosis of the eternal Son? Certainly for myself I find in the study of Lenin's concrete definition of the revolutionary idea, in his achievement, the source of a continual impulse to engage anew with the doctrine of the Incarnation.[169]

Apprehending Christology afresh via historical figures such as Lenin is certainly an eccentric and controversial move from the vantage point of twenty-first-century Britain, but it shows the way analogical and parabolic imagination coalesces with historical criticism in MacKinnon's thought to provoke therapeutic disruption, as well as highlighting again his tendency to break ranks with any form of reductionist empirical historicism. MacKinnon's sympathetic reading of Merleau-Ponty's *Humanism and Terror* shows him to be conscientized to the horrors suffered by Soviet citizens in the wake of the revolution and his point is never to see Lenin as being a 'second Christ'.[170] Furthermore, we would do well

---

168. Ibid., 19.
169. Ibid., 21.
170. *BT*, 159. Additionally, Muller has drawn my attention to this excerpt from a forward that MacKinnon wrote for one of Marcel's books: '[Marcel] reveals to us (and I am myself a member of the Labour Party) how the Left no less than the Right can count in its

to read MacKinnon's provocative reflections alongside the 1966 essay 'Some Reflections on Secular Diakonia', in which he locates parables of sacrificial service in the contemporary political sphere over several case studies. For MacKinnon, the universal significance of Christ's life and sacrifice is apprehended by the fact that it is refracted in parabolic stories of individuals who have spent themselves for humanistic social reform. His references to Lenin must be interpreted (and moderated) by reference to this wider logic.[171]

MacKinnon's emphasis on the tragic throughout these discussions precludes the imaginative exercise from falling into what Ramsey labelled as Illingworth's 'naïve optimism' when the latter claimed that 'secular civilisation is ... in the Christian view, nothing less than the providential correlative and counterpart of the incarnation'.[172] Darwell Stone criticized Charles Gore in 1890 because he felt that the writers Gore had assembled to compile *Lux Mundi*, 'treated revelation as differing only in degree from the natural man's knowledge of God and blurred the line between the distinctive inspiration of Scripture and the phenomenon of genius in the human race'. MacKinnon may be vulnerable to this charge, but he would have probably dismissed it as a philistine inability to engage the analogical and parabolic imagination.[173]

In the next chapter I will show that MacKinnon did attempt to break down a sacred divide between the text of scripture and texts of the wider literary canon, a move that shares the same originating impulse as the discussion of Lenin in relation to Christology. In his references to Lenin, MacKinnon pointed to a historical persona that renders Christian talk of the incarnation as one that is also native to a modern, secular epoch after all. If the life of Christ illuminates our apprehension of even the most atheistic of individuals, then claims pertaining to its universal significance continue to bear meaning. What becomes apparent here is the presence of elements in MacKinnon's thought that run alongside the empiricist emphasis on the 'particular' and moderate the rejection of idealism so prominent throughout his oeuvre. There *is* a narrative dimension to history; the identification of certain structures, recurrent questions and the linking of particular events through analogy in a way that proves illuminative for realizing what is at stake in both. Again, a 'scissors and paste' approach to history is rejected and the empiricism of the poets is enjoined, but it all pivots, for MacKinnon, on the particularity of Christ.

Do MacKinnon's reflections on Lenin and Christology represent a genuinely creative theological enterprise, expressing a courageous vulnerability to key

---

ranks men ready to apologize for, if not to justify, every form of brutality and foulness which "progress" (the Left's counterpart to "tradition") can somehow justify.' Gabriel Marcel, *Men against Humanity* (London: Harvill Press, 1952), n.p.

171. D. M. MacKinnon, 'Some Reflection on Secular Diakonia', 67–76.

172. Ramsey, *From Gore to Temple: The Development of Anglican Theology between Lux Mundi and the Second World War, 1889-1939*, 4–5.

173. Ibid., 9.

conversation partners in the wider historical milieu, or do they suggest an eccentric obsession that undermines aspects of MacKinnon's Christology as it is developed elsewhere? The answer is probably affirmative on both counts and such explorations left MacKinnon particularly vulnerable to the critiques by Hart and Milbank in as far as they harbour deep reservations about MacKinnon's use of the tragic motif.[174] For, in what I have described above, it seems that the analogical invocation of 'incarnation' is one grounded in a shared participation in the tragic dimension of history, as the tension between freedom and determinism crushes and frustrates the work of otherwise noble, visionary individuals. Indeed, just as MacKinnon sought to purge evasions of the historical particular in others, so there is concern that the same might be said of MacKinnon's invocation of the tragic as a kind of structural component to history or an irreducible presence in Trinitarian ontology.[175] In light of this, Hart makes explicit what remains implicit in MacKinnon's project: the resurrection must shatter the analogy between Christ and Lenin just as soon as it has been invoked. One can easily imagine MacKinnon conceding this point, but stubbornly insisting on the therapeutic value of the analogy all the same.[176]

Conclusion

In this chapter I sought to examine the ways in which the therapeutic methodology identified in Chapter 1 and the key influences on MacKinnon's intellectual formation explored in Chapter 2 are brought to bear on Christological themes. What emerged was an insistent call for a focus on the historical particularity of the incarnation as part of a wider commitment to realism. This was coupled with a conviction that imaginative construction and projection can potentially enhance rather than detract from such realism. A relentless submission of all theologizing to the reality of Christ's historic existence is coupled with an exposure to contemporary historical realities in order to apprehend the meaning of this existence afresh. While this approach helped MacKinnon to avoid some of the excesses of mid-century non-realist theology on the one hand, it also resulted in daring forays into Christological analogy on the other. In the next chapter, I will explore the way in which MacKinnon saw literature as a therapeutic resource towards moral realism in ways that parallel and deepen many of the themes raised above.

---

174. I will return to these in Chapter 5.

175. MacKinnon does seem to be aware of the temptation and I return to this question in the following chapters.

176. Considering the prominence MacKinnon gives to the tragic motif, it must be remembered that the profession of the resurrection 'is the *prius* of Christian construction'. *ET*, 83.

Chapter 4

MACKINNON AND THE LITERARY IMAGINATION

Introduction

MacKinnon once observed that

> it has been very often (though not exclusively) in the medium of imaginative literature that the questions which refuse to be answered in terms of a facile teleology have persistently intruded themselves.[1]

This chapter will focus on MacKinnon's use of literature as a therapeutic resource that serves his primary commitment to moral realism. MacKinnon may be placed in the company of Iris Murdoch, Peter Winch and Gilbert Ryle, all of whom explored the frontiers between literature and moral philosophy from the 1960s, perhaps anticipating the acceleration of the discussion in the 1980s, with figures such as Martha Nussbaum leading the discussion in Anglo-American philosophy.[2]

MacKinnon's literary interests stem from his early realization that Kant's moral formalism needed to be supplemented by means of descriptions which brought out the irreducible complexity of particular human lives.[3] As has become clear from previous chapters, this was a concern that MacKinnon had not only in relation to the Kantian legacy but also positivist utilitarianism, deductive Christian natural law approaches, deconstructive non-realist ethics, or any school of moral philosophy that began by establishing universal principles or overarching theories of moral obligation which were then to be applied casuistically.[4] In each case the formal principle comes into relentless questioning under the exposure of the 'particular' and this pressure inevitably causes moral theories to fail under the weight of their own qualifications and contradictions. The moral discourse struggles to escape the realm of hypothetical abstractions and the temptation is always to generalize and simplify concrete moral dilemmas so as to make them descriptively accessible, even 'solvable'. For MacKinnon, certain kinds of literature can play a corrective role in animating and complementing a kind of historical realism that avoids this

---

1. *ET*, 194.
2. Nora Hämäläinen, *Literature and Moral Theory* (London: Bloomsbury, 2017), 4–18.
3. *SET*, 115–20.
4. Ibid., 56–60. And 'Natural Law', 120–9.

temptation. To the degree to which literature can help us perceive moral conflict inherent in historical events and apprehend the universal in the particular, it also becomes a site where the 'problem of metaphysics' arises.

A moral realist reads literature

MacKinnon acknowledged no foundational metaphysical bedrock that would secure moral realism, or provide it with unassailable positive content. In an agnostic tone he continually associated invocation of a metaphysical register with the persistence of a certain kind of interrogation, rather than any solid answers from which we can secure subsequent concepts and proposals.[5] In this vein, MacKinnon spoke of the intersection of general and special metaphysics or, perhaps translated analogously to the ethical sphere, the universal moral imperative(s) and the demands of a concrete historical situation as discerned by a particular, fallible human being or a community. He argued that

> if there is a *metaphysica perennis,* it is found more in the strange immunity to the acids of criticism of a programme rather than in a positive body of achievement. Where there is achievement it resides more in the deepened awareness of what such a programme involves, and of understanding of the conceptual tools we need for its advancement – and here of course I refer to the interplay of *metaphysica generalis* with *metaphysica specialis:* an interplay that we are immediately aware of in the classical authorities, Aristotle and Kant. Over against this we have to reckon with the Hegelian incorporation into the body of speculative philosophy of the cry for redemption. It is through literature (which Plato so vigorously censured) that the bitterness of that cry is caught.[6]

For MacKinnon, literature does have usefulness: it captures a 'cry'. Literature is an avenue for the most pertinent expressions of the question that traditional theodicy has sought to answer and, compared with many of these efforts by theologians and philosophers, it has provided a more truthful response. It can present us with situations in which agents are confronted by moral demands and a means by which we might be rehabilitated from the kind of self-deception which clouds our moral perception and dulls the capacity for judgement. In this vein, when works such as Shakespeare's *Julius Caesar* present extreme situations of political upheaval, excruciating moral compromise and tragic self-deception, they enable

> us to see what it is that may confront us. In its action we are enabled, in fact, imaginatively to understand the actuality of human action; we are prevented from treating it as something which we can look at from a distance, as if the stuff

---

5. *ET*, 106–12.
6. Ibid., 104.

of individual life were not often at stake in its accomplishment. To write in these terms is not to allow a kind of existential self-indulgence to inhibit action; rather it is to protect ourselves against the sort of self-deception to which, in our action, we may find ourselves exposed, and indeed from which we may suddenly seek to escape by turning aside from what we must do, by passing by on the other side lest, by our intervention, we imperil not only ourselves, but those who have none other than ourselves to give them succour.[7]

MacKinnon spoke about literature in which he identified a relentless pull towards a kind of moral realism and, in some cases, schooling in the prevention of the kind of self-deception that he associated with an ever-present tragic possibility. The tone here is sceptical, confessional and therapeutic: we do not know ourselves nearly as well as we might like to think and we are perennially tempted to shift our gaze from the complex and morally ambiguous particular.

Is MacKinnon's engagement with literature in this way justified? The literary critic S. L. Goldberg criticized philosophers who in their approach to literary texts assume

> that moral philosophy is the centre ... the place where truth and reason are to be found, and that literature is simply the application of moral ideas and feelings, somewhere on the periphery.[8]

The alternative Goldberg advocates is a position which holds that

> literature and literary criticism form a distinctive and irreplaceable way of thinking about certain crucial aspects of Socrates' question ['how to live?'] – a way which is outside the scope of philosophy but complementary to it, which is no less subject to requirements of truth and reason, and which makes some kinds of literary judgement not just like moral judgements, nor just connected with them, but actual moral judgments in their own right.[9]

Goldberg makes mention of Bernard Williams, a contemporary of MacKinnon, attributing to him the view that 'all that literature and literary criticism can offer is perhaps no more than a kind of phenomenology', a representation of the ways

---

7. Ibid., 186.
8. Goldberg, *Agents*, xiiii. Nussbaum concurs, noting that a lot of ethical writing about literature is given a 'bad name, by its neglect of literary form and its reductive moralizing manner'. Although Nussbaum goes on to argue that a reaction concentrating 'on the form to the neglect of the work's sense of life and choice is not a solution, only violence of a different sort'. Martha Nussbaum, 'Perceptive Equilibrium: Literary Theory and Ethical Theory', in *A Companion to the Philosophy of Literature*, ed. Garry Hagberg and Walter Jost (Oxford: Blackwell, 2010), 242–3.
9. Goldberg, *Agents*, xiv.

we experience ethical life that is then taken up into philosophical discourse.[10] Goldberg argues that something more constructive is happening in literature, that literature does its thinking in 'the particulars it imagines' and in doing so it can 'do something which moral codes and moral philosophy cannot', which is to draw together both a notion of the human person as a voluntary agent confronting, exemplifying and responding to moral imperatives, and the notion of the human person as one 'whose particular qualities and trajectory in time are, in quite crucial ways, not like others, nor by any means a matter of voluntary actions'.[11]

Like Bernard Williams, MacKinnon approaches literature with the agenda of a moral philosopher, and perhaps this would be enough to rouse suspicion from the literary critic. His motive, however, is the task of philosophical repair, rather than mere adornment. He considered certain examples of literature as embodying insights that could not have been mediated by means of another form. One example is seen in White's analysis of MacKinnon's approach to parables where he argues that 'for Dodd and Jeremias the realism of the parables is put in the service of using human stories to *illustrate* the divine, whereas in MacKinnon it is time and again put in the service of *exploring* the divine'.[12] Indeed, Dodd and Jeremias are taking what MacKinnon identified as a typical path for philosophers:

> When the philosopher recalls Freud's words ['The poets knew it all already'], he is inclined by reason of his professional commitment, to suggest that the poets 'knew it all' only in the sense of a vague, intuitive perception which must yield place to effective articulation in terms of general concepts. [Here,] … the philosopher in the condescension towards the poets marks his reception of Freud's words, is of course more than he may realize the heir of the ancient quarrel between the poets and the metaphysicians.[13]

By describing MacKinnon as one who did not maintain such a posture of 'condescension', we should take him at his word when he expressed his own temptation and that of others to embark on the 'familiar enterprise of seeking to reduce the bewildering to terms other than itself'.[14] Having affirmed literature as a site where genuine moral factuality is revealed, he also stresses that any serious reading of literature will result in forms of inarticulacy as well, which

---

10. Ibid.

11. Ibid., xv.

12. Roger White, 'MacKinnon and the Parables', in *Christ, Ethics and Tragedy: Essays in Honour of Donald MacKinnon*, ed. Kenneth Surin (Cambridge: Cambridge University Press, 1989), 63.

13. D. M. MacKinnon, 'Theology and Tragedy', *Religious Studies* 2, no. April (1967): 165.

14. *ET*, 180.

philosophy may help to clarify.[15] The discussion of 'substance' in Christology (above) is one such example. MacKinnon's invocation of terms such as 'realism' when considering the irreducible complexity of human motivation and agency, paired with conflicting moral imperatives, provides another. This is not about one form of discourse failing and then looking for completion in the other, but two modes of describing and re-describing the moral task which enrich each other through continual interaction. MacKinnon's aim was to rehabilitate the literary imagination in as far as it had been depreciated in various ways by Plato, Hegel Hobbes, Berkeley and Ryle.[16]

MacKinnon's conviction that literature is an indispensable component of a necessary therapy cannot be understood without reference to George Steiner, Gabriel Marcel (and other expressions of existentialism) and Collingwood.[17] He never offered a worked-out theological aesthetics or a hermeneutical theory that systematically explored literature's relationship to philosophy and theology. Yet for all that, MacKinnon's literary interests were not indiscriminate and the type of distinction Coleridge made between 'imagination' and 'fancy' looms large.[18] The kind of literature which he considered most salient included works that capture the complexity of a realistically portrayed scenario, allowing readers to appreciate the emotional depths of interpersonal relationships, conflicting allegiances, and the ways individual agency may be tragically and fatally compromised. An example of this conviction is found in MacKinnon's essay

---

15. Fiddes explores the dialectic between narrative, imagination and doctrine in ways that parallels and makes explicit some of the issues that remain opaque in MacKinnon's work. Paul S. Fiddes, *Freedom and Limit: A Dialogue between Literature and Christian Doctrine* (Basingstoke: Macmillan, 1991), 27–46.

16. Douglas Hedley, *Living Forms of the Imagination* (London; New York: T&T Clark, 2008), 46–55.

17. The influence of Steiner and Collingwood was noted in the previous chapter. Marcel's influence is evident by the fact that he was hosted at Aberdeen by the MacKinnons to give the 1949–50 Gifford Lectures at a time when MacKinnon was the Professor of Moral Philosophy. These lectures were published as Gabriel Marcel, *The Mystery of Being 1, Reflection and Mystery*, Gifford lectures (University of Aberdeen) (London: Harvill Press, 1950) and *The Mystery of Being 2, Faith and Reality*, Gifford lectures (University of Aberdeen) (London: Harvill Press, 1951). MacKinnon writes about Marcel in an essay 'Drama and Memory' and wrote forwards for two of Marcel's books. D. M. MacKinnon, 'Drama and Memory (1984)', in *Burden*, ed. John C. McDowell (London: T&T Clark, 2011). Muller has further outlined the significance of his influence. Muller, 'True Service', 335–44.

18. MacKinnon, 'Coleridge and Kant', 188. Quoting from Coleridge's *Biographia Literaria*, Hedley encourages his readers to 'consider Coleridge's much-discussed distinction between fancy as 'an aggregative and associative power' and imagination as a 'shaping and modifying power'. The imagination is linked to the unconscious as well as to the will. It is more primordial and inscrutable than fancy. Fancy is a 'mode of memory emancipated from the order of time and space'. Hedley, *Living Forms of the Imagination*, 52.

'Tragedy and Ethics', where he agrees with the Labour politician and journalist R. H. S. Crossman that there is no better explication of the dilemmas confronting those involved in the July 1944 conspiracy to kill Hitler than Shakespeare's *Julius Caesar*. Following Crossman's suggestion, MacKinnon interweaves descriptions of the 'bare historical facts' and Shakespeare's drama in a way that bestows a greater vividness and deeper attentiveness to the moral conflict occurring in the lives of individuals as they navigate the ambiguous choices before them.[19]

In SET, one finds passing references to Albert Camus, Charles Dickens, William Blake, Dostoevsky, George Eliot, George Orwell, Wordsworth and Sophocles. Likewise, PM contains references to Cézanne's reflections on art, as well as to Conrad, Dickens, Euclid, Goethe, Pericles, Plutarch, and again, Shakespeare and Sophocles. Further to this, MacKinnon invokes D. H. Lawrence's 'vehement polemics against falsely spiritual religiosity in the account of the visit to Lincoln Cathedral in *The Rainbow*': a theme repeated in *The Man who Died*.[20] He speaks of *Nostromo* as 'Joseph Conrad's great political novel … not only one of the greatest novels in the English language, but a major contribution to the fundamental anatomy of politics'.[21] Recalling an emphasis within the preceding chapter, MacKinnon speaks of the way in which Conrad's *Under Western Eyes* 'has given us a profound study of [the 1917 Revolution's] ethos … one that penetrates its sombre depths'.[22] Elsewhere he speaks of the 'remarkable modern novel', William Styron's *Lie Down in Darkness* in the midst of his technical foray into the theme of the irreversibility of time, and refers at some length to T. S. Eliot's poetic meditations on time and eternity in his essay 'On the Notion of a Philosophy of History'.[23] Additionally, while a professor at Cambridge, MacKinnon contributed to a book marking the bicentenary of Coleridge's birth, displaying an awareness of various contemporary controversies surrounding the poet and a willingness to make connections with his own philosophical interests.[24]

Like his one-time mentor A. E. Taylor, MacKinnon showed himself to be more than superficially engaged in the reading of 'serious' literature, although his actual examination of texts in published works is rarely deeply exegetical. Even so, behind the passing invocations there is ample evidence that he engaged in reading serious literary criticism too, including Nicholas Brook on *King Lear*, Phillip Vellacott on *Oedipus*, Victor Ehrenberg's monograph on Sophocles and Pericles,[25] Kermode's essays on literary criticism,[26] and as noted above, Steiner and Marcel.[27] If we add

---

19. *ET*, 182–5.
20. MacKinnon, 'Natural Law', 116.
21. MacKinnon, 'Some Reflection on Secular Diakonia', 70.
22. *ET*, 18.
23. Ibid., xi. See also *BT*, 164–5.
24. MacKinnon, 'Coleridge and Kant', 183–203.
25. *BT*, 101.
26. MacKinnon, 'The Evangelical Imagination', 189–93.
27. MacKinnon, 'Theology and Tragedy', 163–9.

MacKinnon's abiding concern with the theological interpretation of Christian scripture to this list, there is no exaggeration in the proposition that engagement with literary culture is an important structural component to MacKinnon's project.

When there is a move towards critical self-awareness of this fact, a word that appears with frequency is 'imagination'. The 'Evangelical Imagination' (1986) and 'Intellect and Imagination' (1991) are two essays in which the cognitive status of the imagination and its relationship to historical realism is explored, albeit with MacKinnon's characteristic brevity and open-endedness.[28] A chief concern is the way in which the notion of the imagination might help us escape forms of empiricism and idealism that have failed in the task of adequately accounting for the moral demands of concrete historical situations. In the essay 'Intellect and Imagination', MacKinnon, in less than six pages, attempts the titanic task of establishing a speculative link between concepts of the imagination in Hume and Kant, with the distinctive literary characteristics of St. John's Gospel.[29]

What MacKinnon took from Hume's Treatise is that there are 'habits of the imagination' that are 'permanent, irresistible and universal' as well as those that are 'changeable, weak and irregular'.[30] The first pertains to the philosophy of causation where imaginative effort is used to explicate the relationship between cause and effect or effect and cause; the second is when people begin to deploy this practice of inference to establish the influence of spiritual forces as explanatory agents. Without the working of the imagination to make the inference, human life would become unintelligible. Yet, the capacity to make inferences can also lead us away from reality into a self-created world that is a projection of our own ignorance and fears. MacKinnon observes a healthy ambivalence about the imagination in Hume, with his stipulation that the only good use of the imagination is 'naturalistic'. This is a point which anticipates aspects of Kant's use of the notion according to MacKinnon:

> For Kant ... the imagination was the 'understanding working blind', its activity associated particularly with the second synthesis in the subjective 'deduction of the categories' (named 'synthesis of reproduction through imagination'). Later in the structure of the *Critique of Pure Reason* imagination is treated as the effective agent of the schematism of the categories, whereby in fact the forms of understanding are transmagnified into the conditions of objective awareness, the pure category of ground and consequent, for instance, into that of cause and effect. The latter is vindicated in the 'second analogy' as the assumption that we must bring to the manifold of our experience if we are able to consider an objective time-order, wherein before and after are not matters of our caprice or situation, but following one another with the inevitability of night or day.[31]

---

28. MacKinnon, 'The Evangelical Imagination', 189–99 and 'Intellect and Imagination', 29–35.
29. MacKinnon, 'Intellect and Imagination', 29–35.
30. Ibid., 29.
31. Ibid.

The point to take from this is twofold. First, MacKinnon assented to a thread of argument in Hume and Kant holding that there is a faculty related to our apprehension of causality which is a crucial enabler of our apprehension of the world. Secondly, it is also the case that this faculty must come under the most rigorous scrutiny and discipline if it is to support reliable claims to knowledge. MacKinnon noted Kant's concern that the 'understanding' risked 'the indulgence of sheerly undisciplined extrapolation of its resources to achieve no longer the conditions of objective experience, but to delineate in ways that would outrun any procedure of confirmation or falsification, the ultimate secrets of the universe'.[32] This is an eventuality which the whole argument of the *Critique of Pure Reason* sets out to prevent. MacKinnon was of the view that Christian theologians might see something analogous to what Kant is describing at work in their own system of 'projection', particularly when it comes to their engagement with the gospels. While acknowledging the imaginative stretch that may be required to accept such an analogy, MacKinnon nonetheless makes reference to the supper discourses of St. John's gospel, arguing that

> the very unnoticed richness of perceptual experience with the inter-penetrating resources that make it what it is, are wonderfully uncovered by Kant in his quest for the conditions of objectivity. We are not in bondage to sense-awareness in the manner suggested by the uncritical empiricist, who disdains skills enabling us [to] transcend the immediate, and for whose conceptual activity is reduced to a mere *Vorstellung-ablauf*. So in the fourth gospel faith demands a reference point; it does not disdain ostentation whether by sight, hearing or touch. Yet that reference point by itself is insignificant, even as Kant judged sense without conceptual activity to be blind.[33]

Here, MacKinnon was developing his own trajectory within a tradition that Hedley associates with Kant, Coleridge and Collingwood – an 'anti-empiricist polemic' in which 'perception of an object always involves more than sense data: it involves the imagining of properties which are not disclosed to the senses, or noticing, i.e. looking at or attending to, what is seen'.[34] When it comes to the disciplining of the imagination in the theological realm, MacKinnon seems to draw upon two sources: the historical critical approach to the text and the work of the Holy Spirit. In the case of the former, it became clear in the preceding chapter that the relationship is not unidirectional. It is not just a matter of empirical historical methodology taming the imagination, but an interaction of greater mutuality in which imagination enhances historical realism, while a commitment to the empirical draws the imagination back from a flight to the unreal.

32. MacKinnon, 'The Evangelical Imagination', 202.
33. Ibid., 203.
34. Hedley notes here a 'continuity between the imaginative component in habitual perceptual experience and in artistic vision'. Hedley, *Living Forms of the Imagination*, 61.

After discussing the use of imagination in Milton's and Luke's versions of Christ's temptation, MacKinnon raised a nagging question; a question which arose whenever it was clear that description of the event and imaginative theological embellishment were inextricably wedded: 'Are we engaged with, that which is somehow factually referential?'.[35] MacKinnon's answer was affirmative: 'We need the tools of literary study, above all the discipline of close reading, to enable us to reach through the apparent flight from fact to fantasy, back towards the coldly factual basis.'[36] MacKinnon could see the imagination as an ally for realism because the notion of 'cold factuality' with which he worked was rather more expansive than that of many positivists and empiricists, as noted in previous chapters. With Marcel, 'cold factuality' is not seen as antithetical to notions of transcendence; with Barth, it is not antithetical to a Divine act and with Taylor and Sorley, it is not antithetical to moral realism.

In as far as MacKinnon had a pneumatology, it would seem that one of the guises of the Holy Spirit is to act as a limit on the imaginative excess: an aspect of Divine agency which undermines any 'unchecked aspiration that will bend the deliverance of sense to confirmation of its own ill-disciplined fantasy'.[37] The mythological and typological are essential, and when limits are placed on the imagination by philosophers, historians and the Holy Spirit, what we encounter is not a flight away from factuality but 'a standing protest against failure to take seriously the sheer concreteness of God's self-incarnating'.[38] The Spirit draws the theological imagination back to the historical figure of Christ, but is also present in that same history. From MacKinnon's vantage point, any hard distinction between historical fact and the interpretation of that fact becomes problematic, especially when 'imagination' becomes a word applied to the former and 'hard factual knowledge' to the latter. Here we see a mirror or analogy of MacKinnon's refusal of any strict fact/value distinction in the realm of moral theory.

On scripture as literature

MacKinnon upheld continuities between the Bible and other forms of 'canonical' literature. He noted 'curious similarities' between the book of Job and Aeschylus's *Prometheus Vinctus* and saw Milton's writings on the temptation of Jesus as entirely in-keeping with an imaginative trajectory or hermeneutic tradition found in St. Luke's gospel.[39] On Milton he notes that

---

35. MacKinnon, 'The Evangelical Imagination', 195.
36. Ibid., 196.
37. Ibid., 203. He points to John's narrative about Mary Magdalene's growing realization of the identity of the risen Jesus as a case in point.
38. MacKinnon, 'The Evangelical Imagination', 196.
39. Ibid., 195.

he himself was responding to what Luke had done with the tradition before him. We do well to heed the fact that we are dealing with great literature, where the imagination of a creative artist has transcended the limitation of bare factual record, in Luke's case an imagination liberated by freedom to indulge in acceptance of the miraculous as part of the furniture of the world in which he lived.[40]

Christian Scripture contains literary achievements to aid realist therapy although MacKinnon is adamant that it is unevenly the case. In a way that may provoke the prudishly conservative, he spoke of the book of Acts as 'markedly inferior … in theological and spiritual perception' compared to the Gospel commonly attributed to the same author'.[41] When MacKinnon does make reference to the Bible, his focus is almost entirely on the gospels, with John seen as the pinnacle achievement of the genre because of its penetrating perception beyond mere 'events' and towards 'actions'. In the attention he gave to biblical narratives, MacKinnon, at a minimum, discerned another purgative resource to further aid moral discernment, but more besides, he placed its claims about the incarnation at the centre of his intellectual striving.

In observing strong continuity between scripture and other forms of literature, MacKinnon found at least a modicum of shared sensibility with liberal theologians such as Hick and Cupitt, as well as literary critics such as Steiner. Where he departs from these figures is in the way he wants to pair this commonality with a radical discontinuity, the source of which is an appreciation of Jesus's life and death as an act of salvific revelation, together with an insistence that, unlike literary fiction, an absolute commitment to realist historical referents and a dialectic of 'correspondence' must be upheld. To explore this discontinuity more fully, one might be tempted to go back to the underdeveloped invocation of the Holy Spirit in MacKinnon's writings. As noted above, he understood the Spirit in terms of a check on the imagination: an agent preventing self-delusion and dissolution into groundless religious fantasy. A developed pneumatology remains a yawning gap in MacKinnon's work, yet its brief appearance in discussions about transformative encounters with gospel narratives are indicative of an effort to distinguish himself from those who saw Scripture as *merely* one form of morally 'improving' literature interchangeable with others.[42]

Within the gospel genre, and aside from the betrayal and crucifixion, it was the parables that most captivated MacKinnon's imagination as a moral philosopher

---

40. Ibid., 193.

41. MacKinnon is particularly incredulous at the story of Ananias and Sapphira, describing their slaying as 'pitiless and self-righteous', against the grain of pious commentary that dulls any sense of discomfort or moral outrage. Ibid., 195.

42. At issue here is what Janz identifies as the task of 'a genuinely empirical response to the demand for theological reference – one that demonstrates Christological continuity', Janz, *God, the Mind's Desire*, 185.

and theologian. White observes that 'if we engage ourselves seriously with the parables, we are continually invited to tread strange and offensive paths of thought'.[43] He was supervised as a student by MacKinnon and notes his teacher's plain acknowledgement of parable's 'perverse, offensive and even blasphemous' suggestions, their 'intense human realism' and their irreducible complexity.[44] White sees MacKinnon's approach as emerging in the wake of 'the tradition of parable interpretation inaugurated by Adolf Jülicher and modified and developed by authors such as Dodd and Jeremias', and indeed MacKinnon does mention these three whenever he is trying to give some representation of contemporary scholarship about the genre.[45]

The theme of the parabolic makes a strong appearance in PM, and in essays such as 'Parable and Sacrament'.[46] The latter is typical of his style: suggestive and creative, with insightful comparisons and alluring intimations of barely grasped depths, yet conceptually underdeveloped and frustratingly open-ended.[47] MacKinnon described the 'openness of texture' as the chief benefit of the parabolic, and it is no surprise that his essays disorient readers in analogous ways.[48] This 'texture' 'subsume[s] under it … pieces of discourse as different one from another as the parables of the sower, the tares, the ten wise and ten foolish virgins, the marriage feast, the labourers in the vineyard, the talents, the lost sheep, the lost coin, the two brothers, the good Samaritan, the prayers of the Pharisee and tax-gatherer, the unjust steward etc'.[49] One is invited to see the work of God in the manifold diversity of human lives and daily struggles, yet more than offering simple moral and theological object lessons, they often obscure as much as they clarify and continually undermine assumptions made about God rather than securing readers against the assaults of doubt and perplexity. MacKinnon saw parables as non-prescriptive, therapeutic and confessional resources that held vital lessons for the way the moral theologian understood and carried out their task.

MacKinnon made two suggestive connections in 'Parable and Sacrament'. The first was between the distinctive character of the parabolic and the theological projects of Bonhoeffer and Barth. Along with many other readers of Bonhoeffer, MacKinnon noted a very particular kind of secularization of theological sensibility under the discipline of the incarnation, and in Barth, a relentless concern for the factuality and concreteness of revelation.[50] An emphasis on a qualified secularity

---

43. White, 'MacKinnon and the Parables', 69.

44. Ibid., 54.

45. Ibid., 49.

46. White overstates the case when, referring to PM, he calls it 'one of the central themes of the book', however. Ibid.

47. ET, 166–81.

48. Ibid., 169.

49. Ibid., 168.

50. Ibid., 181.

and realism is what MacKinnon sees in the parables, and I will return to this point as this chapter unfolds. The second connection arises between the parabolic form and Eucharistic practice. Again, in a qualified sense, MacKinnon took the sacrament to be (in part) an enacted parable. Both parable and sacrament involve narrations that drive a participant towards a type of 'historical realism'. Yet, in both, narratives are imaginatively pressed and expanded in such a way that the possibility of a continually renewed quest for meaning goes together with a deeply personal, potentially transformative and destabilizing mode of participation. There is a dynamic and disruptive dimension that undermines the inevitable forces of stagnation, sentimentality or ideology from corrupting discourse about God or moral obligation. On the connection between parable and sacrament, MacKinnon makes the following observation:

> In the upper room on the threshold of his betrayal, Jesus performed actions whose manifestly symbolic character demanded that they should be understood in ways comparable to that in which a highly contrived parable might be said to demand understanding, or more simply in ways comparable to those in which we understand or fail to understand ... what a person is saying who for instance is deliberately rendering himself vulnerable in our presence by self-revelation, or what we ourselves are actually doing when by promise or other verbal performance we commit ourselves in the future or arouse in others expectations concerning our behaviour which we bind ourselves to fulfil with only a partial discernment of what is involved.[51]

MacKinnon's engagement with key debates in biblical scholarship of the mid-twentieth century (noted in Chapter 3) paved the way for such speculations and convictions to develop. Jülicher became known for an argument by which he sought to pit the historical Jesus who told simple parables, with simple moral messages to simple people, against the Jesus of the gospel writer's imaginations, particularly that of Mark, in whose gospel Jesus is seen to deliberately court obscurity and misunderstanding by means of the parabolic form.[52] According to White, while Jeremias and Dodd shift the emphasis of the debate, they

> take their starting point in Jülicher. ... For now the idea that moves into the foreground is that the parables as we encounter them in the Gospels are frequently obscure and difficult to understand, and hence the task of the New Testament critic is to restore them and recover their original setting so that we may be able to see them in their full simplicity.[53]

---

51. Ibid., 177–8.
52. William R. Herzog, *Parables as Subversive Speech: Jesus as Pedagogue of the Oppressed* (Louisville, KY; London: Westminster/John Knox Press, 1994), 7–39.
53. White, 'MacKinnon and the Parables', 53.

And MacKinnon sees the work of Jeremias and Dodd as important:

> We must reckon with the arguments advanced in such works as C.H. Dodd's *The Parables of the Kingdom*, and Joachim Jeremias' the *Parables of Jesus*, which have insisted on the distinction between the setting of the parable's actual delivery by Jesus (frequently irrecoverable) and the context in which their delivery is recorded in the individual gospel.[54]

As MacKinnon came under the influence of Collingwood's views on historical method, however, and also the developments of redaction criticism, he moved away from Dodd's and Jeremias's focus on uncovering (what was thought to be) the simplest and most original form of a parable. The problem was that such efforts tended to result in reduction of the parables to pithy moral or theological object lessons, with exegesis tasked to remove the 'husk' of subtlety, complexity, and obscurity, with these characteristics thought to be accretions overlaying what was presumed to have been an original simplicity. For MacKinnon, 'if the parable counsels simplicity, it is a simplicity of which *simplisme* is the mortal foe'.[55]

One might say that Dodd and Jeremias represented a particular epistemological presupposition about the nature of factuality which motivated their approach to the parables; they wanted to discipline the imagination in a way that for MacKinnon undermined their literary power and therapeutic potential. The alternative route was to see the complexity and obscurity of the canonical parables as the optimal form of the text, not because entering speculation on original forms and asking the question of their historical context is invalid or irrelevant – quite the opposite – but because the complexity and obscurity render them potentially more realistic and historically vivid, not less. On this point MacKinnon noted that

> the texture of the concept of parable is open; but it is of the nature of the parabolic, not simply to disturb or break the stale cake of long-ago backed moral custom, by pointing to unnoticed possibilities of well-doing, but to hint, or more than hint, at the ways in which things fundamentally are. Parables are true or false; we do not mean true or false in the sense of correspondence, which we use in connection with a passport photograph or a newspaper report of an air disaster.[56]

Here we see notions of 'correspondence' emerging in MacKinnon's thought but 'not as we knew it' in the hands of the classical empiricists. I will return to this issue in the next chapter.

For MacKinnon, it is a genre by which the historical referent of Jesus's teaching ministry and imaginative construal are fused on many interweaving levels,

---

54. *ET*, 171.
55. Ibid., 169.
56. *PM*, 79.

resulting in purgative moral intensity. He argues that parables set us free from 'the illusion of supposing that the sacred could be isolated or set apart from life as a whole, treated as the object of special experience or quality of special time and place'.[57] MacKinnon was drawn in by

> their total freedom from any quasi-numinous quality, the kind of quality that one believes one finds in, for instance, great liturgical texts. Again, they are totally free, *for the most part*, from the sort of pregnant religious imagery, of the kind with which traditional preaching is saturated.[58]

Similarly in PM he argues that the parables have

> an unquestioned advantage of focusing in completely concrete terms the central metaphysical concern – that of reaching through the familiar to its alleged transcendent ground, without evacuating that familiar of its own proper dignity, without treating it, for instance, as if *alles Vergängliches ist nur ein Gleichnis*.[59]

There is a resonance here with Bonhoeffer's later writings on 'religionless' Christianity; an outworking of an already well-established humanistic sensibility which recognized the potential for the purgation of a stagnant Christendom by internalizing the challenge of secularization. It might, after all, force the church to a renewed appreciation of the all-to-often ignored shattering of the sacred/secular dualism enacted in the incarnation. Speaking of Bonhoeffer, MacKinnon observed that his criticism of religion

> was the criticism of a man who found that certain sorts of religious concentration, in consequence of their intense preoccupation with the supposedly special experiences that brought men before God, neglected the wide-ranging complexity of the human reality. In his teaching by parable, Jesus illustrated ways in which very various aspects of this reality could, if seen aright, convey, with devastating effect, the ways of God to man. [MacKinnon then adds that] … it is Barth's prophetic utterance which helped make possible this sort of response to the parabolic, this sensitivity … to its profoundly theological, yet deeply non-religious dimensions.[60]

Barth's rejection of the trajectory represented by Schleiermacher and Ritschl was part of his insistence that 'we must not set frontiers to the sort of human situation or experience through which God may declare himself', and with this came intense scrutiny of a generic notion of religion popular with liberal theology and the quest

---

57. *ET*, 180.
58. Ibid., 171–2.
59. *PM*, 82.
60. *ET*, 170.

to explicate a common underlying element of religious experience.[61] This point becomes explicit in an essay MacKinnon wrote to honour Barth on his eightieth birthday, in which he explicated the theme of 'secular *diakonia*', mentioned in the last chapter.[62] Here MacKinnon's sensibility to the Marxist critique of quietist religion was evident. Yet further, he points to a paradoxical dynamic at the heart of dialectical theology in which an unrelenting focus on particular moments of revelation paved the way for a renewed expression of intellectual catholicity; a broadening or secularizing of expectations as to where divine action might occur and in what form it may take. The Bonhofferian resonances are palpable and Janz's commentary in this regard is worth quoting:

> The call to this-worldliness (*Diesseitigkeit*) is by no means a call to the profane over the sacred (as some questionable readings of Bonhoeffer's 'non-religious Christianity' suggest), since for Bonhoeffer all of these kinds of conceptual dualities have been overcome in Christ. Rather it is again the same call to empirical reality, in the full and integrated Kantian sense that I have described above. For it is precisely in drawing attention to the empirically real that 'this-worldliness', far from closing off the promise of meaningful reference to the transcendent, actually reopens the way to it, since empirical history is the only place that a finality of non-resolution can be encountered.[63]

In this vein, the secularizing trajectory that MacKinnon takes in his *Festshrift* essay for Barth, and in engagements with secular history and literature, should not be seen as a distraction from a Christological focus. The same trajectory is present in Jesus's life and teaching.[64] The parabolic is more likely to engender a contemplative attentiveness to the concrete tasks and moral dilemmas of daily life, rather than specifically religious experiences. Nonetheless they do contain a sort of 'factuality' which includes the self-interpretation of Jesus and 'his Father's interpretation of him' in so far as these have become part of the 'secular' history of the incarnation.[65] The gospels use imaginative means to enable us to draw 'back toward the coldly factual', yet MacKinnon quickly adds: 'I say coldly factual; I am, of course, referring to the unique, unrepeatable presence of the transcendent in and to the world around us. To capture even the outskirts of that drawing near demands every resource of imagination that we possess.'[66]

---

61. Ibid., 167.
62. MacKinnon, 'Some Reflection on Secular Diakonia', 69.
63. Janz, *God, the Mind's Desire*, 184.
64. Thus MacKinnon's rejected Maritain's negative reception of Barth, whereby the revival of reformed theology was thought to present a position opposed to 'integral humanism'. Maritain, *True Humanism*, 88–120.
65. MacKinnon, 'The Evangelical Imagination', 196.
66. Ibid.

There is a paradox here and it is one at the heart of the parables: the greater the immersion in the concrete particular, with its inevitable moral imperatives and dilemmas, the greater the need to articulate a notion of transcendence that destabilizes and interrogates, not MacKinnon would insist, as a function of human projection but rather *apprehension*. Here we see something analogous in the Christian imagination which perceives the utterly unexpected possibility of transcendent love in the midst of a crucifixion. Imagination is the key to the recognition of transcendence and where transcendence is at issue tragedy is never far away from MacKinnon's concern:

> For the authentically human can be lost if we fail to allow our imaginations to be opened by the frightening possibilities of the transcendent that presses upon us, if we belittle the dimension of contemplation where we are schooled to perceive tragedy without loss of hope.[67]

'To perceive tragedy without the loss of hope' is to look upon the crucified one as the ultimate parable. And for Christians subsequently, there is no training ground for such a demanding form of purgative contemplation than the Eucharist. If MacKinnon could be said to have a sacramental theology, it would have at its centre a conviction as to the way healthy Eucharistic participation leads to a greater immersion in the coldly factual, in the particular, the local and the concrete in the very same way that the parables do.[68] There is to be no fetishization of a cultic act and sacramental theology must go hand in hand with an intense scepticism of Otto's claim that *mysterium tremendum atque fascinosum Deitatis* should be the defining feature of quintessentially religious experience.[69]

In this vein, MacKinnon registered his concern about the non-realist temptation contained in the realm of the liturgical: in the past the churches have been tempted to render the liturgy an end in itself, 'by erecting the sacred into a place of allegedly triumphal authority over the human', and presumably also over the freedom of God in a way that offended MacKinnon's Barthian sensibilities.[70] And yet, just as the parables of Jesus are given coherence and find consummation in the liturgy enacted by Jesus at the Last Supper, so the Eucharist guards us against an atomizing, reductionist, 'scissors and paste' approach to the text that was noted in a different context in the last chapter. Yet again, MacKinnon is holding a number of perspectives and practices in dramatic, mutually correcting, tension:

> without liturgy, without religion, we too quickly lapse into a mood that trivialises parable by making what it would communicate an easy lesson, somehow

---

67. *ET*, 179.
68. See for instance D. M. MacKinnon, 'Sacrament and Common Meal', in *Burden*, ed. John C. McDowell (London: T&T Clark, 2011), 77–82.
69. *ET*, 169.
70. Ibid., 179.

complete in itself, not requiring continually to be complemented, even corrected by reference to authentic human existence.'[71]

The liturgy fires the imagination, drawing out the full drama of historically embedded moral agency in an analogous way to what a play might allow in another context. Crudely speaking, it represents an idealist pole in a dialectic that leads us back to greater realism: a move in which one risks distortion, excess and the accusation of indulging fancy for the sake of a greater contemplative attentiveness. MacKinnon's development of these connections is woefully underdeveloped, but it would seem that there was a tacit return to an elusive pneumatology and muted ecclesiology occurring here.[72] Yet, there is no space for a confident ecclesiastical or liturgical consummation. The incompleteness of parables is of their essence and any participation in the Eucharist shares this characteristic: 'If it is the place of understanding, it is also the place where misunderstandings of many sorts may assume an obstinate permanence in the life of the spirit.'[73]

In light of human limitation and obstinacy, MacKinnon acknowledged that the Word must become the determinative presence in the hermeneutical circle, but it beckons us towards the tragic *via dolorosa* rather than diverting us to a more surefooted route.[74] The 'intense human realism of these little fictions' (the parables) causes a crisis for conventional religiosity and rationality in an analogous way to the incarnation itself.[75] The parables, like the Eucharist which played such a central role in MacKinnon's devotional life, confront us with the sort of transcendent referent which has echoes in Kant's agnosticism and Barth's observations about the divine Word, but with the former's moral seriousness and the latter's uncompromising commitment to the action of God's self-revelation. Parables have a role in opening the way to unexpected apprehensions of transcendence because, as Jesus understood,

> one of the major functions of a fiction [is] to force us to consider matter afresh by presenting cases in such a way that our normal prejudices, self-deception and complacency are not allowed to operate.[76]

---

71. Ibid.
72. MacKinnon, *The Church of God*, 71. MacKinnon's invocations of ecclesiology after the *Church of God* are more pessimistic and sceptical, focused on purging self-preoccupation and aggrandisement, than they are building a doctrinal edifice.
73. *ET*, 181.
74. Janz, *God, the Mind's Desire*, 188. It seems to me that this insistence also lies at the heart of the more recent defence of theological realism mounted by Moore, *Realism*, 1–20.
75. White, 'MacKinnon and the Parables', 54.
76. Ibid., 60.

MacKinnon and tragic literature

Like MacKinnon, Stanley Cavell was a moral philosopher who perceived lessons to be learnt in Shakespeare's tragedies. In his essay on King Lear, Cavell writes,

> It is said by Dr Johnson, and felt by Tom Jones's friend Partridge, that what we credit in a tragedy is a possibility, a recognition that if we were in such circumstances we would feel and act as those characters do. But I do not consider it a very live possibility ... and if I did ... I haven't any idea what I would feel or do. – That is not what is meant? Then what is? That I sense the possibility that I shall feel impotent to prevent the object I have set my soul on and won, from breaking it; that it is possible that I shall trust someone who wishes me harm; that I can become murderous with jealousy and know chaos when my imagination has been dried and then gutted and the sense of all possibility has come to an end? But I know, more or less, these things now; and if I did not, I would not know what possibility I am to envision as presented by this play.[77]

As noted in the exploration of MacKinnon's Christology in Chapter 3, part of his strategy of protest against objectionable trends in contemporary theology was to invoke the tragic motif.[78] He embraced it as a tool for his therapeutic endeavour, anticipating, at least in part, the inevitable accusations of fatalism and quietism that would follow.[79] In many ways, this was just a continuation of Plato's 'ancient quarrel'.[80] Karl Jaspers made a forceful argument for the incommensurability of Christian theology and the category of 'tragedy', noting that

---

77. Stanley Cavell, *Disowning Knowledge in Seven Plays of Shakespeare* (Cambridge University Press, 2003), 101–2.

78. In the face of the sort of optimistic attitudes towards the future that grips theologians such as Teilhard, 'we may well find ourselves driven to a more tragic appraisal of the human scene, but [MacKinnon adds a qualification] let us be sure that the appraisal is tragic – something very different from the mood of tired impatience which finds nothing new under the sun, which thinks quite wrongly that one only grasps *la misère de l'homme* by depreciating *la grandeur*; whereas it is only against the background of a true estimate of human creativity and genius that we see human weakness, frailty and sin for what they are'. *ET*, 6.

79. MacKinnon argued that 'recognition of the tragic must not be allowed to inhibit action, even if it must deepen perception and, in consequence, purify the motives and intentions from which men act'. MacKinnon, 'Some Reflection on Secular Diakonia', 70.

80. MacKinnon, 'Theology and Tragedy'. See also Anthony Cascardi, 'Tragedy and Philosophy', in *A Companion to the Philosophy of Literature*, ed. Garry Hagberg and Walter Jost (Oxford: Blackwell, 2010). 161–4.

Christian salvation opposes tragic knowledge. The chance of being saved destroys the tragic sense of being trapped without chance of escape. Therefore no genuinely Christian tragedy can exist.[81]

Tragedy's association with pessimism and the exultation of a heroic yet flawed individual are often seen to disqualify it as a resource for positive theological construction.[82] Yet the tragic is MacKinnon's way of identifying perspectives within the Christian tradition that have been underplayed.[83] More particularly, it is a way of bringing to the fore the intractability of the problem of evil, the experience of moral conflict, and what he, in the spirit of Bonhoeffer, saw as the abject failings of the church in the context of modernity generally and fascism in particular.[84] I have already mentioned that Steiner was developing an interest in the tragic genre at around the same time; invoking it as a way of giving voice to the existential shock and intellectual challenge posed by the holocaust. Alongside Steiner, whose book *The Death of Tragedy* MacKinnon read with interest, the influence of Raymond Williams's *Modern Tragedy* looms large, particularly in its attempt to break down barriers between 'high' and 'low' tragic art, making connections between historical, theatrical and journalistic invocations.[85] Raphael prefigured these two and his lectures published as *The Paradox of Tragedy* (1960) attracted MacKinnon's praise. He saw them as a watershed in the contemporary interchange between literary criticism and moral philosophy. To this end, they warranted mention in essays entitled *The Euthyphro Dilemma* and *Theology and Tragedy*, as well as in his Gifford Lectures. MacKinnon lamented that Raphael's work

> has suffered the neglect from British moral philosophers which is so often the lot of writings which attempt something at first sight (though not on deeper consideration of the very best contemporary work) unrelated to dominant habits of thought. While I differ a great deal from Professor Raphael's book, I am deeply indebted to him for writing it. This whole topic will receive extended treatment in my forthcoming Gifford Lectures.[86]

---

81. Karl Jaspers, *Tragedy Is Not Enough* (London: Gollancz, 1953), 38. In a similar vein, Raphael argued that 'tragedy glorifies human resistance to necessity, religion praises submission'. Raphael, *The Paradox of Tragedy*, 51.

82. Dan O. Via, *The Hardened Heart and Tragic Finitude* (Eugene, OR: Cascade Books, 2012), 1–29.

83. There are parallels with Fiddes' questioning of the dominance of a 'U-Shaped curve' reading of Christian narrative and history, '…which we may describe as Paradise, Paradise Lost and Paradise Regained'. Fiddes, *Freedom and Limit: A Dialogue between Literature and Christian Doctrine*, 47–63.

84. The latter point is no more evident than in D. M. MacKinnon, *The Stripping of the Altars: The Gore Memorial Lecture*, Fontana library (London: Collins, 1969).

85. *BT*, 101–3.

86. Ibid.

While he did not spell out disagreements with Raphael here or in the Gifford Lectures, it seems obvious enough that his most pronounced departure is on the former's insistence that the category of tragedy is entirely incommensurate with the Christian tradition. Speaking of the approaches of Hegel, Schopenhauer and Nietzsche, Raphael argues that

> the metaphysical problem from which they fashioned their Procrustean beds for Tragedy, is the problem of evil – by which I mean the existence of unmerited suffering. I have already allowed that a villain may be a tragic hero. Nevertheless, it seems to me, the poignancy of tragedy comes out chiefly in the misery of innocence. All tragedy deals with the presentation of evil, but some of the greatest works of tragic drama are concerned especially with the metaphysical or theological problem of evil. If one already has some metaphysical theory of the world, some rational scheme into which all human experience is to be fitted, one approaches the problem of evil with an explanation ready-made. The great tragedians do not inscribe evil under a prepared rubric.[87]

For the most part, Raphael saw the Christian tradition as routinely seeking to 'inscribe evil under a prepared rubric', whether it be in systematic theodicies emphasizing an all-embracing divine providence or those that looked to eschatology to repair, compensate or somehow relativize the horrors of history. He also saw the opposition springing from his observation that one of the reasons for the perennial attraction to tragic art is the pleasure readers (or audiences) get from 'regarding the tragic hero as more sublime than the power he opposes'.[88] Raphael presumes that there would be something potentially blasphemous about a person resolving to fight against the will of providence within the Jewish and Christian traditions. He notes that even though Job was given space to vent his protest, he submitted to God's inscrutable will in the end. Raphael also gives examples of texts from other parts of the Hebrew Bible which, along with Job, are seen to contain genuinely tragic themes: the lament Psalms and Isaiah 53. Yet in all of these, he finds reasons as to why they differ in kind to anything resembling a full-fledged tragedy. In texts expressing lament and describing the lot of the 'suffering servant', it becomes clear to Raphael that for the most part,

> as soon as the existence of unmerited evil is recognised, the religious spirit finds in it a heightened goodness and a means to good. The moral order of the universe is not dimmed, but shines with a more brilliant light than before.[89]

It is interesting and perhaps instructive from MacKinnon's perspective, that Raphael does not mention Jesus's crucifixion at any stage. In any case, one

---

87. Raphael, *The Paradox of Tragedy*, 24.
88. Ibid., 41.
89. Ibid., 46.

presumes that Raphael would see the resurrection as undercutting any free rein of the tragic motif. Indeed, where he did observe authors trying to compose 'Christian tragedies' or to reconcile the notion of tragedy to Christian theology, he also detected a failure to replicate some crucial aspect of classical tragedy, or a departure from orthodoxy. Milton's *Samson Agonistes*, Corneille's *Polyeucte* and two plays from Racine including *Athalie* and *Phèdre* are considered. In the case of the first of Racine's works, 'A Christian standpoint allows pity for her fate but not admiration for her defiance of God'.[90] In the latter work Racine 'reaches tragic sublimity' yet only renders Phèdre into a tragic figure because she is a 'victim at once of Greek fate and Jansenist predestination'.[91] According to Raphael, Racine's Christianity meant Jansenism, complete with reference to an inscrutable yet essentially a-moral divine providence undercutting any pity we might have for the damned or admiration for them when they try to escape their fate. Apparently, the capacity for such pity is essential to the tragic ascription and this is always

> liable to conflict with orthodox Monotheism, in which absolute goodness and justice are combined with absolute power in one God. ... A tragic hero may display some of the typically Biblical virtues – righteousness, love, and patience. But humility is not easily made heroic; and if the tragic hero strives against omnipotence, admiration of his heroism is impious for a theology which unites omnipotence with absolute goodness.[92]

MacKinnon picked up on the stream of Raphael's analysis which identified the partial presence of tragic motifs within scripture in addition to modern dramas billed as 'Christian tragedies', yet he resisted the conclusion that Christianity and tragedy are fundamentally incompatible. I. A. Richards observed that the tragic mood is agnostic or Manichean and MacKinnon may have some tendencies in these directions, as perhaps indicated by the understated role he gives to the resurrection and the Holy Spirit.[93] Having come under the influence of Kant's agnosticism, and like Steiner fuelled by a sense of the existential crisis of the holocaust, MacKinnon rejected any notion that evil is ever inscribable under a

---

90. Ibid., 66.
91. Raphael: 'In Phedre time is frozen, as place is; the action is transfixed by the lucidity which arrays itself against the truth, absorbing its brilliance, and the lucidity which supervenes as truth breaks through.' ... 'In Phedre, we are placed unprotected under heaven, examined by an unblinking light.' Ibid.
92. Ibid., 44–5.
93. Ibid., 43. MacKinnon: 'It is not a chance that the so-called Manichaean heresy awoke in the defenders of Christian orthodoxy emotions of savagery such as received terrible expression in the Albigensian crusade. The questions which that heresy raised in a metaphysically confused and indeed vulnerable form, have never been fully answered. The so-called "problem of evil" remains intractable by any of the methods traditionally employed to solve or dissolve it'. *ET*, 193.

'prepared rubric' and yet did so while claiming that his position remained a Christian one.[94] The only rubric that is available for Christians on this issue is the person of Jesus, and for MacKinnon there is plenty about his demise on a roman cross befitting of a tragic ascription, just as there is nothing about the resurrection which could be described as a 'prepared rubric'.[95]

There is a great deal of debate within literary circles as to how one might categorize the 'tragic' and MacKinnon took full advantage of the ambiguity.[96] In this vein, perhaps he would have accused Raphael of an overly prescriptive approach if he had ever developed his critique further. Indeed, MacKinnon argued that

> it would be a very grave mistake to generalize about tragedy as if there were an 'essence' of the tragic that we could extract and capture in a manageable formula. The word of Racine is very different from that of Shakespeare, and both alike from worlds explored by the ancient Greek tragedians. Yet if one bears in mind Plato's searching criticism of tragic drama as a suitable form for the presentation and exploration of ultimate issues, one finds that the most important aspect of what he repudiated was the sense that from tragedy we continually renew our sense of the sheerly intractable in human life.[97]

Although MacKinnon rejected the search for an 'essence' he did try to explicate 'the fundamental theme of tragic drama' nonetheless, and here we may find some similarities with the extract from Cavell which I discussed earlier in this chapter. MacKinnon argued that

> it is a commonplace of very old-fashioned moral philosophy to insist that 'ought implies can'. A man has an obligation, if, and only if, he has the means of fulfilling that obligation, of fulfilling it without, in fact, jeopardizing himself, as he must, if he finds the act of fulfilment self-destructive. Tragic exploration of the human condition makes men aware of the reality of this jeopardy. What our responses make of ourselves is not what we foresee'.[98]

MacKinnon explored this thought with reference to the Greek tragedians, and on this score the plays of Sophocles were a focus, including *Electra*, *Antigone*, *Trachiniae* and *Oedipus the King* (the last he judged to be 'the greatest and most complex of them all').[99] In *Trachiniae* we confront 'the element of the utterly intractable in the human environment, whereby men and women are tricked into

---

94. The person of Judas is something of a litmus test here. Cane, *The Place of Judas Iscariot in Christology*, 60–86.
95. *BT*, 97–104.
96. Cascardi, 'Tragedy and Philosophy', 166.
97. *ET*, 186–7.
98. Ibid., 185–6.
99. Ibid., 190.

destructive courses by their very virtues'.[100] When it came to *Antigone*, MacKinnon sought to supplement (what he perceived as) the Hegelian tradition of interpreting the 'tragedy as residing essentially in the conflict of "right with right"'; a view which placed the conflict between familial and civic duties at the heart of interpretation.[101] For MacKinnon things were more complex. It *is* the case that Antigone

> explores at a very deep level conflicts of personal duty. [Yet, MacKinnon continues...] The exploration is in the portrayal, compelling the reader and spectator to recognize that not only in the circumstances of actual life does it very frequently prove impossible to reconcile such conflicts by recourse to a formula, but more importantly, when an individual makes a right choice, the motives of that choice may be muddied beyond his or her full, or even partial awareness. Consequently human action comes to seem ambiguous; or it may be that while we continue to applaud what men or women do, we find that in the doing of it they have revealed themselves as flawed, not only in the actual performance, but in the springs of their response to the situation confronting them – springs which we acknowledge to be at least a necessary condition of their acting as they did.[102]

In 1981 MacKinnon's gave the Boutwood Lectures, which he named 'Creon and Antigone', focusing on the vexed issue of Cold War nuclear proliferation. Unlike his discussion of Shakespeare's *Julius Caesar* in relation to the July 1944 Plot, he did not make explicit the way in which the tragedy was thought to illuminate British policies of nuclear armament in the name of deterrence. As noted above, MacKinnon saw deficiencies in Hegel's reading, seeing in Antigone's character many 'obsessive, potentially incestuous and morally blind features', yet at the same time characterizing her as 'markedly Creon's superior as a human being'. Indeed, MacKinnon claimed that 'she activates the very worst in him, compelling him to identify inextricably the welfare of his city, for which he bears executive responsibility, with his own image of himself, which deteriorates as their exchanges proceed'.[103] I suspect that MacKinnon, in a characteristic flight of analogical imagination, found something akin to Antigone in the peace movement, which opposed the development of a nuclear deterrent, questioned the self-evident nature of its necessity and steadfastly refused the utilitarian logic whereby nuclear apocalypse is seriously countenanced as a justified risk in defence of a state. Intimating such a link gave scope for MacKinnon to acknowledge the risks of blindness, obsessiveness and utopianism that may accompany parts of the pacifist

---

100. *ET*, 190.
101. Hegel, it seems, 'does not get at the obsessiveness and frankly, the incestuous undertone of her brother's burial, nor Creon's weakness and his hubris'. Ibid., 188.
102. Ibid., 189.
103. Ibid.

and peace movements, yet to find in them something heroic, needful and true nonetheless.

The final Sophocles play mentioned by MacKinnon is *Oedipus*, where he considered many of the key insights of the tragic genre to be distilled with a high degree of clarity and maturity. In approaching the play, MacKinnon appreciated the work of literary critic Phillip Vellacott, and while not entering into dispute on some of his more controversial interpretive proposals, he nonetheless approved the way Vellacott found an analogy between the types of moral thinking being encouraged in the tragedy and some perennial themes of epistemology. Indeed, present in this play are the 'sorts of epistemological investigations with which students of some of Plato's dialogues are very familiar, i.e. those dialogues concerned with the relations of knowledge and right opinion etc. (e.g. *Meno*, *Republic* V-VII and *Theaetetus*), part of whose impulse came from Plato's reflection on the Socratic imperative "know thyself"'.[104] Further, we may detect a literary approximation of the unresolved tension between realism and idealism; a possibility that is intimated when Cascardi argued that

> Sophocles' interest in politics ultimately revolves around the tragically structured conflict between the force of an utterance (a law) that precedes all inner-worldly speech and the institutionally grounded utterances through which a legislator attempts to bring health and order to the polis.[105]

As well as affirming the presence of a high degree of philosophical sophistication in the play, MacKinnon saw in it a crystallization of quintessentially tragic motifs: a tendency to be blind to key aspects of our situation and its moral claim, scenarios in which conflicting duties and moral demands collide, moral actors whose virtues contribute to disaster just as much as their vices, and people subject to contingency and compelled to act in such ways that the realization of the significance and true moral (or immoral) status of their actions are only possible in retrospect, if ever.[106]

Tragedy offers tools for therapeutic correction, but it is not an ultimate category for Christianity according to MacKinnon.[107] Yet the question remains:

---

104. Ibid., 191.

105. Cascardi, 'Tragedy and Philosophy', 164.

106. If we have in *Oedipus* something of a distillation of the tragic motif, what we *do not* have is some sort of definitional criteria with which to systematically group disparate works together, including some and excluding others from the genre. In all substantive respects, MacKinnon left this debate to the literary critics. Speaking of those works which we might class together as tragedies MacKinnon says that 'they are inherently complex, and various in emphasis; at best we can discern a family resemblance between them, and, in an essay like this, the author runs the risk not only of selecting examples tailor-made to his thesis but also of imposing an appearance of similarity of conception where it is at least equally important to stress differences'. MacKinnon, 'Theology and Tragedy', 163.

107. *ET*, 6.

what then is the substance of MacKinnon's link between tragedy and theology? Here, the focus shifts from literary tragedy to historical tragedy, a move that is never explicitly explained or justified.[108] There are two factors that need to be mentioned by way of answering this question. The first pertains to a purgation of abstraction and triumphalism in Christology. The second relates to the fact that circumstances involving the tragic unravelling of lives, meaningless suffering and insurmountable moral conflict, all struck MacKinnon as locations where attempts by human reason to bring resolution must give way to inarticulacy and evocations of the transcendent.

MacKinnon saw tragic dimensions within the life of Jesus as recorded by the gospel writers and additionally in subsequent tendencies for the significance of his life and death to become enmeshed in ambivalent or openly violent ideological projects. His essay *Atonement and Tragedy* provides some essential insights here and it was discussed in Chapter 3. For MacKinnon, the downfall of Jesus and also later the destruction of Jerusalem in 70 AD, which occurred despite his best attempts to model a way to avert the calamity, contained elements of the tragic just mentioned. I also noted his attempt to resist all efforts to turn the resurrection into any sort of 'resolution' to the problem of the crucifixion. On this point MacKinnon was fond of summarizing his conviction with a quote from the Duke of Wellington, who reportedly reacted to a gushing admirer with the remark that 'a victory is the greatest tragedy in the world, only excepting defeat'.[109]

As well as Jesus's journey to the cross and the very real sense in which MacKinnon insisted on not shying away from the language of 'failure' in Christology, there is also a note of the tragic in the way New Testament narratives have been directly implicated in human suffering. Given his own historical milieu, there is no surprise that the woeful history of Christian anti-Semitism was often at the forefront of MacKinnon's consciousness as he read and re-read the Scriptures, particularly St. John and St. Matthew, as well as the Acts of the Apostles.[110] In this vein, MacKinnon called his essay *Evangelical Imagination* a 'twentieth century footnote to Milton's Paradise Regained', and with this, he moved to identify the fact that present imaginative efforts to speak meaningfully of the crucified Christ in the train of Milton and the Gospel writers cannot be undertaken without a serious realization of this effort taking place in 'the age of the Holocaust'.[111] Evidently, MacKinnon wanted for theology what Zygmunt Bauman sought for sociology,[112] observing 'that the quest for the historical Jesus is complemented very properly

---

108. Janz, *God, the Mind's Desire*, 172.

109. *ET*, 192.

110. MacKinnon spoke in terms of a '…claim that the sanction for such [anti-Semitic] judgement[s] can be extracted from the New Testament'. MacKinnon, 'The Evangelical Imagination', 197.

111. Ibid.

112. Zygmunt Bauman, *Modernity and the Holocaust* (Ithaca, NY: Cornell University Press, 1989).

today by that for the historical Pilate'.[113] Christians have never found a way of drawing near to the 'fact' of Christ and the true significance of his life, without partaking in a betrayal of all that Christ lived and died for. In this vein, Lapide asked,

> Why this wave of hatred, this scarlet thread that reaches from Golgotha to Auschwitz? Why this condemnation of God's biblical people, whose 'perfidy' consists in remaining true to their faith through three millennia – the faith of Abraham, Moses, David, and last not least, Jesus of Nazareth, who, though not the messiah of Israel, like us, longingly hoped for the Messiah's coming?[114]

Perhaps it was such questions that caused MacKinnon to be suspicious of the way certain readings of the *privatio boni* tradition had led to a 'papering over' of theodicy's challenge and led him to argue for a greater realism to be attached to the notions of good and evil alike.[115]

The second dimension of MacKinnon's link between tragedy and theology came in the way he saw the former pointing towards a fissure in human language and a crisis of inarticulacy.[116] This is at least analogous to the inarticulacy that notions of transcendence express in some streams of the Wittgensteinian philosophy of language, and most acutely (at least for MacKinnon) in the domain of Kantian-infused moral philosophies and theologies. In this vein, MacKinnon argued that in the tragic

> we touch the frontiers of the rational, if the rational is identified with the prudential. We also touch the frontiers of the rational where rationality is

---

113. MacKinnon, 'Natural Law', 127.

114. Pinchas Lapide and Ulrich Luz, *Jesus in Two Perspectives: A Jewish-Christian Dialog* (Minneapolis, MN: Augsburg Publishing House, 1985), 51.

115. Milbank criticized MacKinnon on this point: 'Without some notion of evil as ontologically predatory it becomes indeed impossible to grasp that while God may truly have suffered evil, he can yet, in some important sense have 'left it behind'. For if evil is not a surd element outside the world-text which humans beings write, then within this narrative it can be constantly re-enacted, re-presented, shown up as mere subjectivity, and so contained.' John Milbank, '"Between Purgation and Illumination": A Critique of the Theology of Right', in *Christ, Ethics and Tragedy: Essays in Honour of Donald MacKinnon*, ed. Kenneth Surin (Cambridge: Cambridge University Press, 1989), 180. A similar concern to that of MacKinnon's is expressed by Sands in the context of feminist theology, when she notes the import of the tragic ascription as essential for addressing lacunas in traditional attempts to 'rationalise' evil. Kathleen Sands, *Escape from Paradise* (Minneapolis, MN: Fortress Press, 1994), 17–69.

116. Janz has provided a perceptive and critical assessment of this dimension of MacKinnon's evocation of the 'transcendence of the tragic'. Janz, *God, the Mind's Desire*, 81–98.

4. MacKinnon and the Literary Imagination

conceived in the metaphysical sense of a creative Logos, whether immanent, or transcendent, or both at one powerful to make all things expressive of its creative power.[117]

Like Steiner, MacKinnon thought that the intractability of tragedy opened the way to silence. Steiner noted that

> wherever it reaches out towards the limits of expressive form, literature comes to the shore of silence. There is nothing mystical in this. Only the realization that the poet and the philosopher, by investing language with the utmost precision and illumination are made aware, and make the reader aware, of other dimensions which cannot be circumscribed in words.[118]

Both Steiner and MacKinnon acknowledge the 'shore of silence', yet they want to continue probing this silence with experiments of articulation. MacKinnon did this with reference to Christian revelation on the one hand and the firm conviction that empiricists and moral philosophers cannot, in the end, avoid questions of transcendence on the other, at least if they are properly attentive to the moral ambiguities of history and the suffering of individual persons. As noted in Chapter 1, these are issues MacKinnon saw as intertwined with 'the problem of metaphysics' and he detects this thread going all the way back to Plato. One sign that the problem of evil and its tragic manifestation in actual lives is being taken seriously, is that attempts to solve it are avoided.[119] Like the realm of freedom in Kant, Mill and Berlin, one apprehends a 'mystery' in Marcel's sense of the term, meaning ideas whose admission may compel a philosopher to 'revise a conception of the way things are to make room for their reality, or even to subordinate cherished goals of theoretical comprehension in order to establish their pre-eminent dignity'.[120]

Attempts to trace lines between tragedy, the metaphysical task of the philosopher and notions of transcendence, became particularly prevalent in MacKinnon's Gifford Lectures, where sections on 'Empiricism and Transcendence' and 'The Transcendence of the Tragic' appear in successive chapters. A strong moral focus is evident at the heart of both discussions, as well as a continual 'moving to and fro' between insights from the artist and those of the philosopher. What MacKinnon sought to explore here was a perceived affinity between the work of a moralist, informed by the empiricist's demand for a disciplined focus on the concrete particular, and the portrayal of the rise and fall of particular individuals

---

117. *ET*, 187.
118. George Steiner, *Language and Silence: Essays 1958-1966* (London: Faber, 1967), 112.
119. MacKinnon admired Hick's book on the subject: 'Evil and the Love of God'. D. M. MacKinnon, 'The Justification of Science and the Rationality of Religious Belief (Book Review)', *Epworth Review* 19 (1992): 108.
120. D. M. MacKinnon, 'Mystery and Philosophy (Book Review)', *Philosophical Quarterly* 9, no. July (1959): 284.

by the tragedians. Both can leave us torn between wanting to make realist claims to knowledge in terms of absolute good and evil, right and wrong, yet finding the reality of particular situations continually undoing our best efforts to secure these ascriptions with any neat resolution or finality. Both domains reach for the same frontier and approach it via different routes, in which we know the unavoidability of the moral enterprise and the in-built limits to our knowledge. In this vein, Janz observes,

> Orientation to the tragic – to the sheerly discontinuous in human life – allows us to project our questioning to the transcendent like no other form of discourse because it gives us *factual, tangible* examples in *real empirical* human experience, of the finality of non-resolution that we must encounter in the transcendent.[121]

For MacKinnon, this is a move which takes us beyond the idiom permitted to those who favour either a naturalistic reduction of ethical concepts, or who follow an alternative route of finding in our ethical language before all else a sort of method whereby we 'comment on human behaviour, stylise it, seek to modify it for good or for ill, to awaken in ourselves this or that response to this or that situation confronting us, but who deny it any factual import'.[122]

In tragedy, we apprehend a particular circumstance that demands a value judgement; a distinction between good and evil, human flourishing and dissolution that resists simple labelling in terms of 'naturalistic' or 'constructed', and which for MacKinnon, calls forth – however inadequately – a realist ascription. In the Spirit of Wisdom's *Paradox and Discovery*, the limits reached here are not pointing to a deficiency in knowledge that can be filled by further analysis of the situation or the invocation of God in a facile way. Like Kant, MacKinnon is pointing to in-built and permanent limits in our capacity to understand key dimensions of reality as we experience it.[123] On this point, Janz observes that

> tragedy-as-discourse is capable of accommodating or 'representing' the fact that real suffering and evil can exist in such intrusive and discontinuous particularity, or in such 'ruthlessness of interrogation', that in the end it can only be apprehended as calling attention to itself irresolvably, confronting us on its own terms with a kind of sui generis authority or finality, which is at one and the same time both undeniable and unspeakable.

There is more than a loose overlap with MacKinnon's Christological convictions here, if we accept his claim that a tragic ascription is appropriate for aspects of how the revelation played out in history. There are also resonances with the type of project that Rowan Williams sought to undertake in his 2013 Gifford

---

121. Janz, *God, the Mind's Desire*, 175.
122. *PM*, 109.
123. Cf. Janz, *God, the Mind's Desire*, 173–4.

Lectures, even though Williams adopted a much broader focus examining why the limitations and excesses of human linguistic practice may furnish a renewed and much qualified natural theology. After a sympathetic discussion of the work of the Dominican Cornelius Ernst and Arthur Gibson, Williams outlines a project that resonates with, enlarges and deepens a sensibility that is evident in MacKinnon's evocation of the transcendent: [124]

> A defensible natural theology, then, … would be a discourse that attempted to spot where routine description failed to exhaust what 'needed to be said' (however exactly we spell out the content of this phrase). This is emphatically not about spotting explanatory gaps in the usual sense (this would be to look only for extra descriptive resources that happen not to be available as yet). It is more like the recognition that a faithful description of the world we inhabit involves taking account of whatever pressures move us to respond to our environment by gesturing towards a context for the description we have been engaged in – not as a further explanatory level, but as a cluster of models and idioms and practices working quite differently from the discourse we have so far been operating, without which our 'normal' repertoire of practice would not finally make sense.[125]

Williams draws on Wittgenstein's legacy for this project, and I will leave the examination of MacKinnon's relationship with this legacy until the next chapter. Before moving onto that, I would like to note, albeit briefly, the way Janz also provides a helpful expansion of MacKinnon's examination of the 'transcendence of the tragic' in conversation with Bonhoeffer in a way that intensifies MacKinnon's own therapeutic sensibility.

At the heart of Janz's exploration is a conviction that the question 'Who are you?' is posed by 'transcendence', whereas 'How?' is the question of 'immanence'.[126] In this way the question of transcendence is not one that calls for a rational account, but the type of exposure to the interrogative question which is part and parcel of all therapeutic and confessional activity; a point with clear connections to the projects of Kierkegaard and Cavell.[127] The advent of the transcendent indicates more than just the irresolvable intellectual problem of 'structural' inarticulacy, but also a rupture at a most personal level. This can be mitigated by genuine acknowledgement (Cavell's term) of the presence of another person, our own

---

124. It is no coincidence that MacKinnon wrote the foreword to this book. Cornelius Ernst, *Multiple Echo: Explorations in Theology* (London: Darton, Longman and Todd, 1979). Arthur Gibson, *Metaphysics and Transcendence* (London: Routledge, 2003).

125. Rowan Williams, *The Edge of Words: God and the Habits of Language* (London: Bloomsbury, 2014), 8.

126. Janz, *God, the Mind's Desire*, 204.

127. Unsurprisingly, Levinas joins Bonhoeffer in Janz's account. Ibid., 205–7.

untapped depths and the self-disclosure of God. Williams articulates the heart of MacKinnon's insistence with characteristic insight when he notes that

> the tragic ... is not simply the order of the world that must be accepted (tragedy is not accident ...): it is one's own appropriation of the limits of possibility, in protest against a polity and a culture that lure us to sink our truthful perceptions in a collective, mythologized identity that can shut its eyes to limits (and so can talk of mass annihilation without pain).[128]

Conclusion

In this chapter, I have explored the literary dimension of MacKinnon's project. MacKinnon claimed to be working in the 'borderlands' and this is a reference to his location 'between' philosophy and theology. Yet another dimension of this borderland-dwelling vocation has been revealed in the links he made and tensions he observed between sacred and secular literature.

As noted earlier, MacKinnon saw Kant as providing a therapeutic treatment for anthropomorphism and the positivists a remedy for the excesses of idealism. He saw literature as a sphere in which the purgation may continue and deepen. Positively, the literary sphere exemplifies for MacKinnon the perennial Kantian tension between the receptive and creative dimensions of reason and it can furnish the kind of realist commitment that MacKinnon learnt in Moore's school. Additionally, MacKinnon found resources in literature that can help us move beyond the limitations of the moral philosophy encouraged by Kant and the positivists alike. Indeed, as we have seen, certain types of literature provide a remedy against the various pitfalls of formalist and systematic modes of moral philosophy, by evoking the irreducible particularity of persons and the complexity and compromise inherent in history. It is in the literary sphere and specifically in tragic literature where MacKinnon sought to articulate what he meant by moral realism, where he located the impetus for a style of humanism, and where he perceived a dimension of human life which reached a point of inarticulacy-toward-mystery in a way that is analogous with classical Christian narrations of the significance of Jesus's life and death.

In the next chapter, the themes of inarticulacy and transcendence in the wake of Kant return, but this time in the form of Wittgenstein's project; Wittgenstein was another thinker who provided purgative resources, without which our appreciation of MacKinnon's approach to moral philosophy would be incomplete.

---

128. Williams, 'Trinity and Ontology', 86.

Chapter 5

MACKINNON, WITTGENSTEIN AND MORAL REALISM

Introduction

The motivation for this chapter came from reading Kerr's essay *Idealism and Realism: An Old Controversy Dissolved*, which appeared in the 1989 *Festschrift* compiled in honour of MacKinnon's seventy-fifth birthday.[1] A crude summary of Kerr's argument is that MacKinnon was too caught up in the antiquated conflict between idealism and realism in a way that caused him to turn his back on Wittgensteinian philosophical resources that would have made his project more tenable.[2] It *is* true that MacKinnon did not wholeheartedly embrace the resources that the later Wittgenstein apparently provided for theologians and philosophers of religion to counter the scepticism of A. J. Ayer and Antony Flew, among others.[3] To investigate why this may be, the focus, at least in the first instance, must be on reckoning with the debate that surrounds Wittgenstein's relationship to idealism and realism. This may seem a circuitous way to proceed, but MacKinnon's reaction to Wittgenstein was closely linked with his convictions regarding these categories. In so many ways MacKinnon's project cohered with Wittgenstein's desire to return philosophy to the discipline of the 'concrete particular', yet in the end, MacKinnon did not find in Wittgenstein a reliable ally for the kind of catholic humanism and moral realism he saw as indispensable.

On Wittgenstein and ethics

The claim of Chapter 1 that MacKinnon was something of a philosophical 'therapist' whose work encouraged participation in a kind of confessional moral discipline was made with Wittgenstein in mind. Maurice O'Connor Drury recalls

---

1. The chapter title is a play on the title of MacKinnon's 1976 essay 'Idealism and Realism: A Controversy Renewed'. Fergus Kerr, 'Idealism and Realism: An Old Controversy Dissolved', in *Christ, Ethics and Tragedy: Essays in Honour of Donald MacKinnon*, ed. Kenneth Surin (Cambridge: Cambridge University Press, 1989), 15–33.
2. Ibid., 26–8.
3. Joseph Incandela, 'The Appropriation of Wittgenstein's Work by Philosophers of Religion: Towards a Re-Evaluation and an End', *Religious Studies* 21, no. 4 (1985): 457.

a conversation in which Wittgenstein stated that he considered St. Augustine's *Confessions* 'to be the most serious book ever written'.[4] Additionally, Thompson agrees with Cavell when the latter argued that in the *Investigations* Wittgenstein drew on a form of confessional therapy analogous to that employed by Augustine to address the problem of 'illusion'.[5] In explicating this claim, Thompson points to Wittgenstein's statement in §110 of the *Investigations*:

> 'Language (or thought) is something unique' – this proves to be a superstition (not a mistake!), itself produced by grammatical illusions.

Thompson goes on to interpret Wittgenstein's purpose, noting that

> when we are in the grip of such grammatical or linguistic illusions, we think that we are using language meaningfully, when in fact we are not. We have disconnected words from their contexts – the language-games – in which they have meaning. Such misuses of language are not 'mistakes' since we have moved outside the context in which mistakes (of fact, say) could be identified and criticized. …To break the grip of illusion, to come to see that one is using words without meaning, one must force oneself to look carefully at how one's words are ordinarily used. … [The *Investigations*] is confessional because … in talking about ordinary language … I am inevitably saying something about myself, about what I say. But the *Investigations* is also confessional because this struggle to find clarity goes on, 'despite an urge to misunderstand' (§109).[6]

A crucial insight into the character of the purgative activity going on here can be seen in the shift from the early to late works, for Wittgenstein realized that he had been captivated by certain illusions himself. This is particularly the case when

---

4. Rush Rhees, ed., *Recollections of Wittgenstein*, Oxford Paperbacks (Oxford: Oxford University Press, 1984).

5. Thompson, 'Wittgenstein's Confessions', 4–5. And Stanley Cavell, *Must We Mean What We Say? A Book of Essays* (New York: Scribner, 1969), 71.

6. Thompson, 'Wittgenstein's Confessions', 3. Cavell expresses the crux of Wittgenstein's diagnosis with characteristic insight: 'Wittgenstein finds philosophers attempting to explain the workings of the mind by appealing to psychological mechanisms about which they know nothing, rather than to the noticeable inner and outer contents in which the mind takes the forms which puzzled them in the first place (and these are the forms which physiological mechanisms will have to explain), or when he finds a philosopher supposing that he is *pointing* to a sensation by *concentrating his attention* on it, or finds him citing "evidence" for the "hypothesis" that other people "have" feelings "similar" to "our own", or finds him attempting to locate the essence of a phenomenon (say of intention, or meaning, or belief, or language) by stripping away all the characteristics which could comprise its essence, he does not say of them that they are making *mistakes* – as though greater attention and care could have gained them success.' Cavell, 'Existentialism and Analytical Philosophy', 970.

it came to his conviction that the kind of analysis undertaken in the *Tractatus* was compatible, indeed, would contribute to, the realization of 'a complete and general set of conditions of language, namely the correlated notions of logic, world, and subject'.[7] Christenson links this to an idealized view of 'language as representation', where scientific verification is seen as the commanding paradigm for epistemology and statements of value are seen to be 'transcendental', that is, 'non-factual'; they are related to the mystical, to that which cannot be put into words but that which 'shows itself' (6.4-6.421 and 6.522).[8] On this point, and as noted in Chapter 2, there seems to be more than superficial similarities between Wittgenstein's early philosophy and that of A. J. Ayer. According to the *Tractatus*, ethics is the domain of the subject's will; the domain addressed by psychology (6.4-6.421).[9] Christianson observes that as his philosophical position matures

> Wittgenstein gives up the idea of a unified set of conditions for all instances of language use; he now investigates ethics as one possible perspective amongst others, a particular way of using and addressing language. … What does not change is Wittgenstein's view of ethics as the subject's relationship with the world, as well as his idea that all forms of language use may have an ethical point, at least in principle.[10]

While not amounting to 'knowledge' per se, ethics remained a core aspect of his *Tractatus*. It was not the subject of a dogmatic construction, but appeared in the midst of 'elucidations', 'clarification', and 'perspicuous representation of our use of language' (4.112). In Wittgenstein's lecture on ethics, he described his endeavour vaguely as 'the enquiry into what is valuable, or into what is really important … into the meaning of life, or into what makes life worth living, or into the right way of living'.[11] Both here, and in the *Investigations*, Wittgenstein rejected certain inherited modes of ethical theorizing; he avoids debates in constructive meta-ethics and rejects any temptation to lay down a metaphysical ontology to ground

---

7. Anne-Marie S. Christensen, 'Wittgenstein and Ethics', in *The Oxford Handbook of Wittgenstein*, ed. Oskari Kuusela and Marie McGinn (Oxford: Oxford University Press, 2011), 802–5.

8. Ibid. See Ludwig Wittgenstein, *Tractatus logico-philosophicus* (London: Routledge, 1981).

9. Wittgenstein was similarly dismissive of attempts at subsuming 'evil' into an explanatory framework; it can be described but not analysed because 'good and evil only enter through the subject. And the subject is not part of the world, but a boundary of the world. … As the subject is not part of the world, but a presupposition of its existence, so good and evil are predicates of the subject, and not properties in the world. Ludwig Wittgenstein, *Notebooks, 1914-1916* (Oxford: Blackwell, 1961), 79.

10. Christensen, 'Wittgenstein and Ethics', 805–7.

11. Ludwig Wittgenstein, 'A Lecture on Ethics', *The Philosophical Review* 74, no. 1 (1965): 5.

judgements of value.[12] In the *Investigations*, Wittgenstein describes his methods as not offering solutions to problems but rather treatments, 'like different therapies' (§133).

Diamond and Peterman both see Wittgenstein's project in its differing phases as consistently and irreducibly charged with ethical themes.[13] Even if inherited controversies between competing moral theories are seen as having little value, language use in communities of action and discourse has an integral moral dimension that warrants philosophical representation and interrogation. The question that inevitably arises at this point for anyone under MacKinnon's influence is this: does Wittgenstein turn out to be a realist or idealist when it comes to ethics? Discussing this point, Fergus Kerr notes that the idealist–realist distinction has been a reoccurring theme in Western philosophical history:

> Since Plato's 'ideas', in the theory of Forms, are 'real' it has been argued, with brilliance and plausibility, that ancient philosophy should be described as 'realism'. The term 'idealism' is then available for the spread of mentalist-subjectivist themes in post-Cartesian philosophy where ideas have taken up residence in the head. That accords well enough with Wittgenstein's few references to idealism, because he always links it to solipsism: his idealists are tempted to say that we never know what is in each other's mind.[14]

These pejorative remarks about idealism have not prevented a long-standing debate as to whether or not Wittgenstein was, in fact, guilty of something analogous. The problem is the way in which Wittgenstein sought to articulate the 'conditions of meaning' and on this basis Thomas Nagel mounted what is probably the most sustained and influential accusation of 'idealism'.[15] At the heart of the ascription is a focus on the way Wittgenstein's linguistic turn places primary emphasis on our knowledge being limited within 'boundaries set by our human form of life', yet as Cerbone notes this is never adequately reconciled with another dimension of Nagel's analysis of Wittgenstein, which concerns the fact that the language of boundaries implies something lying beyond them, which might suggest something of a realist dimension.[16] What is clear to a number of interpreters, particularly those who examine Wittgenstein on the question of the language of pain, is

---

12. Christensen, 'Wittgenstein and Ethics', 805.

13. Cora Diamond, 'Wittgenstein, Mathematics, and Ethics: Resisting the Attractions of Realism', in *The Cambridge Companion to Wittgenstein*, ed. Hans D. Sluga and David G. Stern (Cambridge: Cambridge University Press, 1996), 230–1.

14. *TAW*, 120.

15. Thomas Nagel, *The View from Nowhere* (New York: Oxford University Press, 1986), 105ff.

16. David R. Cerbone, 'Wittgenstein and Idealism', in *The Oxford Handbook of Wittgenstein*, ed. Kuusela Oskari and Marie McGinn (Oxford: Oxford University Press, 2011), 322–5.

that this opposition to idealistic solipsism is more robust in Wittgenstein's later works than Nagel suggests *and* it has a crucial ethical dimension.[17] Wittgenstein demanded that one should not look beyond articulations of pain to some inner dimension, but that the concrete body of the other is to be given the fullest moral weight possible 'on its own terms'. That is, Wittgenstein did not appear to allow for the type of sceptical luxury that might lead one to agonize over the 'problem of other minds' when someone in their midst is expressing pain (§293, §295).[18] To the extent that some expressions of idealism lay down epistemological conditions that obfuscate the moral demand represented by an 'irreducible other', MacKinnon would surely agree.

According to Kerr, if one looks for the heart of the distinction between realism and idealism as it continued to be evoked by figures such as MacKinnon, one will find the lingering presence of the Cartesian subject.[19] The relation of the self to the external world is conceived as a self-evident problem, with idealism and realism providing competing and incommensurable answers as to how such a relationship might be managed. Kerr notes,

> In terms of the older story, realists and idealists divide over the intelligibility of the external world. For idealists, things only have the intelligibility that we give them. Clearly, the dispute revolves round our understanding of the place that the subject occupies in the world.[20]

Elsewhere he argues,

> The idealist has identified a profound and terrifying problem: my thoughts and feelings may be radically incommunicable, my inner life may be totally unsharable. But the assurances of the realist, while they take drama out of the predicament of epistemological solitude, leave the metaphysical picture of the self undisturbed.[21]

In response to this,

> Wittgenstein, and Heidegger more clearly, are out to destroy the picture of the self which sustains the whole dispute. [Kerr adds that Wittgenstein] ... is neither realist nor idealist: the gap between the subject and the world is simply not admitted. It is not bridged, for it never existed in the first place.[22]

---

17. Cavell, *Claim of Reason*, 341ff.
18. *TAW*, 132–41. See also Norman Malcolm, 'Wittgenstein's Philosophical Investigations', *The Philosophical Review* 64, no. 4 (1954): 530–5.
19. *TAW*, 206–11.
20. Kerr, 'Idealism and Realism', 27.
21. *TAW*, 138.
22. Kerr, 'Idealism and Realism', 17.

To demonstrate the character of this realism Nagel offers the case study of 'perpetual nine-year olds' and emphasizes the intelligibility of a perspective and a set of truths existing beyond the capabilities of these individuals to which they could conceivably come to realize in time. Thus, there is a linear hierarchy of truths, with people of differing capacities having differing levels of apprehension of the 'real'.[23] Perhaps Wittgenstein proposed something similar when he reflected on 'feeble-minded persons' (§371), but conceived the relationships between persons of differing perspectives and capacities quite differently from Nagel's 'linear' approach, at least according to Cerbone:[24]

> Wittgenstein's 'more fruitful' way of looking at the feeble-minded interrupts this way of picturing things, since it invites us to think of the feeble-minded as *alongside* our way of being minded, as another, perhaps 'queer', way of being minded rather than an 'essentially incomplete' version of our own. When Wittgenstein famously declares that 'what has to be accepted, the given, is – so one could say – *forms of life*', his more fruitful way of looking at the feeble-minded may be one form of that acceptance.[25]

While there may be ethical gains in the assumption that foreign or unusual forms of life may need to be accepted in their irreducible difference, rather than being subsumed as a subordinate and partial perspective into a universal epistemological whole occupied by 'us', the impression may be given here that Wittgenstein's proposal leaves the field of human knowledge strewn with incommensurate subjectivities. Such a concern is certainly close to the heart of Nagel's negative portrayal of Wittgenstein's idealism. Indeed, related to this point, Wittgenstein has been accused of fostering moral relativism. Christenson notes that Wittgenstein

> seems to accept a radically relativistic view of ethics, where there are – at least in principle – just as many ethical positions as there are people. This ready acceptance of the possibility of relativism appears to challenge the objective and imperative character of ethics, especially as Wittgenstein at the same time refuses to provide a shared foundation from which we may evaluate the value of different ethical viewpoints.[26]

Whether it is the accusation of idealism or relativism, Kerr and Cerbone are unwilling to let the charge go unanswered. Incandela joins them, calling it a 'pseudo-problem' based on a misreading which turns Wittgenstein's emphasis

---

23. Cerbone, 'Wittgenstein and Idealism', 314ff.
24. Ludwig Wittgenstein, *Zettel* (Oxford: Blackwell, 1981).
25. Cerbone, 'Wittgenstein and Idealism', 314ff.
26. Anne-Marie S. Christensen, 'Wittgenstein and Ethics', 796–7.

on 'forms of life' into a detached philosophical principle.[27] With Wittgenstein's rejection of the 'private world' of the Cartesian subject comes the rejection of a whole style of epistemology – one which sees the subject as having the capacity to take on 'some extra-mundane perspective from which observer-independent knowledge of things as they really are would become available'.[28] This subject gives priority to 'things' or alternatively 'our conception of things', depending on whether one has realist or idealist leanings, with the result that 'the realist, just as much as the idealist, marginalizes "life", the real thing', 'the given'.[29] Kerr argues that Wittgenstein's solution is to abandon what he sees as the philosophical presuppositions that gave rise to the problem:

> For Wittgenstein ... it was not a matter of reviving the realist versus idealist controversy in the hope of resolving it but rather of recovering a sense of the place of the subject in the world which would render the controversy superfluous.[30]

As Wittgenstein developed his position beyond his early period, the old controversy is seen to be more and more redundant. Both terms are taken by Wittgenstein as 'belonging to metaphysics' – pejoratively understood.[31] Indeed, Kerr observes that metaphysics is completely redefined by Wittgenstein, now related to any attempt to make observations regarding the shared view of 'the way things are', which is a function of shared embodiment; the basis for the possibility of coherence of language among speakers. This redefinition seeks to avoid a certain type of damage:

> We damage the intelligibility of our readings of the utterances of others when our method of reading puts others into what we take to be broad error. We can make sense of differences all right, but only against the background of shared belief – this is 'the method of truth in metaphysics'.[32]

As one becomes attuned to language use in everyday situations, the greater the pressure on epistemological distinctions between an abstract subject with his or

---

27. Incandela, 'The Appropriation of Wittgenstein's Work by Philosophers of Religion: Towards a Re-Evaluation and an End', 460.
28. Kerr, 'Idealism and Realism', 22.
29. Ibid.
30. Ibid., 24. Here Lovibond's observation about the later Wittgenstein is also pertinent: Wittgenstein's view of language implicitly denies any metaphysical role to the idea of 'reality'; it denies that we can draw any intelligible distinction between those parts of assertoric discourse which do, and those which do not, genuinely describe reality. This is an instance of the principle that 'if the words "language", "experience", "world", have a use, it must be as humble a one as that of the words "table", "lamp", "door"' (PI I 97): the "humility" in question here consists in an absence of metaphysical pretension'. Lovibond, *Realism*, 36–7.
31. Kerr, 'Idealism and Realism', 25.
32. *TAW*, 108 (Kerr is quoting Wittgenstein).

her private cognitive sphere and an external object with some essence beneath or beyond its appearance.[33] Rather than a subject who responds to the problem of scepticism with realist or idealist solutions, there is rather a 'form of life' (§19).[34] The practice of language in its holistically conceived cultural and communal context becomes the only reference point for determining the failure or success of an utterance, and with it the failure or success of a life. A commitment to this vantage point means that there is literally no sense in attempting to find a depth of meaning, or an unanswered philosophical riddle, in positing a 'gap' between linguistic utterance and external objects.[35] In this vein, Cavell notes that

> [In the *Investigations* Wittgenstein] says: 'What we do is to bring words back to their everyday uses.' Presumably, then, he felt that in philosophy words were unhinged from their contexts; it now became a problem for him how this could have happened and why it happened, what there is about philosophy that makes it happen and how language can allow it to happen. None of the criticisms of the tradition produced by Moore or the Oxford philosophers or the positivists seems to him to be right, to do justice to the pain, the pervasiveness, even the mystery of that conflict. He could not, for example, be content to say that in this conflict philosophy had been playing tricks or spoken with lack of seriousness, because he had had the experience of producing his first book, and he knew that such criticisms were not true of it.[36]

The problem being identified is a 'representative' view of language, whereby the gap between our language and the objects to which it is being applied becomes yet another proxy for the underlying problem of the gap between the Cartesian self and the world.[37] What is needed is a recognition of the subject's full immersion in the world, the irreducible 'situatedness' which renders what is usually taken for granted explicit. The romantic tradition offered one means of doing this; Wittgenstein offered another.[38] On this point Mulhall notes that

> if a grammatical investigation displays what it makes sense to say about something (what it is for any talk about something to count as, to be, talk about

---

33. A. J. Ayer, *Ludwig Wittgenstein* (Harmondsworth: Penguin, 1993), 71–8.

34. Ludwig Wittgenstein, *Philosophical Investigations*, Third edition (Oxford: Blackwell, 1968).

35. Mulhall observes that 'whereas traditional philosophers tend to conceive of the essence of things as hidden from view, hence as having to be revealed, say by penetrating the veil of mere appearance, Wittgenstein suggests instead that essence finds expression in grammar – in the kinds of statement that we make about the relevant phenomenon'. Stephen Mulhall, 'Wittgenstein on Religious Belief', in *The Oxford Handbook of Wittgenstein*, ed. Oskari and McGinn Kuusela, Marie (Oxford: Oxford University Press, 2011).

36. Cavell, 'Existentialism and Analytical Philosophy', 956.

37. *TAW*, 84–90.

38. Kerr, 'Idealism and Realism', 28.

that kind of thing), then the grammar thereby made manifest is not itself a kind of talk about that thing, and so cannot be saying anything false or otherwise misleading about it – any more than it can be saying something true.[39]

Grammatical analysis allows for a style of immersive philosophical observation, which may give rise to judgements of truth and falsity, meaning or meaninglessness within linguistic communities, but is itself neither true nor false. The accusation of idealism comes in the impression given that what is true can never be conceived apart from present or future extensions of our often-faltering capacity to express ourselves in language. As noted above, the charge of relativism soon follows.

Yet on the first count, Wittgenstein may reply with a counter-question regarding how we might possibly conceive a truth without a self-awareness of our location and limits as language users. Clearly, he believed there to be a way of acknowledging this fact without conceding to an epistemology which saw our apprehension of reality as merely constructive rather than receptive. Further, Wittgenstein's approach would sound like an affirmation of idealism rather than a denial *if* language was not 'public' in the way Wittgenstein believed it to be; that is, a dynamic effort of self-understanding and expression continually transgressing any fixed boundary between subject(s) and object(s).[40] His rejection of the possibility of untranslatable language would be relevant here too.[41] While there is the possibility of language arising from alternative life contexts striking us as strange or incorrect, there is a confidence in the possibility of mutual comprehension, however fallible.[42]

The final point to make against the pejorative ascription of idealism pertains to Wittgenstein's conviction that concepts pertain to facts:

> It is a fact of experience that human beings alter their concepts, exchange them for others when they learn new facts; when in this way what was formerly important to them becomes unimportant, and vice versa.[43]

On reading this claim, Cerbone states,

> The image Wittgenstein encourages here is a kind of ongoing engagement with the world, where new facts may be learned (not created, stipulated, or 'imposed' by the mind) that sometimes push and prod us to alter how we think about the world, even at the basic level of our conceptual repertoire.[44]

---

39. Mulhall, 'Wittgenstein on Religious Belief', e-book.
40. *TAW*, 94–100.
41. Cerbone, 'Wittgenstein and Idealism', e-book.
42. Incandela, 'The Appropriation of Wittgenstein's Work by Philosophers of Religion: Towards a Re-Evaluation and an End', 460.
43. Wittgenstein, *Zettel*, 67.
44. Cerbone, 'Wittgenstein and Idealism', electronic source.

It may now seem that Wittgenstein is countering a potential idealist accusation with a realist claim, yet, once again, this would be to ignore the extent to which our conception of the bounds of language and its limits are inconceivable outside the language games that pertain to the subject's form of life. There is no sense of Wittgenstein advancing or defending the sort of correspondence understanding of the subject's entanglements with these facts favoured by the empiricist, but nor can these comments rule out the suspicion that something analogous to correspondence does come into play, perhaps on the margins of Wittgenstein's thought, by which can describe the way language evolves and purifies itself in relation to the world.

Applying these insights more specifically to his ethical approach, it would seem that Wittgenstein's response is two-pronged: he seems to reject any accusation that his approach destroyed the possibility of seeing qualitative differences between ethical claims, while insisting that these can be established by the description of language use, not a matter of accessing ethical claims via a 'view from nowhere'.[45] Even *if* Wittgenstein's proposal did have relativistic implications, anyone who made such a claim should tread carefully, if only for the fact that for Wittgenstein, 'ethical relativism' would undoubtedly represent the embrace and articulation of an overarching ethical theory – something which he rejected as neither useful nor possible.[46] Furthermore, it is not evident that such a claim displays an adequate appreciation of the development of Wittgenstein's later thought particularly as it developed during the war years. Over this period, Wittgenstein expressed a conviction that ethics begins with dependence on other people and must acknowledge the moral claim that their existence represents.[47] He also employed language of God, particularly in his journals, when addressing the need for some goal in the quest for ethical perfection, even though nothing by way of positive content can be given to this word beyond the language games that we have, together with a general sense that the way in which the limits and excesses of language open a way to the mystical.[48] This does not indicate a radical departure: to the extent that Wittgenstein participated in any sort of moral realism, it was the realism of another human being, our linguistic 'embeddedness' and the reality of our own quest for self-knowledge and moral improvement.[49]

---

45. Wittgenstein, 'A Lecture on Ethics', 5–9.
46. Christensen, 'Wittgenstein and Ethics', 810–15.
47. Rupert J. Read, 'Wittgenstein's Philosophical Investigations as a War Book', *New Literary History* 41, no. 3 (2010): 6–7. Cavell develops this line of thought, claiming Wittgensteinian inspiration for his notion of 'acknowledgement'.
48. Christensen, 'Wittgenstein and Ethics'.
49. A. Bowyer, 'Moral Philosophy after Austin and Wittgenstein: Stanley Cavell and Donald MacKinnon', *Studies in Christian Ethics* 31, no. 1 (2018): 49–64.

MacKinnon's response to Wittgenstein

The therapies that Wittgenstein and MacKinnon offered shared a sceptical stance towards realist metaphysical ontologies, associated deductive moral epistemologies and attempts to vindicate religion 'rationally'. They shared an approach to the philosophical task which sought to enact purgative disciplines by which abstract universals were avoided and concrete particulars took centre stage. It is the difficulties of realism and the centrality of a kind of ethical intensity where the similarities become most evident. Lovibond observes,

> Wittgenstein writes in RFM VI §23: 'Not empiricism and yet realism in philosophy, that is the hardest thing.' The difficulty is presumably this: we wish to purge our critical concepts (such as 'truth', 'rationality', 'validity') of the absolutist or transcendent connotations attaching to them in the context of a foundational epistemology; but we do not wish, in the process, to find ourselves abolishing those concepts altogether. What is difficult is to pursue the twofold aim of showing, on one hand, that it does not make sense to look for a source of authority external to human practice which would certify as true (e.g.) those propositions that we call true; while, on the other hand, resisting the proffered alternative to our former, metaphysically contaminated use of those concepts – an alternative which would consist simply in jettisoning the concepts in question and replacing them by others. (Thus it might be argued that we should replace 'true' by 'assertible', and 'rational' by 'in keeping with the prevailing intellectual norms'.)
>
> [Lovibond goes on to note that] Wittgenstein evidently feels there is something paradoxical about the program indicated by the words, 'not empiricism and yet realism'. The appearance of the paradox is dispelled, however when we come to consider that programme in its application to ethics. For in ethics, and in evaluative discourse generally, any move toward realism – that is, towards the view that the assertibility conditions of evaluative sentence are truth conditions – is ipso facto a move away from the empiricist position, which involves a denial that moral judgement is answerable to truth.'[50]

Lovibond's engagement with Wittgenstein contains much that rings true to the tensions and concerns of MacKinnon's project. This is especially the case regarding observations about the persistence of certain terms after their association with metaphysical excess has been addressed, and the way in which a commitment to the notion that 'moral judgment is answerable to truth' may motivate one to embark of a struggle towards realism *and* cause tensions with the empiricist legacy. Yet, as noted in Chapter 1, if there was an underlying philosophical loyalty it was given to Kant, and this inevitably shaped MacKinnon's reception of Wittgenstein.

---

50. Lovibond, *Realism*, 45. The abbreviation 'RFM' refers to Wittgenstein's *Remarks on the Foundations of Mathematics*.

MacKinnon understood Kant to have achieved a high level of sophistication in his account of the rational subject, at one point referencing 'a celebrated passage in the Analytic of Principles as refuting what he called 'idealism' encountered in 'dogmatic' form in Berkeley, and in 'problematic' form in Descartes'.[51] For MacKinnon, Kant showed that key insights from idealism and realism need not be mutually exclusive, but rather the tension must be perpetually re-articulated; held despite the extreme difficulty this will cause the philosopher.[52] Importantly, MacKinnon did not think it possible for a philosopher to escape the sort of tension that the idealist–realist discourse was attempting to capture, Wittgenstein included. Additionally, he thought that some of Wittgenstein's chief concerns, such as his 'private language argument', were not necessarily antithetical to those of Kant. In this vein, MacKinnon noted that

> Kant certainly did not see the growth of human knowledge as a movement from the private to the public; for him the world of which we spoke was by that fact alone the public world; the categories were vindicated as indispensable conditions of communication, the notion of causality itself being proved as the *sine qua non* of the dating of events in a public time order. Moreover, as has been constantly insisted, the problem of metaphysics, of the validity of men's [*sic*] attempt to orientate themselves in respect of the unconditional was fundamental for him; it was the status of that enterprise that he was concerned.[53]

---

51. *ET*, 138.

52. Michael Dummett's work was an encouragement to MacKinnon to persist with this argument. Ibid., 138–9. I presume one of the key texts in this regard was the essay 'Realism' in Michael Dummett, *Truth and Other Enigmas* (London: Duckworth, 1978), 145–65. Janz holds MacKinnon in high regard as an interpreter of Kant, crediting him with a nuanced reading that avoided the temptation of turning him into an arch realist or idealist (or with Strawson, both at the same time). Janz argues that 'there are two basic and fundamentally opposing ways that the *Critique of Pure Reason* has been standardly – and devastatingly – misconstrued. The first is when its essential character as a *critique* is *ignored* and it is made into a thoroughgoing *defence* of "pure" reason. The second is when its essential character as a *critique* is *radicalized* and it is made into an all-out assault on metaphysics per se.' [Janz goes on to argue that] 'Idealism (anti-realism) enquires "into things" based on mind-dependence, realism based on mind-independence, and so on. So now, configuring this in an admittedly oversimplified way … we can say basically, along with Kant, (a) that scepticism is the fate of all philosophical enquiries "into things" that give priority to the senses, and (b) that, likewise, dogmatism is the fate of all philosophical enquiries "into things" that give priority to the intellect.' According to Janz, Kant's 'therapy' is not to choose sides between idealism and realism, or accept their respective 'undersides' – scepticism or dogmatism – but to reject the metaphysical system on which both are based, with its self-construal as the foundation of an enquiry 'into things'. Janz, *God, the Mind's Desire*, 130–5. MacKinnon saw parallels with Wittgenstein's project, yet sides with Kant on the question of whether the tension can or should be dissolved.

53. *SET*, 158.

In the same way that MacKinnon avoided a mischaracterization of Kant as either realist or idealist he avoided common simplistic and polarizing interpretations of Wittgenstein. That is, MacKinnon did not see the early Wittgenstein as engaging in quintessential expressions of positivism in any simple sense, nor his later work as tending towards idealism in any stereotypical way.[54] A case for Wittgenstein-as-idealist was certainly made by Dummett, yet MacKinnon's sympathetic engagements with John Wisdom probably counteracted any naïve acceptance of this assessment. It was Wisdom who introduced MacKinnon to the contrast between Moore and Wittgenstein; a discussion which convinced him that the latter had an insight that could not be ignored. Wisdom helped MacKinnon realize

> the crucial importance of Wittgenstein's contention that we are obsessed by the habit of supposing the meaning of a word to be an object, and in consequence are impatient of the sheer hard work involved in understanding a word or expression, by mastering its role or use.[55]

By submitting to Wittgenstein's purgation, MacKinnon thought that it was possible to grow in awareness of

> the perilous consequences of asking questions aimed at establishing the essential nature, for example, of discovery concerning matters of fact, as if there were not a whole multitude of different procedures involved in factual investigation on different occasions, which we must acknowledge as valid in appropriate context, refusing to fetter the flexibility of our understanding by acceptance of a definition endowed with sovereign authority.[56]

MacKinnon's attitude to the early phase of Wittgenstein's project is evident in an address given to the Christendom group in 1939. It indicates that MacKinnon was aware of differences between Wittgenstein and the logical positivists with whom his views were often conflated subsequently. Here, he made an extended reference to the *Tractatus*:

> Wittgenstein's *Tractatus Logico-Philosophicus* ... furnished the impulse of the logical positivist movement. But both in that work, and more definitely, in his later unpublished writings, there are traces of a difference in method. His work lacks

---

54. *BT*, 207–21. While MacKinnon did not engage in deep exegesis of Wittgenstein's project, recent compilations of his essays by Muller allow us to see more engagement than Kerr's critical essay would suggest. Essays such as *Metaphysical and Religious Language* (1953), *On the Notion of a Philosophy of History* (1954) and *Absolute and Relative in History* (1971) show a ready consciousness that there are demands for exercises of language posed by our apprehension of history that cannot be adequately accounted for by Wittgenstein's approach alone. *ET*, 54–69; *BT*, 152–68.
55. *BT*, 223.
56. Ibid.

the vigorous application of phenomenalistic attitudes. For him *all* philosophy is nonsense. Yet it may be helpful nonsense. There is really no problem there – none at all, and certainly nothing to get excited about. Philosophic bewilderment is a form of disease. Remember – 'everything is what is and not another thing' (to borrow from Butler an aphorism often quoted by Wittgensteinians). If only we understood our language, if we grasped its oddities, its flexibility, its looseness, there would be no philosophy. As it is, we don't, and there is, and therefore philosophy must go on, or rather that heir of the historic subject of philosophy, which is Wittgensteinian therapy. For to Wittgenstein and his disciples analysis is a form of therapy. We can say what we like. That is the next important fact about language, and philosophy will prevent us from forgetting it. Wittgenstein's philosophy seems to me to be one of the most remarkable essays in nominalism that the history of philosophy discloses.[57]

At a minimum, MacKinnon clearly discerned a vehement rejection of all Platonic vestiges coupled with a suspicion of deductive epistemologies in Wittgenstein's early work.[58] He saw the 'verificationist position' of the early Wittgenstein as 'the rational outcome of Kant's attitude to knowledge'.[59] That MacKinnon was cognisant

---

57. D. M. MacKinnon, 'And the Son of Man that Thou Visitest Him', *Christendom* 8, no. September and December (1938): 187. Wittgenstein, it seems, was aware of the charge of nominalism and seeks to distance himself from it in his later work: 'We do not analyse a phenomenon (for example, thinking) but a concept (for example, that of thinking), and hence the application of a word. So it may look as if what we were doing were nominalism. Nominalists make the mistake of interpreting all words as names, and so of not really describing their use, but only, so to speak, giving a paper draft on such a description.' Wittgenstein, *Philosophical Investigations*, 383.

58. Simon Blackburn, 'Religion and Ontology', in *Realism and Religion: Philosophical and Theological Perspectives*, ed. Andrew Moore and Michael Scott (Aldershot: Ashgate, 2007), 50–52.

59. MacKinnon, 'Kant's Agnosticism', 31. In the review of Wisdom's paradox and discovery – MacKinnon seems to have been influenced by Erik Stenius's work on the *Tractatus*, particularly the similarities he perceives between it and Kant's project. MacKinnon, 'John Wisdom's Paradox and Discovery', 65. Lovibond also makes a connection between Wittgenstein and Kant on the following question: 'Can our proposed realism accommodate the idea of a moral circumstance which would transcend the awareness of the entire community of speakers?' Lovibond responds: 'We can think of Wittgenstein's position here as comparable to that of Kant, for whom the phenomenal realm as such transcends the totality of propositions that we believe, as of now, to be true. Kant's view … is that we are far from the full truth about the world of appearances; that is what we should have if science were completed – completed in accordance with the principles that govern human thought. [Lovibond continues…] …Wittgenstein, however – unlike Kant – points us towards a naturalistic account of the mind's constructive activity. Lovibond, *Realism*, 73–4. Cavell also makes the connection between Wittgenstein and Kant. Goodman describes Cavell

of the dramatic shift which took place between Wittgenstein's early and later periods is evident, not so much by a direct analysis of Wittgenstein's works, but by changes in the way MacKinnon related Wittgenstein to Kant in essays from the 1940s compared to those of the 1970s. When MacKinnon made the connection, both are seen to be engaged in a comparable metaphysical purgation:

> Any reader of Wittgenstein's *Tractatus*, for all the difference of inspiration, receives continual reminders of the Kantian distinction of the form and matter of knowledge, from which the critique of metaphysics inevitably springs.[60]

MacKinnon understood Wittgenstein's earlier work as an extreme manifestation of a trajectory launched by Kant, and in his later writings, he began to identify elements of the two projects that were differently analogous:

> Kant's refutation [of Berkley's idealism] is interesting in itself; but in his work it is a necessary part of his subtle and strenuous effort to have the best of both worlds, to hold together a view which treated learning about the world as a finding, with one that regarded such learning as a constructive act. It is partly in response to this dual claim that the analogy between his work and that of Wittgenstein is to be found.[61]

as 'the first writer to point out the Kantian background to Wittgenstein's thought and to take seriously the therapeutic nature of his method'. Russell B. Goodman, *Contending with Stanley Cavell* (Oxford: Oxford University Press, 2005), 3. Quoting Wittgenstein, Cavell notes that the 'the problems of philosophy are not solved by "[hunting] out new facts; it is, rather, of the essence of our investigation that we do not seek to learn anything *new* by it. We want to *understand* something that is already in plain view. For *this* is what we seem in some sense not to understand"'. Thus, according to Cavell, the sort of answers the later Wittgenstein is seeking to uncover with his approach are not meant to provide us with 'more knowledge of matters of fact, but the knowledge of what would count as various "matters of fact". [Cavell then asks]: Is this empirical knowledge? Is it a priori? It is a knowledge of what Wittgenstein means by grammar – the knowledge Kant calls "transcendental"'. Cavell sees similarity between Kant's description of those intuitions or concepts that can be 'employed or are possible purely a priori' and Wittgenstein's position when he argues in §90 that 'our investigation ... is directed not towards phenomena, but, as one might say, towards the "possibilities" of phenomena'. Cavell also notes that they are both concerned with analogous types of illusion: 'And where Kant speaks of "transcendental illusion" – the illusion that we know what transcends the conditions of possible knowledge – Wittgenstein speaks of the illusions produced by our employing words in the absence of the (any) language game which provides their comprehensible employment. Cavell, *Must We Mean What We Say?: A Book of Essays*, 65.

60. MacKinnon cites Prof. R. B. Braithwaite's Herz Lecture as the source of this observation. *BT*, 212. See also MacKinnon, 'Kant's Influence on British Theology', 362.

61. *ET*, 138.

And yet the comparison has its limits, as MacKinnon also notes,

> If [Wittgenstein's] similarity to Kant is seen, the differences light up the nature of the problems Wittgenstein sets himself. For Wittgenstein, it would be an illusion that we do not know things in themselves, but equally an illusion that we do (crudely, because the concept of "knowing something as it really is" is being used without a clear sense, apart from its ordinary language game).[62]

MacKinnon viewed Wittgenstein as *tending towards* something like a coherentist position, one in which 'it is in the stream of life that expressions have meaning'.[63] In this way, the later Wittgenstein was seen to have swung from positivist nominalism to a kind of idealism that was analogous to that of Kant. Yet, Kant still retained the distinction between our conception of a 'thing' and a 'thing in-itself' and it was Wittgenstein's mission to purge this sort of talk from the philosophical canon.

Despite these efforts the distinction continued to appear at the centre of debates among Wittgenstein's interpreters. For example, in 1983 Lovibond could still offer a reading of Wittgenstein as developing a position which easily fitted within MacKinnon's standard definition of idealism, while Cora Diamond offered a riposte.[64] Lovibond argued that 'Wittgenstein's view of language implicitly denies any metaphysical role to the idea of "reality"; it denies that we can draw any intelligible distinction between those parts of assertoric discourse which do, and those which do not, genuinely *describe* reality'.[65] The difference of perspective between Diamond and Lovibond is representative of a much wider fissure identified by Cerbone, who observes,

> Of the many sources of interpretive conflict in Wittgenstein's philosophy, one of the most recalcitrant is surely the question of his philosophy's ultimate commitment to *idealism*. Many readers of Wittgenstein (for example G. E. M. Anscombe (1981), David Bloor (1996), Michael Forster (2004), Jonathan Lear (1982), Thomas Nagel (1986), and Bernard Williams (1981) have detected at least some affiliation with, if not outright endorsement of, some form of idealism, while other readers, such as Cora Diamond (1991), Ilham Dilman (2004), Norman Malcolm (1995), John McDowell (1998), Edward Minar (2007), Stephen Mulhall (2009), Barry Stroud (1984), and Michael Williams (2004), have offered persuasive considerations *against* any such affiliation.[66]

---

62. Ibid., 65.
63. Ibid., 143.
64. Diamond, 'Wittgenstein, Mathematics, and Ethics: Resisting the Attractions of Realism', 226–7.
65. Lovibond, *Realism*, 36. For Cora Diamond's response see Diamond, 'Wittgenstein, Mathematics, and Ethics: Resisting the Attractions of Realism', electronic source.
66. Cerbone, 'Wittgenstein and Idealism', electronic source.

Dummett is not mentioned here, yet Kerr refers to Dummett's 1959 review of Wittgenstein's *Remarks on the Foundation of Mathematics*, as 'fateful' in as far as the former portrayed the latter as

> such an extreme anti-realist, as regards mathematical statements, that [Dummett] speaks of [Wittgenstein's] 'constructivism' and 'full-blooded conventionalism'. In old fashioned terms Wittgenstein's philosophy of mathematics is interpreted as a form of subjectivist idealism. … Dummett's review lends authority to a now widespread belief that Wittgenstein's later work licences anti-realist inclinations in every disputable domain.[67]

Kerr proceeds to note arguments made in Cupitt's *Sea of Faith* to demonstrate the degree to which theologians adopted what he saw to be the pernicious and inaccurate conclusions of Dummett's review.[68] That MacKinnon was a sustained critic of the kind of non-realist theistic revisionism developed by Cupitt may point to the fact that he did not fall into the trap that Kerr identifies.[69] Indeed, speaking of Wittgenstein's lectures on the foundations of Mathematics, MacKinnon claimed that 'he seems to ground every sort of necessity in an arbitrary fiat of the subject. Yet what he is doing only begins to become clear when viewed in relation to language as a whole'.[70] Signs that MacKinnon was perceptive enough to avoid

67. *TAW*, 129–30.
68. Ibid., 129. Kerr also seeks to demolish Nagel's accusation pertaining to Wittgenstein's supposed 'idealism'.
69. As noted in Chapter 1, MacKinnon was also critical of what he characterized as the non-realist approach of D. Z. Phillips. He was sceptical about Phillips's appropriation of Wittgenstein's legacy, arguing that 'Wittgenstein's attitude is a great deal more complex than that of his supposed follower [i.e. Phillips]. If he could not attach any sense to the notion of a first all-originating cause, he yet felt deeply the authority of an ultimate judge. Professor G. H. von Wright rightly discerned a kinship with Pascal, and the fascinating similarities between the structure of the *Tractatus* and the work of Immanuel Kant have often been remarked (e.g. by Professor Erik Stenius). MacKinnon, 'The Justification of Science and the Rationality of Religious Belief (Book Review)', 108. McCutcheon has recently advanced a similar argument. Felicity McCutcheon, *Religion within the Limits of Language Alone: Wittgenstein on Philosophy and Religion* (Aldershot: Ashgate, 2001). Moore's analysis helps to clarify the strengths and weaknesses of MacKinnon's (possibly simplistic) characterization of Phillip's work. Moore, *Realism*, 80–4.
70. *ET*, 143. When it comes to the later Wittgenstein, MacKinnon has some sympathy for Dummett's characterization of the 1939 lectures on the foundations of mathematics as showing forth a 'strict finitism', yet this does not provide the basis for the accusation of thoroughgoing idealism for the former as it did for the latter. 'Finitism' here represents a form of epistemology by which the subject's creativity is emphasized and becomes the horizon within which knowledge is being circumscribed: 'We have many illustrations of the way in which Wittgenstein himself obeyed his own prescription in treating such problems

Dummett's misreading are also evident in an essay from 1968, where he noted the fact Wittgenstein 'learnt from Moore of the philosopher's duty to be concerned with what is the case, and what we can properly say to be the case'.[71] MacKinnon continued with the following qualification:

> To say this is not, of course, to suggest that such concern is absent from Wittgenstein's later work; it is not, but a careless reading of, for example, some of the things he says concerning mathematical discovery and invention go some way to encourage such tendencies among lesser men.[72]

MacKinnon did not see Wittgenstein as an idealist in the way he has sometimes been accused, yet under the influence of Wisdom, he still viewed Wittgenstein's later work as needing supplementation by figures such as Moore in as far as the latter continued to point to the necessity of correspondence notions of truth.[73] MacKinnon took Wittgenstein as holding to a 'holistic' theory of meaning, and to the extent that this did not equate with a coherentist or an idealist position in any simplistic or reductionist way, MacKinnon was open to learning from him. And yet what concerned MacKinnon was the possibility that

> both [holistic and coherentist theories of meaning] agree in a determination, if not to abandon, at least radically to depreciate concern with what is or is not the case in the sense in which such concern if affirmed as central by those who identify truth fundamentally with correspondence: this though they realize the need for the utmost sophistication in analysis of that correspondence.[74]

This emphasis and insistence is something that has been noticed by Janz, and it is worth quoting him at length

as those of the sense in which we can properly speak of the existence of natural, rational, irrational and transfinite numbers of the relations of pure to applied mathematics. He has much to say moreover of the central crux in the philosophy of mathematics, namely whether a new piece of mathematics is to be regarded as an invention or as a discovery.... [Wittgenstein] worked out in detail the consequences of Brouwer's rejection of the so-called "law of the excluded middle", [and his] standpoint in this period has been characterized as '"strict finitism"'. *ET*, 152.

   71. *ET*, 226.
   72. Ibid.
   73. D. M. MacKinnon, 'Karl Barth: An Introduction to His Early Theology (Book Review)', *Journal of Theological Studies* xiv (1963): 556–9. MacKinnon's concern with correspondence, coherentist and 'pragmatist' theories of truth is evident as early as 1948. 'Christian Understanding of Truth', *Scottish Journal of Theology* 1, no. 1 (1948): 19–29.
   74. *ET*, 146.

MacKinnon insists that those who, like himself, want to 'identify truth fundamentally with correspondence ... [must] realize the need for the utmost sophistication in analysis of that correspondence'. He is thus, as a *realist*, repeatedly at pains to distance himself from what he calls 'a *simpliste* model of correspondence' which buys into the 'logical mythology of "atomic propositions" corresponding with "atomic facts", and the implied ontology of ultimate simples'. Of course, what MacKinnon is referring to here is precisely the straw-man version of 'metaphysical realism' (or more correctly, atomic realism) repudiated by Putnam, a realism that in his words contends that 'the world consists of some fixed totality of mind-independent objects', that 'there is exactly one true and complete description of "the way the world is"' and that 'truth involves some sort of correspondence relation between words or thought-signs and external things and sets of things'. MacKinnon refers to such a *simpliste* construal of realism or correspondence as the 'picture theory' of truth. All of the characterizations of realism we have been considering so far (i.e. 'atomic realism', 'metaphysical realism', the 'One True Theory' view, the 'God's Eye' point of view and so on) are for MacKinnon versions of the 'picture theory', and as such they all represent a fundamental misconstrual of the true import of correspondence.[75]

What then is the 'true import'? To make any headway here we must remember that MacKinnon saw the 'constructive' and 'imaginative' dimensions of reason as potentially enhancing realism; a point made in the previous chapter's focus on the literary imagination and historical analogy. MacKinnon sought a sophisticated position that avoided pitting coherentist and correspondence approaches against each other in a blunt opposition: both can forget what Janz calls the 'anthropocentric challenge', which is essentially a therapeutic determination not to ignore the person who is attempting to philosophize their historical embeddedness and their moral successes and failures.[76]

As we have seen time after time, MacKinnon never abandoned the realist insistence that part of any claim to coherence must be a reference to facts independent of human cognition and subjectivity. Yet, he drew on examples of Newton's Inverse Square Law and Russell's comments on the 'coherentist' nature of pure mathematics to emphasize the necessity of speaking in terms of coherence as well.[77] MacKinnon clearly noticed that Wittgenstein combined 'holism' with a correspondence approach *of sorts*: there is a world to which language must continually adapt itself even if his way of expressing this courts the idealist charge as it seeks to avoid perceived missteps of the empiricist. Together with

---

75. Janz, *God, the Mind's Desire*, 84–5. Discussing MacKinnon's position, Williams observes: 'If picture theories must go, are we left with any option but something like this: a realism which shows itself in the halts and paradoxes, shifts and self-corrections of language itself as a material and historical reality.' Williams, 'Trinity and Ontology', 76.
76. Janz, *God, the Mind's Desire*, 83.
77. *ET*, 74–5.

him, MacKinnon adopted 'a kind of openness to holism and coherence that any properly integrated correspondence theory (or realism) will have to manifest'.[78] Yet MacKinnon, contra Wittgenstein and to the apparent frustration of Kerr, was determined to maintain an empiricist's purposive and explicit distancing of the rational subject from objects of knowledge; a move that is perhaps loosely analogous to Cavell's post-Wittgensteinian reassertion of scepticism.[79]

MacKinnon never countenanced an absolute parting with the Enlightenment tradition; aspects of the 'Cartesian subject' and a correlationst approach to truth are seen as indispensable, despite the temptations they bring.[80] Such a move is seen to allow a kind of reflexivity in the midst of the concrete particular, allowing one creative space to speak (contra Wittgenstein) of a 'philosophy of history', to mount 'a study of ethical theory' and to continue to raise the 'problem of metaphysics' in the form of a set of perennial questions which demand the invocation of the realist / idealist tension.[81]

With Wittgenstein, MacKinnon held that purgation is needed to drive philosophers from fruitless abstractions and faux-controversies into the concrete circumstances of everyday life, but this immersion led to a return to metaphysical questioning rather than silence. Most of all, MacKinnon refused to concede that discussion centred on realist and idealist labels had reached an *unproductive* impasse. What might *seem* like an impasse is a nest of permanent difficulties intrinsic to the philosophical task and unavoidable for any attempt to apprehend the moral complexity of the human condition. Indeed, part of MacKinnon's argument, which Kerr does not mention in his *Festschrift* essay, is the former's contention that Wittgenstein's philosophy revives questions that gave rise to the distinction, despite Wittgenstein's best efforts.[82] This may be a case of a naïve reading of Wittgenstein on MacKinnon's part, yet if we look at the debate that emerged in assessing Wittgenstein's legacy it seems MacKinnon had a point.[83]

---

78. Janz, *God, the Mind's Desire*, 86.

79. MacKinnon maintains a tension articulated by Hedley: 'The error of Cartesianism is to present the *cogito* as theoretically autonomous, whereas the self requires mediation through a context and relations with other selves. But Cartesianism preserves the commonsense intuition that a substantial part of human identity eludes physiology, society and circumstance. And it is this sense of the human soul underlying the variations of culture, race and creed that founds the proper task of the humanities – of intelligent and critical empathy with the great cultures of the past'. Hedley, *Living Forms of the Imagination*, 60.

80. As we will see, this is an aspect of MacKinnon's project that attracts criticism from Milbank. Milbank, 'Between Purgation and Illumination', 161–96.

81. Williams is surely right to point out that MacKinnon's hints at a doctrine of analogy become relevant at this point. Williams, 'Trinity and Ontology', 76.

82. *ET*, 143–5.

83. Insole has developed a critique of the Wittgensteinian legacy that could be read as a more systematic development of the anxiety MacKinnon tried to express in the wake of the *Philosophical Investigations*. Insole, *Realist Hope*, 11–69.

I suggested above that at the heart of Kerr's criticism of MacKinnon is the way the latter maintained strong sympathies for the philosophical predilections of British empiricism as he sought to explicate a type of realism.[84] Kerr learns from Wittgenstein that realists of this ilk just as much as the idealists they opposed

> fail to acknowledge that *das Leben* is 'the given': these *Lebensformen* that, in a later and more celebrated formula, are what has to be accepted. (PI, 226) In effect, Wittgenstein implies here, realists are as oblivious as idealists to 'the real thing', *das Eigentlich*, which, again in a much later phrase, he refers to as 'the bustle of life', *das Getriebe des Lebens*. (RPPII, 625). Obsession with representing reality makes the unrepresentable bustle of life seem contingent and marginal. The 'stenographer', in Bukharin's phrase, takes the place of 'the real subject', i.e. social and historical man.[85]

By Kerr's reckoning, MacKinnon was a realist, or at least someone who 'conducted an anti-idealist campaign throughout his career'.[86] My argument is that MacKinnon's position is subtler. His realism entailed forms of purgation that paralleled those put forward by Wittgenstein, at least to the extent that he pursued a project that was weary of the dualistic tendencies of realism and its temptation to develop – inadvertently or otherwise – a 'metaphysical antipathy to the body'.[87] As I will note below, there were ways in which MacKinnon can be criticized for countenancing certain 'abstractions', yet such failures often *derive from* an otherwise admirable attempt to account for the historical subject, rather than avoid it. Indeed, attentiveness to the very particular character of human action in history is what remedies temptations towards dualism, antipathy to embodiment or flights of metaphysical abstraction for MacKinnon, who can write that it is

> at the level of action that men and women engage themselves, suffer and make others to suffer. It is where informed choices serve carefully conceived policies of individual or collective conception that men and women achieve what they do achieve, break others and themselves are broken in pieces. It is at the level of raw human existence, where we make play, not with ideas but with the substance of our lives, that for good or ill we make our mark upon the sands of time. We cannot trivialize such achievement and such suffering by suggesting that, for the historian, it is nothing apart from the significance which he himself gives it. There is an element of creativity to be reckoned with in the human situation, -creativity for good and for ill … but in the background there lies the actual work of men [sic], and it is this that gives significance to what we recollect, and to our

---

84. *TAW*, 121–41.
85. Ibid., 134. Kerr is quoting from Wittgenstein's *Remarks on the Philosophy of Psychology*, Vol. 2.
86. Kerr, 'Idealism and Realism', 15.
87. *TAW*, 137.

efforts as disciplined historians, to reshape the raw material of our recollection, more in accordance with actuality.[88]

If it is a crime that 'our *life* has traditionally been regarded as accidental and marginal to the great metaphysical debates about words and things, thought and reality, self and world',[89] can MacKinnon be declared 'not guilty'? The answer, I think, is broadly affirmative. He sought to perpetuate the 'great metaphysical debate', yet in the tradition of Butler he also insisted on a textured and immersive moral epistemology, and under Collingwood's influence, saw a renewed focus on the category of history as a locus for the continual re-positing of questions that justify efforts towards a revisionary metaphysics.[90] While someone like John Caputo 'opposes correspondentism by insisting that access to objects is always mediated by historically contingent concepts', MacKinnon wanted the best of both worlds: a type of correspondence that was compatible with a historical immersion of a self-aware subject.[91] This is evident in MacKinnon's appreciation of Bultmann's close reading of Collingwood in the context of an otherwise hostile review of the former's *Gifford Lectures*. MacKinnon noted that

> for Collingwood, sometimes history and metaphysics were identified; and it is clear that one of the things which Bultmann deeply admires in Collingwood are those elements in his conception of history which enable him practically to identify the historian's task with the achievement of existential self-knowledge. In the passages in his concluding lectures, in which Bultmann meditates on Collingwood's writings, his readers can watch him moving on beyond anything Collingwood explicitly said to the point of identifying history with a peculiar kind of self-awareness, which belongs to and indeed shapes the sort of decisions that the responsible individual must make. History; self-awareness; decision; these notions gradually pass into one another.[92]

Collingwood was seen by MacKinnon as having made 'his own signal contribution' to the trajectory of modern approaches to history represented by Hegel, Marx and Dilthey, in distinction from the trajectory represented by the 'logical revolutions

---

88. *ET*, 60–1.
89. *TAW*, 134.
90. MacKinnon, 'Ethical Intuition', 101. Kerr acknowledges that alongside Dummett, Collingwood was major influence on MacKinnon's 'historicization' of metaphysics. Kerr, 'Idealism and Realism', 18. See also, *BT*, 169.
91. Kevin Hector, *Theology without Metaphysics God, Language, and the Spirit of Recognition* (New York: Cambridge University Press, 2011), 27.
92. This becomes the prolegomena to reflection on Jesus Christ as 'the eschatological event'. MacKinnon, 'History and Eschatology', 207.

of Frege and Russell'.[93] Yet, just as MacKinnon appreciated that Marxist approaches to history potentially offered provocations towards purgation which themselves needed subsequent purging towards greater realism, so it was with Collingwood's proposals.[94] Collingwood can be cited, along with Kant, as an influence that led MacKinnon to differentiate himself from Wittgenstein, yet he also resisted any depreciation of the significance of the historical event 'in itself' or any excessive idealistic scepticism that he detected in these figures.

Yet, for all this, Collingwood's historically informed 'moral seriousness' left a lasting impression on MacKinnon. Such a capacity to speak about history in terms of free agency, narrative and ultimacy was important, as was the ability to adequately factor into his philosophy movements of 'absolute' historical breakthrough, suffering, tragedy and evil in a way that could call on the language of 'factuality'. In addition to Collingwood (and Kant), the source of MacKinnon's resistance to Wittgenstein can also be traced to the kind of Christological reflections that constituted Chapter 3.[95] In this vein, he perceived that history's interrogation of us, via events like the incarnation and the holocaust, demanded bolder attempts to test the 'correspondence' of moral language to 'the given', even if this meant courting failure and the continuous fragmentation of language. MacKinnon felt this was required for a more explicit, more forceful, articulation of humanism beyond that which Wittgenstein provided for. The freedom exercised to create and to destroy moral possibilities, alongside a historical apprehension of non-negotiable moral limits, drove MacKinnon to persist beyond the point where Wittgenstein thought a boundary of silence was reached.

In the end, MacKinnon's continued probing arises from and leads towards an uneasy combination of intuitionism and 'natural law' approaches. These ideas appear in disconnected parts of his corpus; they are never reconciled and this is deliberate. They are, in MacKinnon's own slippery idiom, 'moves in a game', but observing these moves is the closest we can come to 'placing' MacKinnon.[96]

MacKinnon's unsystematic proposal for moral philosophy: Intuition and natural law

MacKinnon desired to articulate a version of moral realism that went beyond both Kantian formalism and Wittgenstein's attempts to circumvent the realist / idealist distinction and ethical theorizing per se. In earlier chapters I noted MacKinnon's

---

93. *BT*, 169. This is an insight shared by Vanheeswijck who notes Collingwood's identification with the 'objective idealist' label and the Hegelian tradition. Guido Vanheeswijck, 'Robin George Collingwood on Eternal Philosophical Problems', *Dialogue: Canadian Philosophical Review/Revue canadienne de philosophie* 40, no. 3 (2001): 566.

94. *BT*, 163.

95. Ibid., 152–68.

96. MacKinnon, 'Ethical Intuition', 113–14.

preference for utilitarianism over emotivism when it came to articulating possible alternatives to Kantian moral philosophy. Indeed, MacKinnon *did* value ultilitarianism if it was tempered by intuitionism and vice versa. Both have the potential to take debates about conduct away from the concrete particular in distorting ways; both can harbour an 'impulse to escapism' just as they both can provide a means for greater realist apprehension and a more robust defence of humanistic values.[97] Unlike Pritchard, who built a theory of intuitive ethics as part of a crusade against utilitarianism, MacKinnon *could* see that the utilitarian held to a vital 'realist impulse'.[98] Even so, there was something that the utilitarian needed to hear in the intuitionist's emphasis on the 'subjective aspect' within debates about conduct.[99] At the same time, MacKinnon could be weary of the pull of subjectivism within the work of the intuitionists in as far as grounding for moral factuality was being sought in an increasingly a-historical and non-empirical interiority.

Mackie saw forms of intuitionism as the insidious intellectual compromise at the base of attempts to defend moral realism.[100] Intuitionism was a position which for many years was dominated by debates between the Moore, Pritchard, Ross and their respective followers.[101] In one of his most famous papers on the topic, Ross argued (quite awkwardly it must be said) 'that good is objective in the sense of being independent of being attended to and of rousing any sort of experience in a mind, but not independent of mind, since it belongs only to minds and to their states and qualities'.[102] This leaves us with an explanation for direct (as opposed to inferential) judgements of good that holds something like this: 'If our intuition of some proposition is to (defensibly) justify our judgment, then intuitions must be understood as nondoxastic, nonfactive states.'[103] In a paper that MacKinnon read with some sympathy, A. C. Ewing developed a reading of Ross's argument that countered those of Stevenson and Ayer.[104]

---

97. Ibid., 111–14.
98. *SET*, 41.
99. MacKinnon, 'Ethical Intuition', 111–14.
100. Mackie, *Ethics: Inventing Right and Wrong*, 38–9.
101. Ewing, 'Recent Developments in British Ethical Thought', 70–5. Warnock describes Prichard's preference for the 'subjective view', referring to the fact that obligation depends on how we think of a situation rather than characteristics of the situation itself. Warnock: '[Pritchard's] progress towards this conclusion is typical not merely of his technique, but of the method of intuitionism as a whole.' Warnock, *Ethics since 1900*, 36.
102. W. D. Ross, 'The Basis of Objective Judgments in Ethics', *International Journal of Ethics* 37, no. 2 (1927): 118.
103. Philip Stratton-Lake, 'On W.D. Ross's "The Basis of Objective Judgments in Ethics"', *Ethics* 125, no. 2 (2015): 523.
104. D. M. MacKinnon, 'British Philosophy in the Mid-Century (Book Review)', *Church Quarterly Review* CLIX (1958): 112–14.

5. MacKinnon, Wittgenstein and Moral Realism

Warnock and A. E. Taylor variously interpreted intuitionism as a revised form of Kantian deontology.[105] In an early essay from 1956 MacKinnon developed a highly qualified defence of intuitionism, beginning with the observation that 'the philosophical intuitionist is concerned to argue, in some way, for the view that fundamental principles of morality or of value are self-evident and irreducible.'[106] He then went on to explicate what can and cannot be defended in the notions 'self-evident' and 'irreducible': the first pertaining to the way we come to know, and the second pertaining to the relation between moral principles and other principles from which philosophers have often attempted to ground or explicate moral knowledge, such as 'my concern as a human being for the welfare of my fellows'.[107] MacKinnon saw the attempt of the intuitionist to continue probing the nature of such principles as important and he does so in a way that suggests both sympathy and resistance to the Wittgensteinian project. His argument:

> What is irreducible is underived, and it was insisted that the absence of derivation must be epistemic as well as ontological. And it may indeed be argued that with the advent of modern linguistic methods, this sort of artificial to and fro between what we know and the way in which we know it, has been abolished; something of this sort may seem to have been admitted in the earlier paragraphs of this essay, where the notion of irreducibility was analysed in terms of the way in which we argue. Some might actually go as far as to suggest that such phrases as 'we know directly', 'we are certain', occurring in ethical contexts, simply conveyed emphasis, adding nothing in content of assertion, but simply advertising the speaker's temper of adherence to what he said. Yet I suspect that however confused their idiom, the intuitionists were calling attention to something important by their anxiety to speak about the manner of our knowing as well as concerning the status of what we know.[108]

Here, I perceive moves on MacKinnon's part both to reinterpret key intuitionist doctrines via Wittgenstein, but also to see the intuitionists as keeping alive insights that might otherwise be lost in the face of Wittgenstein's purgation and the rise of aggressive forms of non-realism from other quarters. As noted in Chapter 2,

---

105. Warnock, *Ethics since 1900*, 30–46. And Taylor, 'The Right and the Good', 272–5.

106. MacKinnon, 'Ethical Intuition', 99–100. In an early book review, MacKinnon sees parallels between Burke and Butler in respect to their 'criticism of a morality of abstract benevolence' and a commitment to a certain form of ethical intuitionism 'which neither follow the fashion of Richard Price or W.D. Ross on the one hand, nor that of the Romantics on the other, but which rather take shape as critical rejections of a proposed single formula definitive either of the whole duty of man, or of the whole content of human virtue'. D. M. MacKinnon, 'Burke's Political Thought (Book Review)', *Philosophical Quarterly* 9, no. April (1959): 183–4.

107. MacKinnon, 'Ethical Intuition', 100.

108. Ibid.

MacKinnon avoided committing to anything like Moore's moral intuition of the good, which the latter took to be a simple, indefinable, non-natural property, but which can be apprehended through careful analysis of key terms.[109] Value judgements must still be reasoned-through by inference, yet terms such as 'good' offer a window onto a dimension of rationality that securely links particular judgements to a truth-tracking notion of value.[110] MacKinnon's appropriation of the positivists' sceptical spirit made him hesitant at the invocation of such a mysterious grounding for moral judgements.

For all this, MacKinnon saw the intuitionist as the keeper of the creative and imaginative potential of moral agency at a moment in history. This was important for the way he wanted to maintain loyalty to a Kantian emphasis on the incommensurability of ends with present empirical history, taken together with an enduring hope that the gap may be lessened or abolished, even if contested notions such as God and the resurrection become the only way to imagine the overcoming of tragic separation. MacKinnon observed that 'if the realm of nature must be separated from that of ends in order that the peculiar dignity of the latter shall be established, we yet need sometimes to invoke the imagery of their reconciliation'.[111] In the meantime, and as noted earlier, Butler and St. Paul are invoked to counter Kant's 'formality', in as far as they refused to overlook the 'passional side of human nature' while still advancing the intense introspective self-scrutiny of the *Gesinnungsethiker*.[112] Yet was there a final choice to be made between the paths set out by Butler and St Paul over and against that of Kant? Wittgenstein is surely lurking behind the scenes when MacKinnon claimed that

> we cannot have it both ways. If 'ought' implies 'can', then morality is independent of anything we can call metaphysics, ontology, religious revelation, what you will, even hostile to them. Morality is that in whose light we see everything else whatever; and the task of the critical philosopher is to enable us to see and measure the consequences of this. The many-levelled model of human nature, of which Butler offers us one example … belongs to different universes of discourse

---

109. Moore, *Principia Ethica*, 60–4. On this point, Hare observes that 'to say that it is non-natural is to distinguish it [i.e. the moral intuition of goodness] both from natural properties (like producing pleasure) and supernatural ones (like being commanded by God)'. Hare, *God's Call*, 5. MacKinnon wants to steer a course that avoids the same, yet finds Moore's proposal wanting. *SET*, 10–15.

110. Ewing, 'Recent Developments in British Ethical Thought', 69.

111. *SET*, 274. We must look to figures such as Bachelard and O'Donovan to challenge MacKinnon's reticence to commit to more constructive efforts to show how and why the resurrection points to or enacts a reconciliation of fact and value, tragic history and the ultimate good, at the centre of the Christian ethical task. Oliver O'Donovan, *Resurrection and Moral Order: An Outline for Evangelical Ethics*, Second edition (Leicester: Apollos, 1994); Sarah Bachelard, *Resurrection and Moral Imagination* (England: Ashgate, 2014).

112. *SET*, 252.

which, for all differences one from another, agree in a kind of empiricism, and in an admission of the authority of styles of self-discipline, touching intellect, evolution, and imagination, that cannot be admitted by Kant. They cut across his formalism, even though ... those who think in such terms have a 'form of life' which beckons and commands them in ways analogous to the universal moral order of Kant.[113]

Even with the import of the intuitive and the existential with Butler and St. Paul, Kant is never discarded.[114] Moral complexity, the subjective dimension of moral deliberation and the 'freedom of open possibilities' or 'the simple truth that men [sic] could have done otherwise' are points that the intuitionist, however inadequately, tries to keep within the purview of moral theorizing.[115] Indeed, speaking of intuitionism was MacKinnon's way of expressing his commitment to something like the irreducible dignity of persons which was sustained by his early reading of Maritain and bolstered by his conviction that both Kant's denial of metaphysics and the purgation promised by the utilitarian were effectively moves in a wider programme of the 'vindication of humanism'.[116] The emphasis also

---

113. Ibid., 265–7.

114. Milbank provides an explanation for why this might be the case: 'Both in Butler and Mansel there is an absence of the Kantian rationalist notion of access to a non-phenomenal realm of "pure reason", and this means that, correspondingly, the grounding of natural law becomes more vague: appeal is made to universal "dictates of conscience", as well as (in Butler) to considerations of benevolent utility .... Given the positivity, and at the same time the derivational vagueness, of the principles of natural law in this tradition, it becomes easy to understand revelation as a supplementary legal system of essentially practical injunctions regarding both morality and worship ... . The new "facts" and ordinances belonging to revelation give us no more knowledge than does natural law about the content of the infinite.' Milbank, 'Between Purgation and Illumination', 175.

115. In this regard, MacKinnon was impressed with explorations such as that offered by Roderick Chisholm, particularly in regard to the favourable judgement of Kant's notion of freedom, compared to that of Hobbes. MacKinnon, 'The Justification of Science and the Rationality of Religious Belief (Book Review)', 107–9. MacKinnon is referring to Roderick Chisholm, 'Human Freedom and the Self', in *The Lindley Lecture* (Lawrence: Department of Philosophy, University of Kansas, 1964).

116. *SET*, 212, 233. MacKinnon: 'The intuitionism that I have defended is, itself, a defence of the rights, of the peculiar status of self-knowledge, if you like, of the peculiar dignity of spiritual experience. But [he goes on to qualify] it is, and must be recognised as, *only a move in a game*'. MacKinnon, 'Ethical Intuition', 105, (italics mine). Whether Milbank missed the force of this nuance, and the Christological foundation proposed for this humanism, is an open question. Milbank: 'MacKinnon appears to convert the categorical imperative itself into something very like the view that it is only in tragic perplexity that we know we are free, and at the same time are brought up against the very margins of the humanly responsible world. When we do not any longer know how to act, then we discover ourselves

resonates with Berlin's writings on historical inevitability; refusing any tendency to declare 'good' 'that which would have happened anyway', and resisting any temptation to look for a realm beyond the historically embedded subject to secure the possibility of value judgements.

When comparing the intuitionist's attempts to keep a certain interior conception of the human moral consciousness alive in the midst of the empiricist focus of the utilitarian, MacKinnon did not see a battle from which one or the other must emerge as unrivalled victor, but 'an analogy between the antinomy of freedom and causality' in Kant's philosophy.[117] The analogy remained undeveloped, but the approach of the utilitarian to bring the rigour of law-like regularity to ethics is taken to mirror something of the closed causal account of nature to which Kant contrasts the exercise of freedom. The intuitionist's focus mirrors the exercise of a generative causal agency of the domain of freedom. Intuitionism points to a form of self-awareness and self-questioning that may be identified as another dimension of the therapeutic theme that I have attempted to apply to MacKinnon, who noted that 'sooner or later in serious discussion of ethical intuition we face the problem of self-knowledge, the problem, I might dare to say, of our presence to ourselves'.[118]

Here we come upon the positive tension which drives MacKinnon's approach to moral theory: greater self-apprehension will lead us to draw on metaphors of 'reception' rather than those of 'construction' alone. In this vein, when exploring the ethical import of 'apostleship' in 2 Corinthians, MacKinnon noted that

> both apostle and contemplative alike agree in their realism, in their sense of the appropriateness of the language of correspondence; what they try to affirm in conduct, to seek through self-discipline, is there to be affirmed and sought. ... Both alike within the context of such a realism take up the standpoint of a *Gesinnungsethiker*.[119]

The intuitionist, who plumbs the depths of a rather extreme interiority in order to embody the supreme struggle and dignity of moral agency, should at the same time never lose sight of the fact that 'we are men and women, and particular men and women at that'.[120] In this vein, MacKinnon noted that it is

---

as transcendent subjects standing 'above' our usual narratively instantiated characters. But this has to be read as an extremely subtle version of the aesthetics of the sublime, of the liberal discourse of modernity'. Milbank, 'Between Purgation and Illumination', 178.

117. MacKinnon, 'Ethical Intuition', 112.

118. Mackinnon admits that it is 'abundantly true that the intuitionist usually fails to bring out that what (in his language) we immediately knew when we knew an ethical fact, was something about ourselves; [yet, MacKinnon goes on to claim that] Butler and Kant were both very much wiser here'. Ibid., 111.

119. *SET*, 162.

120. Ibid.

paradoxical to speak of bringing into being what we accept, representing what we create somehow as already real. Yet it is to the necessity of this paradoxical stretching of our language that the intuitionists are inviting our attention. In morality we are active and bring into being a moral universe by our actions; yet even as we do this we are constrained to represent that universe as something in some sense, already *there*, and commanding us to embody its pattern in our daily dealings.[121]

Intuitionism represents for MacKinnon what might be called the 'qualified idealist pole' of his moral philosophy, whereas the utilitarian tradition and language of 'contemplation' and 'natural law' provide a 'qualified realist pole'. To say with the intuitionist that an 'immediately discerned moral universe is its own justification, seems to mean, if it means anything, that by speaking such a language, we create the state of affairs to which it refers'.[122] Yet, in a way analogous to the discussion of imagination and history in Chapter 4, this creative capacity is hemmed in by the demand for correspondence; a fact that becomes clear as MacKinnon mounted an exploratory argument to stave off the non-realist and supplement the intuitionist by showing that an empirical moral temper that takes historical immersion seriously will begin to encounter something like a given 'law'. Reference to social consensus, contract or 'rights' are not enough on their own to ground what MacKinnon sees as the possibility of speaking about actions which serve good and evil in concrete cases.[123] This role needs to be given to natural law; a law which is less like a set of unambiguous commands, and more like the fact that we find ourselves in a world not created by us.[124] The posture is one of contemplation rather than explication

---

121. MacKinnon, 'Moral Freedom', 109.
122. Ibid.
123. MacKinnon, 'Natural Law', 120-2. At least one early source of inspiration on this point were essays in Jacques Maritain's *Redeeming the Time* which MacKinnon reviewed: D. M. MacKinnon, 'The Thought of Jacques Maritain (Book Review)', *Christendom* 13, no. December (1944): 248-51.
124. There is evidence that MacKinnon's interest in natural law stems from his early engagements with the Christendom group. D. M. MacKinnon, 'Prospect for Christendom', *The Student Movement* 48, no. November-December (1945): 29-31. V. A. Demant's *The Religious Prospect* was also an important early influence on MacKinnon's allegiance to the notion. D. M. MacKinnon, 'Christianity and Justice', *Theology* 42, no. June (1941): 348-54. Additionally, in a review of a work by Ian Henderson in 1950, MacKinnon notes, 'In discussing the idea of natural law, it is important to attend to the nuances of medieval teaching as well as to the theories of the Enlightenment. As writers like Canon [V. A.] Demant and Professor [A. P.] d'Entrèves insist, although the "rights of man" of the Enlightenment have the inspiration of Christian tradition behind them, "natural law" for Aquinas was much more than a catena of such claims. It was the sense of an overarching universal hand by which human life was circumscribed, of bounds men must not pass, of order not imposed but discovered woven into the fabric of things. Such an idea persists clearly in Edmund

or construction. Plato is an inspiration here along with Moore, Butler and Kant.[125] Indeed, MacKinnon argued that

> with Plato's speculations (and for Whitehead, all subsequent Western philosophy is a 'footnote to Plato') we are in the presence of the work of an extraordinary, if unbalanced genius, who had the supreme merit of raising for his readers, in subsequent generations, the question of how this supposed 'natural law' was discovered and established, how indeed the vague, fleeting impressions men [sic] had of its over-arching, wide-embracing authority, related to other precarious, yet persistent acknowledgements of a vantage point from which the obscure and fragmentary circumstances of human life might be reviewed, in the light of a vision of the origin and source, the sense and sanction of all. 'We are not our own.' If Jean Paul Sartre argues that men are alone in their freedom to give sense to the world, he has to reckon with those who claim that the idiom of discovery, finding, acceptance belongs to the vocabulary of the moralist, as essentially as inescapably that of invention, devising and even sometimes deciding.[126]

In the same essay, MacKinnon goes on to argue that

> the issue of a 'natural law' ethic, raised at a place where practical and theoretical perplexity meet, is that in fact of the possibility of metaphysics. To say this is not to retreat from the problems of international politics into abstract philosophy; it is rather to advertise the former as raising for us the issues of the latter. The practical man [sic] will, of course, be eager to stress the urgent primacy of his concerns; but the Western world has need maybe of finding new ways to redress the balance of action and contemplation.[127]

MacKinnon speaks of St. Paul's apostleship as an 'ethico-religious category' operating in ways that are analogous to this 'law', and this indicates the slipperiness of the notion MacKinnon was straining towards.[128] The character of, and balance between, self-assertion and contemplation may take on a number of different guises; one can only study an individual biography to see how it has played out in a life.[129] Yet one thing is certain: the contemplative will continue to probe the paradox inherent in moral life and they will, MacKinnon avers, encounter the problem of metaphysics sooner or later. And here we return to MacKinnon's sense

---

Burke, one of the most severe critics of the 'inalienable, imprescriptible rights of man'. D. M. MacKinnon, 'Can Two Walk Together? The Quest for a Secular Morality (Book Review)', *Scottish Journal of Theology* 3, no. March (1950): 94–6.
   125. *SET*, 247.
   126. MacKinnon, 'Natural Law', 181.
   127. Ibid., 193.
   128. *SET*, 262. He may have been influenced by Max Scheler on this point.
   129. Ibid., 261.

that it is the burden of the Christian moral theologian to see the incarnate Christ as a definitive feature of this 'natural law':

> The Christian emphasis on the concrete reality of Jesus as revealer of the Father provides a kind of barrier against the false fashioning of God after the image of our unacknowledged longings; faith is not self-knowledge, but adherence to Christ.[130]

Conclusion

This chapter returned to some of the themes of Chapter 1. Specifically, I sought to achieve a positive account of the realist goal to which MacKinnon's therapeutic method was driving. MacKinnon was not a thinker whose insights can be easily summarized or systematized: one must simply try to keep up with the various twists and turns while attempting to discern patterns emerging over time.

MacKinnon was engaged in a project that mirrored Wittgenstein's in crucial respects. Yet he held back from the kind of Wittgensteinian iconoclasm that sought to jettison continued talk of the 'problem of metaphysics', which for MacKinnon, could be summarized by invoking the perennial tussle between realism and idealism. Transferred to the moral sphere it meant an attempt to reflect on conditions that make for a perennial tussle between styles of philosophy that could be labelled 'natural law' and 'utilitarian' on the one hand and 'intuitionist' on the other. Only such a complex web of proposals could begin to reflect the similarly complex moral domain of historical action and event. In the end, it was MacKinnon's commitment to moral realism, including his sense of what the historical moment of post-war Europe called forth from moral philosophers, that led him to defend notions of correspondence, moral factuality and moral freedom, even if he always did so in highly qualified ways.

---

130. MacKinnon, 'Karl Barth: An Introduction to His Early Theology (Book Review)', 557–8.

Chapter 6

OVERALL CONCLUSION: CONSIDERING MACKINNON'S PROJECT IN RETROSPECT

Applying a 'therapeutic' ascription to MacKinnon's project provides a way of doing justice to his attempt to marry a peculiar mix of pragmatic, existential, confessional and non-foundationalist tendencies with a qualified realism. The specific end to which the therapy drove was a form of moral realism that is discerned in the midst of patient description and re-description. It was Kantian moral philosophy transformed via Wittgenstein, Moore, Collingwood and debates in modern Christology. While the method gave room for God's self-revealing, it never lost a sense of accountability towards, and participation in, a wider humanistic project, forever open to further purgation.

In this final section, I will comment on some of the ways MacKinnon's interests and sensibilities have been perpetuated, and how subsequent developments in British theology highlight the strengths and weaknesses of his approach.

The recurrence of metaphysical reference in the context of a moral argument for the coherence of theism (or perhaps, a theistic argument for the coherence of a certain sort of morality) is one recently revived in British Anglican circles by Angus Ritchie. In a project of ambitious scope, Ritchie examines the way metaphysical language can emerge if one continues to interrogate widely held commitments in support of moral objectivity, particularly if one does not prematurely silence questions as to how such moral capacities are capable of 'tracking truth'.[1] Ritchie examines a host of secular options for defending moral realism and finds the persistence of an explanatory gap relating to the potential of our moral capacities. This occurs in a circumstance where natural selection is seen to have provided explanations for 'truth-tracking' capacities for many other domains of knowledge and Ritchie claims that a degree of arbitrariness enters the discussion when we fail to expect similar explanations from the moral domain.[2] Echoing Moore, he argues that naturalistic approaches have failed (and will always fail) to deliver in the

---

1. Angus Ritchie, *From Morality to Metaphysics: The Theistic Implications of Our Ethical Commitments* (Oxford: Oxford University Press, 2012), 54. This is the problem the intuitionists were trying to address.

2. Ibid., 40–69.

unique case of moral 'facts'.[3] Axiarchism, Neoplatonism and Theism are affirmed as options for metaphysical notions that might yet provide the means to close the explanatory gap.

On this last point, some parallels might be drawn with Douglas Hedley's work in the tradition of the Cambridge Platonists, which perpetuates and substantially bolsters (relative to MacKinnon's attempts) a philosophical defence of the 'imagination' and its relation to the task of the metaphysician and moralist. Against critics, Hedley, like MacKinnon, seeks to reaffirm the ways metaphysical philosophy has been employed to aid theology's coherence, its apprehension of scripture and its articulation of moral realism. Yet in the broadest sense, Hedley and Ritchie join the likes of Moore and Murdoch in the desire (temptation?) to secure moral realism in a substantive metaphysical ontology, whereas MacKinnon was more circumspect; realism never went too far beyond ever deeper descriptions of 'nature' and history, sailing much closer to the pragmatist wind. For all the resemblances between these projects, MacKinnon remained sceptical about the quest for such metaphysical 'grounding', under the force of Wittgenstein's purgation. As noted above, he seeks to articulate a 'negative' revisionary metaphysics of history that emerges from the continuous struggle of human beings to negotiate and express freedom, imagination and dignity in a context of realist constraint and limitation.[4] Together with all these figures, MacKinnon was aware that there were 'very many lessons to be learnt from past failures in threading an authentically human path between e.g. the facile optimism that will not look on historical realities as what they are and a pessimism that has moved too readily from a realistic to a nihilistic posture'.[5]

Ritchie brings theism to the table towards the end of his discussion as an aid to explanation. As such, he is indebted to the tradition of Sorley and Taylor in moving from a commitment to moral realism to theism, even if he does so tentatively and after a more systematic engagement with key advocates of naturalistic reductionism. No such strategies are evident in MacKinnon's project, which lurched between Kantian agnosticism and attempts to apprehend the particularity of divine revelation in history. As claims to moral realism remain enmeshed in unavoidable contingency, ambiguity and the prospect of tragic misapprehension, they provide no clear path to theism. Indeed, after encountering MacKinnon's rather tortured attempts to introduce such nuance to the fact–value distinction, one might speculate that from his perspective, Ritchie is tempted to offer a route to theism that avoids the way of the cross. At the same time, MacKinnon would surely agree with Ritchie when the latter sought to answer the critic who suggested that the 'fact there is more than one possible thing to think' presents an insurmountable problem for the moral realist. To this challenge Ritchie replies that

3. Ibid., 6–7.
4. It is in this respect where comparison with Cavell seems especially warranted.
5. *TT*, 123.

it is not clear why this should be so: one could surely be an 'outright moral realist' and think that competing moral values lead to tragic choices, where agents face irreconcilable claims of, say loyalty and benevolence and will have some reasons for regret whatever choice they make. In some such cases, it may be true that one choice is better than another. In other cases the considerations on each side might objectively have equal amounts to be said for them. 'The world' might then be experienced as a 'void' in that there would be nothing more to be said on the matter, and yet a choice of great moment might need to be made.[6]

Ritchie implicitly perpetuates elements of MacKinnon's project both on the possibility of a 'tragic realism', and in tracing the connections between moral realism, metaphysics and theism. Yet it is Rowan Williams, Paul Janz and John Milbank who are the contemporary British theologians who have been most explicit in attempting to understand what MacKinnon sought to do. Each dissent from MacKinnon to a greater or lesser degree: Williams and Janz see the need for supplementation whereas Milbank judges at least one key aspect of the project as intrinsically flawed and irrecoverable.[7] For Milbank, the 'Kantian backdrop, however much it may be seen as the setting for "something else", always dominates the entire later performance' and this, for him, seems to be a barrier for retrieving and repairing MacKinnon's approach.[8] The key issues include a purportedly a-historical substratum in MacKinnon's project, his overwrought invocation of the tragic and, lurking inchoately behind all this, a lack of clarity in regard the way he understands the doctrine of analogy.

Whatever MacKinnon was doing in his reference to intuition and natural law, the conclusion of all three figures is that supplementation in a broadly conceived Hegelian direction may have aided the attainment of a greater depth of historical realism and perhaps allowed greater coherence to be achieved between the 'intuitive' and 'natural law' poles of his moral philosophy. I suspect that MacKinnon would have remained sceptical at any attempt to build such conceptual linkages for fear of falling into an idealist exercise of 'reconciliation', which would have rendered things suspiciously particularly regarding the problem of evil. Yet acknowledging a greater debt to Hegel may have helped him to avoid the accusation that he not only finds tragedy in history, 'but emplots history within a privileged tragic framework'.[9] Williams understands the humanistic impulse behind the tension MacKinnon tried to hold, noting that 'there can be a

---

6. Ritchie, *From Morality to Metaphysics*, 153.

7. Milbank goes on to explore some features of MacKinnon's thought which 'still retain inescapable value'. Milbank, 'Between Purgation and Illumination', 183.

8. Ibid.

9. Ibid. As noted at the end of Chapter 4. On this critique, Milbank has a lot in common with Hart, who calls the focus of post-war British theology on tragedy as 'the most narcotic metaphysical solace of them all'. David Bentley Hart, *The Beauty of the Infinite: The Aesthetics of Christian Truth* (Grand Rapids, MI: W. B. Eerdmans, 2003), 375. The debate continues in

paralysing obsession with the tragic, but there can also be an attempt to evade the limits of time and particularity through an attempt to bypass or rationalize pain and death'.[10] Milbank seems to think that MacKinnon came close to such paralysis; apparently he was far more influenced by

> the Platonic notion of presence than with the Aristotelian version of telos, and therefore concentrate[d] on tragic indecision which occasions a kind of exit from the narrative instead of remaining in the plot and seeking resolutions.[11]

Janz also appears to be convinced that MacKinnon's focus on 'the tragic' needs to be transcended and that, for all the insight and uncompromising moral seriousness it generated, the intensity and pervasiveness of this focus points to deeper structural limitations in his project.[12] As noted in Chapter 1, Janz saw MacKinnon as an uncommonly perceptive reader of Kant and sought to repair and supplement what he calls 'MacKinnon's conciliatory realism' and use it as a resource in aid of his own constructive suggestion for theological epistemology.[13] Yet, Janz also furnishes the discussion of idealism and realism, externalism and internalism with extended reference to Putnam and Nagel, and then supplements MacKinnon's lack of engagement with Hegel and Heidegger via a chapter dedicated to Bonhoeffer's *Act and Being*. He joins Williams and Milbank in supposing that those who more deeply and critically appreciated the best in Hegel could have assisted MacKinnon in bringing greater coherence to his invocations of natural law and intuition. In the same vein, Kerr is probably right in contending that someone like Charles Taylor provided resources to improve MacKinnon's accounting of the social and political embeddedness of moral discernment and decision.[14] I would add that Gillian Rose's

---

earnest, evident by critical responses to Rowan Williams, *The Tragic Imagination* (Oxford: Oxford University Press, 2016).

10. Williams, 'Trinity and Ontology', 86.

11. Milbank suggests that MacKinnon lost an opportunity to develop a Christian perspective of tragi-comic irony 'rather than unappeased tragedy', and to the extent that this is true, Stanley Cavell and Paul Fiddes provide valuable resources for repair. Fiddes, *Freedom and Limit: A Dialogue Between Literature and Christian Doctrine*. Milbank, 'Between Purgation and Illumination', 179.

12. Janz, *God, the Mind's Desire*, 168–90.

13. With MacKinnon, he takes on a pattern that is common to theologians in the grip of Kant: 'A pained sense of the violence enacted by the thought on the otherness of the object; then … an interest in breaking the pride and autonomy of human thought, usually through some sort of paradox (in Kant's case the antinomies of reason, in Janz's the scandal of God on the cross); finally, there is some sort of gift from otherness that makes human thought, in some transformed way, again possible (for Janz the transformation that comes about through resurrection and salvation).' Insole struggles with 'the slightly arbitrary nature of each of the solutions'. Insole, *Realist Hope*, 162–3.

14. Kerr, 'Idealism and Realism', 31.

exploration of the Hegelian 'broken middle' would be a promising source of purgation and repair as well. Her rejection of postmodern anti-realist ethics, invocation of the tragic, and conviction that the moral task is one of continuous work punctuated by mourning and revelation suggests many points of resonance.[15]

Milbank complains that MacKinnon smuggled into his tragic realism 'an ahistorical assumption about the permanence of the conflict between a public sphere of objective, and strictly equivalent justice, and a private sphere of forgiving cancellation of fault'.[16] Milbank's identification of a lingering, subterranean 'a-historicism' is part of a more general assault on MacKinnon's apparent captivity to the sort of liberal 'theology of right'; an entanglement that results in proposals for moral anthropology and philosophy which both he and MacIntyre find unconvincing. In this respect, Milbank targets MacKinnon's tendency to liken an ethical decision with a creative act, which I noted in the latter's invocation of the intuitionists above. Milbank argues that this act

> is, in regard to formal freedom, 'without grounds'. In this respect he [i.e. MacKinnon] is actually less realist than the Hegelian tradition which sought to remind us how all our values and any possibility of freedom follows from *sein*, from an always already-realized (in some real degree) goodness. On the other hand he tends to prescind from the real site of an 'absolute' human creativity, namely the erection of entire cultural formations which represent 'new types', in no essential way imitative of anything naturally given. Thus while MacKinnon acknowledges the importance of Hegel's attention to the historical, he thinks of historical situatedness in semi-Kantian terms as a further categorical restriction on knowledge and behaviour, and not as the positive fact of the culturally constructed character of theoretical and ethical categories'.[17]

There is broad agreement between Williams, Janz, Milbank and Kerr on the need for a Hegelian supplement of some kind. Yet I wonder whether Milbank's criticism is too pointed. MacKinnon's writings on the moral import of St. Paul's notion of apostleship, his interactions with Marxist thought and his dogged commitment first and foremost to seeing Christian moral agency as grounded in the agency of the 'historical Jesus' suggest that there might be resources to mitigate the criticism, or at least indicate that MacKinnon was not unaware of some of the weaknesses that came with positioning oneself in Kant's orbit. Milbank acknowledges that a sympathetic reading of MacKinnon's illuminations and blind spots can be aided by an appreciation of his biography. His early commitment to Catholic humanism made him perennially cautious of any temptation to slide into a type of ideological confidence that may accompany revelatory positivism, while the experience of the

---

15. Gillian Rose, *The Broken Middle* (Oxford: Blackwell, 1992).
16. John Milbank, '"Between Purgation and Illumination": A Critique of the Theology of Right', 179.
17. Ibid., 182.

social fragmentation of the Second World War and the 'minimal and ambiguous' presence of the church throughout this period made him sceptical that either the church or state (liberal *or* Marxist) could act as trustworthy sites for reliable formation in the virtues.[18] For MacKinnon

> it was from Kant that the theologians were enabled to see that the universalism of the Enlightenment was no facile optimism, but an expression of the need for the devout to submit their aspirations to judgement at the bar of a common humanity – lest indeed they failed to see the Son of Man in the least of his brethren and, failing, forfeited the very faith by which they claimed to live.[19]

Yet, for Milbank, even a sympathetic reading informed by MacKinnon's immediate context is not enough to salvage his project from what he perceives as an enmeshment in

> a secular groundwork in ethics ... [which attempts] to safeguard the absolute disinterestedness of ethics, and the purity of ethical freedom, by stressing agnosticism with regard to transcendence as a counterpart to an existential refusal of any materialist necessitarianism.[20]

Here a real debate opens. Did MacKinnon draw on Kant to supply a 'secular' groundwork for ethics? Even if he did, is it not enough to see this as 'one move in a game' which can be supplemented by a Christ-centred 'natural law', especially given MacKinnon's antipathy to an absolute distinction between sacred and secular, emerging from his Christology. Further to this, was MacKinnon right, together with Hare, Janz, Insole, Michalson and Hedley, to believe that just as there is a danger when 'thinkers bow deeply and uncritically at the Kantian problem, and then pronounce confidently the unique indispensability of their own solution', so there is also danger in failing to see features of Kant's thought that resist the binary Milbank sets up? As it was for many of Milbank's 'radically orthodox'

---

18. Ibid., 190.
19. MacKinnon, 'Kant's Influence on British Theology', 361.
20. Milbank, 'Between Purgation and Illumination', 181–2. Michalson notes that 'Milbank's general appeal to the counter-Enlightenment tradition is supplemented by specific, often arresting interpretive suggestions concerning Kant and others. In his most direct sustained criticism of the Kantian character of modern theology, Milbank clarifies his claim of the "ideological character of transcendentalism" through a provocative comparison of Kant and Aquinas on the use of analogy (John Milbank, *The Word Made Strange: Theology, Language, Culture* (Oxford: Wiley, 1997), Ch. I). [Michalson continues...] Elsewhere, Milbank argues that Kant's liberal ethical programme, far from insuring a person-centred humanist stance, is merely the "great delayer" of the profoundly anti-humanist quality of the post-Nietzschean heritage'. Michalson, 'Re-reading the Post-Kantian Tradition with Milbank', 365.

followers, this Kantian 'curse' was also expunged by neo-Orthodox and revived Aristotelian approaches to Christian virtue ethics, variously associated with Barth, MacIntyre and Hauerwas. Yet, in defending a position that has some resonance with MacKinnon's project, Hedley has argued that

> one might say that Kant's 'critique' (N.B.) of pure theoretical reason and avowal of the primacy of pure practical reason have very little to do with 'secularizing immanentism' but constitute a firmly Christian insistence on both the inferiority of theoretical curiosity and dogmatism and the inherent value of 'good will'. Kant is endorsing Henry More's principle: 'All pretenders to philosophy will be ready to magnify Reason to the skies, and to make it the light of heaven, and the very Oracle of God; but they do not consider that the Oracle of God is not to be heard but in His holy temple – that is to say, in a good and holy man.'[21]

Janz joins Hedley and Michalson in critiquing Milbank's reading of Kant in a way that is broadly affirming of MacKinnon's legacy.[22] I suspect that at the base of this dispute lie deep assumptions about the doctrine(s) of analogy in Aquinas, Kant and Barth. MacKinnon perceived a substratum between the three; a conviction that as disparate as they might be, these different approaches to analogy were themselves strongly analogous, whereas Milbank sees irreconcilable foes and the need for an absolute choice.

I doubt that MacKinnon was anything other than acutely aware of the incommensurability *at one level*: he comments, for instance, on Pryzwara's influence on Balthasar and the impact this had on the latter's reading of Barth on this issue.[23] One source of the sheer tension of MacKinnon's project arose from the fact that he claimed a fickle allegiance to both Kant *and* Barth without wishing to discount the impulse which led theologians to embrace versions of the 'analogy of being'. On the one hand, his philosophical forays adopted Kant's use of analogy, yet tempered the extremity of agnosticism with reference to Thomas. On the other hand, MacKinnon's Christological forays were most influenced by Barth's treatment of analogy and yet with Forsyth, he sought further protection against any charge of fideism by welcoming the influence of Kant's analogical 'theology' to illuminate the moral heart of this domain. Any further attempts to understand

---

21. Douglas Hedley, 'Should Divinity Overcome Metaphysics? Reflections on John Milbank's Theology beyond Secular Reason and Confessions of a Cambridge Platonist', *The Journal of Religion* 80, no. 2 (2000), 289.

22. Additionally, Insole has recently offered a defence of Kant as a 'negative theologian' in a way that critiques MacKinnon's reception of Kantian 'agnosticism' yet resonates with some of MacKinnon's broader intuitions that Kant can provide useful resources for a purgation of Christian doctrines of God. Christopher J. Insole, *Kant and the Creation of Freedom: A Theological Problem* (Oxford: Oxford University Press, 2013), 5, See also chapters 7 and 10.

23. MacKinnon, 'Biblical Faith and Natural Theology (Book Review)', 128–30.

MacKinnon's legacy on this point will have to call upon the help of scholars such as Roger White.[24] Yet, one will look in vain in MacKinnon's *oeuvre* for any systematic treatment of analogy and will have to be content with mere hints and intimations. MacKinnon's vagueness opens the way for Milbank's attack, yet subsequent voices (examined above) suggest that at least some of his intuitions survived and were defended by key philosophical theologians in the subsequent generation.

MacKinnon's theism is entwined with his commitment to moral realism, yet neither could be said to ground, vindicate or necessitate the other.[25] Both are insistences of a realism hard won, with 'facts' not easily discerned and the whole play of our reception and free response ever open to the spectre of the tragic. He is especially insistent that while an emphasis on realism is vital for the continued tenability of Christianity, it is not an apologetic short-cut, indeed

> to speak of ethical facts is to speak of what is chimerical; to create for oneself the illusion of a world that is somehow represented as the superior counterpart of that world of fact wherein statements are verified and hypotheses confirmed, is to invite needless trouble. We may say, of course, that the creation of such a world is only a moment in discourse, something to be understood in terms of what we are trying to bring out by means of it; we are not for a moment supposing that our idiom of finding suggests anything in the way of a geographical exploration of the transcendent.[26]

The Christian is not seen to dwell within a tradition in which the content of moral beliefs and their application is immediately obvious (e.g. the parables), and they will always be 'set on edge' in the presence 'of those who would ignore human limitation to the extent of giving a final and irrevocable force to the passing insights of a particular group in a particular age'.[27]

The type of therapy that I have associated with MacKinnon's borderlands theology is one characterized by interrogation self-apprehension above all else. The goal of confession and purgation is an apprehension of realist moral limits and obligations, all in a wider context of avoiding any simple resolution or distortive imbalance in the relationship between realism and idealism. Whether it was Positivism, Kantianism, Marxism, neo-Orthodoxy or Wittgensteinian philosophy, he saw important therapeutic insights on offer. Each engagement was a 'move in a game' and each represented a historical moment which was related, often in barely expressible ways, to Christ; the one MacKinnon recognized as the ultimate pivot of history, from whom he learnt to 'perceive tragedy without the loss of hope'.

---

24. White, *Talking about God: The Concept of Analogy and the Problem of Religious Language*.
25. Insole makes a similar point. Insole, *Realist Hope*, 193–201.
26. MacKinnon, 'Ethical Intuition', 111.
27. MacKinnon, 'Burke's Political Thought (Book Review)', 184.

BIBLIOGRAPHY

Adkins, Imogen Helen, *Sound, space and Christological Self-giving (with special reference to William Vanstone, Sarah Coakley and Rowan Williams, and Donald MacKinnon)*, Unpublished PhD Thesis, University of Cambridge, 2013.

Allison, Henry E. *Kant's Transcendental Idealism*. New Haven: Yale University Press, 2004.

Anderson, Pamela Sue, and Jordan Bell. *Kant and Theology*. Philosophy and Theology. London: T & T Clark, 2010.

Anscombe, G. E. M. 'Modern Moral Philosophy', *Philosophy* 33, no. 124 (January 1958): 1.

Ayer, A. J. 'Demonstration of the Impossibility of Metaphysics'. *Mind*, no. 171 (1934): 335.

Ayer, A. J. *Ludwig Wittgenstein*. Harmondsworth: Penguin, 1993.

Ayer, A. J. 'The Genesis of Metaphysics'. *Analysis* 1, no. 4 (1934): 55.

Ayer, A. J. 'Verification and Experience'. *Proceedings of the Aristotelian Society* 37, no. 1 (1936): 137–56.

Bachelard, Sarah. *Resurrection and Moral Imagination*. Farnham, Surrey: Ashgate, 2014.

Baldwin, Tom. 'George Edward Moore'. In *Stanford Encyclopedia of Philosophy*, edited by Edward Zalta, 2010. https://plato.stanford.edu/entries/moore/.

Balthasar, Hans Urs von, and Edward T. Oakes. *The Theology of Karl Barth: Exposition and Interpretation* [in Translation of: Karl Barth, Darstellung und Deutung seiner Theologie.]. Communio books. San Francisco, CA: Ignatius Press, 1992.

Bauman, Zygmunt. *Modernity and the Holocaust*. Ithaca, NY: Cornell University Press, 1989.

Berlin, Isaiah. *Historical Inevitability*. Auguste Comte Memorial Trust lecture. London: Oxford University Press, 1954.

Black, Rufus. *Christian Moral Realism: Natural Law, Narrative, Virtue and the Gospel*. Oxford: Oxford University Press, 2000.

Blackburn, Simon 'Religion and Ontology'. In *Realism and Religion: Philosophical and Theological Perspectives*, edited by Andrew Moore and Michael Scott, 47–59. Aldershot: Ashgate, 2007.

Bostock, David. *Russell's Logical Atomism*. Oxford: Oxford University Press, 2012.

Bowyer, Andrew. 'Moral Philosophy after Austin and Wittgenstein: Stanley Cavell and Donald MacKinnon', *Studies in Christian Ethics*, 31, no. 1 (2018): 49–64.

Brink, David O. *Moral Realism and the Foundations of Ethics*. Cambridge: Cambridge University Press, 1989.

Burns, Elizabeth. 'Transforming Metaphysics? Revisioning Christianity in the Light of Analytical Philosophy'. In *Faith and Philosophical Analysis: The Impact of Analytical Philosophy on the Philosophy of Religion*, edited by Harriet Harris and Christopher Insole, 46–60. Aldershot, Hants; Burlington, VT: Ashgate, 2005.

Butler, Joseph. *Fifteen Sermons Preached at the Rolls Chapel and a Dissertation Upon the Nature of Virtue*. London: G. Bell, 1949.

Byrne, Peter. 'Moral Arguments for the Existence of God'. http://plato.stanford.edu/archives/spr2013/entries/moral-arguments-god/.

Byrne, Peter. *The Moral Interpretation of Religion*. Edinburgh: Edinburgh University Press, 1998.

Cane, Anthony. *The Place of Judas Iscariot in Christology*. Aldershot: Ashgate, 2005.

Cascardi, Anthony. 'Tragedy and Philosophy'. In *A Companion to the Philosophy of Literature*, edited by Garry Hagberg and Walter Jost, 161–73. Oxford: Blackwell, 2010.

Cavell, Stanley. *Disowning Knowledge in Seven Plays of Shakespeare*. Cambridge: Cambridge University Press, 2003.

Cavell, Stanley. 'Existentialism and Analytical Philosophy'. *Daedalus* 93, no. 3 (1964): 946–74.

Cavell, Stanley. *Little Did I Know: Excerpts from Memory*. Stanford, CA: Stanford University Press, 2010.

Cavell, Stanley. *Must We Mean What We Say? A Book of Essays*. New York: Scribner, 1969.

Cavell, Stanley. *The Claim of Reason: Wittgenstein, Skepticism, Morality and Tragedy*. Oxford: Clarendon Press, 1979.

Cell, Edward. *Language, Existence and God: Interpretations of Moore, Russell, Ayer, Wittgenstein, Wisdom, Oxford Philosophy, and Tillich*. Nashville, TN: Abingdon Press, 1971.

Cerbone, David R. 'Wittgenstein and Idealism'. In *The Oxford Handbook of Wittgenstein*, edited by Kuusela Oskari and Marie McGinn, 311–30. Oxford: Oxford University Press, 2011.

Chisholm, Roderick. 'Human Freedom and the Self'. In *The Lindley Lecture*. Lawrence: University of Kansas Press, 1964.

Christensen, Anne-Marie S. 'Wittgenstein and Ethics'. In *The Oxford Handbook of Wittgenstein*, edited by Oskari Kuusela and Marie McGinn, 796–818. Oxford: Oxford University Press, 2011.

Coakley, Sarah. *God, Sexuality and the Self: An Essay 'On the Trinity'*. Cambridge: Cambridge University Press, 2013.

Coakley, Sarah. 'Kenosis and Subversion: On the Repression of "Vulnerability" in Christian Feminist Writing'. In *Powers and Submissions: Spirituality, Philosophy and Gender*, 82–111. Oxford: Blackwell, 2002.

Coliva, Annalisa. *Moore and Wittgenstein: Scepticism, Certainty, and Common Sense*. History of analytic philosophy. Houndmills, Basingstoke, Hampshire; New York: Palgrave Macmillan, 2010.

Connor, Timothy G. *The Kenotic Trajectory of the Church in Donald Mackinnon's Theology: From Galilee to Jerusalem to Galilee*. London: T & T Clark, 2011.

Copleston, Frederick C. *Contemporary Philosophy: Studies of Logical Positivism and Existentialism*. London: Burns & Oates, 1956.

Crisp, Oliver. *God Incarnate: Explorations in Christology*. London: T & T Clark, 2009.

D'Oro, Giuseppina. 'The Myth of Collingwood's Historicism'. *Inquiry* 53, no. 6 (2010): 627–41.

Davaney, Sheila Greeve. *Historicism: The Once and Future Challenge for Theology*. Minneapolis, MN: Fortress Press, 2006.

DeHart, Paul. *Aquinas and Radical Orthodoxy: A Critical Enquiry*. Oxford: Routledge, 2012.

DeLapp, Kevin. *Moral Realism*. Bloomsbury Ethics. London: Bloomsbury, 2013.

Desmond, William. *Hegel's God: A Counterfeit Double?* Aldershot: Ashgate, 2003.

Diamond, Cora. 'Throwing Away the Ladder'. *Philosophy* 63, no. 243 (1988): 5–27.

Diamond, Cora. 'Wittgenstein, Mathematics, and Ethics: Resisting the Attractions of Realism'. In *The Cambridge Companion to Wittgenstein*, edited by Hans D. Sluga and David G. Stern, 226–60. Cambridge: Cambridge University Press, 1996.

Dorrien, Gary J. 'Kantian Concepts, Liberal Theology, and Post-Kantian Idealism'. *American Journal of Theology & Philosophy* 33, no. 1 (2012): 5–31.

Dula, Peter. *Cavell, Companionship, and Christian Theology*. New York: Oxford University Press, 2011.

Dummett, Michael. 'Truth and Other Enigmas'. lviii, 470 pages. London: Duckworth, 1978.

Ernst, Cornelius. 'Ethics and the Play of Intelligence'. *New Blackfriars* 39, no. 460–461 (1958): 324–6.

Ernst, Cornelius. *Multiple Echo: Explorations in Theology*. Edited by Fergus Kerr and Timothy Radcliffe. London: Darton, Longman and Todd, 1979.

Ewing, A. C. 'Recent Developments in British Ethical Thought'. In *British Philosophy in the Mid-century: A Cambridge Symposium*, edited by C. A. Mace, 63–94. London: Allen and Unwin, 1957.

Fergusson, David. *Community, Liberalism and Christian Ethics*. Cambridge: Cambridge University Press, 1998.

Fiddes, Paul S. *Freedom and Limit: A Dialogue between Literature and Christian Doctrine*. Basingstoke: Macmillan, 1991.

Ford, David. 'Tragedy and Atonement'. In *Christ, Ethics and Tragedy: Essays in Honour of Donald MacKinnon*, edited by Kenneth Surin, 117–29. Cambridge: Cambridge University Press, 1989.

Forsyth, Peter Taylor. *Positive Preaching and Modern Mind*. London: Hodder and Stoughton, 1907.

Forsyth, Peter Taylor. *The Person and Place of Jesus Christ*. Congregational Union Lecture. London: Congregational Union of England and Wales and Hodder & Stoughton, 1909.

Gibson, Arthur *Metaphysics and Transcendence*. London: Routledge, 2003.

Godlove, Terry F. *Kant and the Meaning of Religion: The Critical Philosophy and Modern Religious Thought*. London: I.B. Tauris & Co., 2014.

Goldberg, S. L. *Agents and Lives: Moral Thinking in Literature*. Cambridge: Cambridge University Press, 1993.

Goodman, Russell B. *Contending with Stanley Cavell*. Oxford: Oxford University Press, 2005.

Graham, Gordon. *Evil and Christian Ethics*. New studies in Christian ethics. Cambridge: Cambridge University Press, 2001.

Hämäläinen, N. *Literature and Moral Theory*. London: Bloomsbury, 2017.

Hare, J. E. *God's Call : Moral Realism, God's Commands, and Human Autonomy*. Grand Rapids, MI: Eerdmans, 2001.

Hare, J. E. *The Moral Gap: Kantian Ethics, Human Limits, and God's Assistance*. Oxford: Clarendon Press, 1996.

Hart, David Bentley. *The Beauty of the Infinite: The Aesthetics of Christian Truth*. Grand Rapids, MI: W. B. Eerdmans, 2003.

Hauerwas, Stanley. *Vision and Virtue: Essays in Christian Ethical Reflection*. Notre Dame, IN: University of Notre Dame Press, 1981.

Hebblethwaite, Brian. *The Incarnation: Collected Essays in Christology*. Cambridge: Cambridge University Press, 1987.

Hebblethwaite, Brian, and Stewart R. Sutherland, eds. *The Philosophical Frontiers of Christian Theology: Essays Presented to D.M. Mackinnon*. Cambridge: Cambridge University Press, 1982.

Hector, Kevin. *Theology Without Metaphysics God, Language, and the Spirit of Recognition*. New York: Cambridge University Press, 2011.

Hedley, Douglas. *Living Forms of the Imagination*. London; New York: T & T Clark, 2008.

Hedley, Douglas. 'Should Divinity Overcome Metaphysics? Reflections on John Milbank's Theology beyond Secular Reason and Confessions of a Cambridge Platonist'. *The Journal of Religion* 80, no. 2 (April 2000): 271–98.

Herzog, William R. *Parables as Subversive Speech: Jesus as Pedagogue of the Oppressed*. Louisville, KY; London: Westminster/John Knox Press, 1994.

Hick, John. *The Myth of God Incarnate*. London: SCM Press, 1977.

Incandela, Joseph. 'The Appropriation of Wittgenstein's Work by Philosophers of Religion: Towards a Re-evaluation and an End'. *Religious Studies* 21, no. 4 (1985): 457–74.

Insole, Christopher. 'A Metaphysical Kant: A Theological Lingua Franca?' *Studies in Christian Ethics* 25, no. 2 (2012): 206–14.

Insole, Christopher. 'Political Liberalism, Analytical Philosophy of Religion and the Forgetting of History'. In *Faith and Philosophical Analysis: The Impact of Analytical Philosophy on the Philosophy of Religion*, edited by Harriet Harris and Christopher Insole, 158–70. Aldershot, Hants; Burlington, VT: Ashgate, 2005.

Insole, Christopher J. *Kant and the Creation of Freedom: A Theological Problem*. Oxford: Oxford University Press, 2013.

Insole, Christopher J. 'Kant's Transcendental Idealism, Freedom and the Divine Mine'. *Modern Theology* 27, no. 4 (2011): 608–38.

Insole, Christopher J. *The Realist Hope: A Critique of Anti-Realist Approaches in Contemporary Philosophical Theology*. Aldershot: Ashgate, 2006.

Janz, Paul D. *God, the Mind's Desire: Reference, Reason, and Christian Thinking*. Cambridge: Cambridge University Press, 2004.

Jaspers, Karl. *Tragedy Is Not Enough* [in Translation of a section of: Von der Wahrheit.]. London: Gollancz, 1953.

Kamenka, Eugene. *The Ethical Foundations of Marxism*. Second edition. London: Routledge and Kegan Paul, 1972.

Kant, Immanuel. 'Critique of Practical Reason'. Translated by Mary J. Gregor. In *Practical Philosophy: The Cambridge Edition of the Works of Immanuel Kant*, edited by Mary J. Gregor, 133–272. Cambridge: Cambridge University Press, 1999.

Kant, Immanuel. *Groundwork of the Metaphysics of Morals*. Translated by Mary J. Gregor and Jens Timmermann. Cambridge Texts in the History of Philosophy. Cambridge: Cambridge University Press, 2013.

Kant, Immanuel. *Kritik der reinen Vernunft* [Critique of Pure Reason]. 2nd ed. London: Macmillan, 1933.

Kerr, Fergus. 'Idealism and Realism: An Old Controversy Dissolved'. In *Christ, Ethics and Tragedy: Essays in Honour of Donald MacKinnon*, edited by Kenneth Surin, 15–33. Cambridge: Cambridge University Press, 1989.

Kerr, Fergus. *Theology after Wittgenstein*. 2nd ed. Oxford: Basil Blackwell, 1997.

Kirkland, Scott. 'Particularity Regained: Kenotically Recovering a Theological Pedagogy in Karl Barth and Donald MacKinnon'. *Irish Theological Quarterly* 80, no. 1 (2015): 56–82.

Lampe, G. W. H., D. M. MacKinnon, and W. E. Purcell. *The Resurrection: A Dialogue Arising From Broadcasts by G.W.H. Lampe and D.M. MacKinnon*. London: Mowbray, 1966.

Lapide, Pinchas, and Ulrich Luz. *Jesus in Two Perspectives: A Jewish-Christian Dialog* [in Translation of: Der Jude Jesus.]. Minneapolis, MN: Augsburg Publishing House, 1985.

Lash, N. '"Up" and "Down" in Christology'. In *New Studies in Theology 1*, edited by Stephen Sykes and Derek Holmes, 33–45. London: Duckworth, 1980.

Lawson, Tom. *The Church of England and the Holocaust: Christianity, Memory and Nazism*. Woodbridge: Boydell, 2006.

Long, Eugene Thomas. 'The Gifford Lectures and the Scottish Personal Idealists'. *The Review of Metaphysics* 49, no. 2 (1995): 365.
Lovibond, Sabina. *Realism and Imagination in Ethics*. Oxford: Blackwell, 1983.
MacIntyre, Alasdair C. *After Virtue: A Study in Moral Theory*. 2nd ed. London: Duckworth, 1985.
Macintyre, L. 'Thinking Legend Still in Search of Answers'. *Glasgow Herald*, 7 November 1989.
Mackey, James P. 'Introduction'. In *Religious Imagination*, edited by James P. Mackey, 1–29. Edinburgh: Edinburgh University Press, 1986.
Mackie, J. L. *Ethics: Inventing Right and Wrong*. Harmondsworth: Penguin, 1977.
MacKinnon, D. M. 'A Note on Sorley as a Philosopher'. In *A History of British Philosophy to 1900*, edited by W. R. Sorley, xvii–xx. Cambridge: Cambridge University Press, 1965.
MacKinnon, D. M. *A Study in Ethical Theory*. London: A. & C. Black, 1957.
MacKinnon, D. M. 'And the Son of Man That Thou Visitest Him'. *Christendom* 8, no. September and December (1938): 186–92, 260–72.
MacKinnon, D. M. 'Aristotle's Conception of Substance'. In *New Essays on Plato and Aristotle*, edited by Renford Bambrough, 69–96. London: Routledge, 1965.
MacKinnon, D. M. 'Ayer's Attack on Metaphysics'. *Royal Institute of Philosophy Supplement* 30, no. 1 (1991): 49.
MacKinnon, D. M. 'Barth's Epistle to the Romans (Book Review)'. *Theology* 65, no. 499 (1962): 3–7.
MacKinnon, D. M. 'Biblical Faith and Natural Theology (Book Review)'. *Epworth Review* 20, no. 3 (1993): 128–30.
MacKinnon, D. M. *Borderlands of Theology, and Other Essays by Donald M. MacKinnon*. Edited by George W. Roberts and Donovan E. Smucker. Eugene, OR: Wipf and Stock, 2011. 1968.
MacKinnon, D. M. 'British Philosophy in the Mid-Century (Book Review)'. *Church Quarterly Review* CLIX (1958): 112–14.
MacKinnon, D. M. 'Burke's Political Thought (Book Review)'. *Philosophical Quarterly* 9, no. April (1959): 183–4.
MacKinnon, D. M. 'Can Two Walk Together? The Quest for a Secular Morality (Book Review)'. *Scottish Journal of Theology* 3, no. March (1950): 94–6.
MacKinnon, D. M. *Christian Faith and Communist Faith: A Series of Studies by Members of the Anglican Communion*. London: Macmillan, 1953.
MacKinnon, D. M. 'Christian Understanding of Truth'. *Scottish Journal of Theology* 1, no. 1 (1948): 19–29.
MacKinnon, D. M. 'Christianity and Justice'. *Theology* 42, no. June (1941): 348–54.
MacKinnon, D. M. 'Coleridge and Kant'. In *Coleridge's Variety: Bicentennary Studies*, edited by John B. Beer, 183–203. London: Macmillan, 1974.
MacKinnon, D. M. 'Does Faith Create Its Own Objects?'. In *Burden*, edited by John C. McDowell, 209–20. London: T & T Clark, 2011.
MacKinnon, D. M. Explorations *in Theology*. London: SCM, 1979.
MacKinnon, D. M. 'Faith and Reason in the Philosophy of Religion'. In *Philosophy, History and Civilization: Interdisciplinary Perspectives on R.G. Collingwood*, edited by David Boucher, James Connelly and Tariq Modood, 79–91. Cardiff: University of Wales Press, 1995.
MacKinnon, D. M. 'History and Eschatology'. *Journal of Theological Studies* 9 (1958): 205–8.
MacKinnon, D. M. 'How Do We Know God? [Book Review]'. *Journal of Theological Studies* 46, no. April (1945): 108–10.

MacKinnon, D. M. 'John Wisdom's Other Minds & Philosophy and Psycho-analysis'. *Aberdeen University Review* 35, no. Spring (1954): 271–3.

MacKinnon, D. M. 'Kant's Influence on British Theology'. In *Kant and His Influence*, edited by G. MacDonald Ross and Tony McWalter, 348–66. Bristol: Continuum, 1990.

MacKinnon, D. M. 'Karl Barth: An Introduction to His Early Theology (Book Review)'. *Journal of Theological Studies* xiv (1963): 556–9.

MacKinnon, D. M. 'Mr Murry on the Free Society (Book Review)'. *The Christian News-Letter* 310, no. May (1948): 9–16.

MacKinnon, D. M. 'Mystery and Philosophy (Book Review)'. *Philosophical Quarterly* 9, no. July (1959): 283–5.

MacKinnon, D. M. 'Natural Law'. In *Burden*, edited by John C. McDowell, 115–30. London: T&T Clark, 2011.

MacKinnon, D. M. 'No Way Back: Some First Principles of Catholic Social Judgment Restated (Book Review)'. *Christendom* 9, no. December (1939): 292–8.

MacKinnon, D. M. *Objections to Christian Belief*. London: Constable, 1963.

MacKinnon, D. M. *Philosophy and the Burden of Theological Honesty: A Donald MacKinnon Reader*. Edited by John C. McDowell. London: T & T Clark, 2011.

MacKinnon, D. M. 'Prospect for Christendom'. *The Student Movement* 48, no. November-December (1945): 29–31.

MacKinnon, D. M. 'Religion and Philosophy by W.G. de Burgh [Book Review]'. *Laudate* 15 (1937): 224–34.

MacKinnon, D. M. 'Revelation and Social Justice'. In *Burden*, edited by John McDowell, 137–60. London: T & T Clark, 2011.

MacKinnon, D. M. 'Some Reflections on Hans Urs von Balthasar's Christology with Special Reference to Theodramatick II/2 and III.'. In *The Analogy of Beauty: The theology of Hans Urs von Balthasar*, edited by John Kenneth Riches, 164–79. Edinburgh: T & T Clark, 1986.

MacKinnon, D. M. 'Some Reflections on the Summer School'. *Christendom* 14 (1945): 107–11.

MacKinnon, D. M. 'Studies in Chistian Existentialism (Book Review)'. *Journal of Theological Studies*, no. xviiii (1967): 294–5.

MacKinnon, D. M. 'Subjective and Objective Conceptions of Atonement'. In *Burden*, edited by John C. McDowell, 289–99. London: T & T Clark, 2011.

MacKinnon, D. M. *The Church of God*. Signposts. London: Dacre, 1940.

MacKinnon, D. M. 'The Concept of Mind (Book Review)'. *Philosophical Quarterly* 1, no. April (1951): 248–53.

MacKinnon, D. M. '"The Fourth Gospel" (Book Review)'. *The Oxford Magazine* 59, no. May (1941): 268–9.

MacKinnon, D. M. 'The Justification of Science and the Rationality of Religious Belief (Book Review)'. *Epworth Review* 19 (1992): 107–9.

MacKinnon, D. M. *The Problem of Metaphysics*. Gifford Lectures. Cambridge: Cambridge University Press, 1974.

MacKinnon, D. M. 'The Thought of Jacques Maritain (Book Review)'. *Christendom* 13, no. December (1944): 248–51.

MacKinnon, D. M. *Themes in Theology: The Three-Fold Cord; Essays in Philosophy, Politics and Theology*. Edinburgh: T&T Clark, 1987.

MacKinnon, D. M. 'Theology and Tragedy'. *Religious Studies* 2, no. April (1967): 163–9.

MacKinnon, D. M., and Mark J. Schofield. 'Taylor, Alfred Edward (1869-1945), Philosopher'. In *Oxford Dictionary of National Biography*. Oxford: Oxford University Press. https://doi.org/10.1093/ref:odnb/36426.

MacKinnon, D. M. 'Drama and Memory (1984)'. In *Burden*, edited by John C. McDowell, 181-8. London: T&T Clark, 2011.
MacKinnon, D. M. 'Ethical Intuition'. In *Burden*, edited by John C. McDowell, 99-114. London: T&T Clark, 2011.
MacKinnon, D. M. *God the Living and the True*. Signposts. London: Dacre Press, 1940.
MacKinnon, D. M. 'Hans Urs von Balthasar's Christology'. In *Burden*, edited by John C. McDowell, 281-8. London: T & T Clark, 2011.
MacKinnon, D. M. 'Intellect and Imagination'. In *The Weight of Glory: A Vision and Practice for Christian Faith: The Future of Liberal Theology*, edited by Daniel W. Hardy and P. H Sedgwick, 29-35. Edinburgh: T&TClark, 1991.
MacKinnon, D. M. 'John Wisdom's Paradox and Discovery'. *Church Quarterly Review* 168, no. 366 (1967): 66-74.
MacKinnon, D. M. 'Kant's Agnosticism'. In *Philosophy and the Burden of Theological Honesty: A Donald MacKinnon Reader*, edited by John C. McDowell, 27-34. London: T&T Clark, 2011.
MacKinnon, D. M. 'Moral Freedom'. In *Burden*, edited by John C. McDowell, 83-98. London: T&T Clark, 2011.
MacKinnon, D. M. *On the Notion of a Philosophy of History: Lecture Delivered on 5 May 1953 at King's College, London*. Hobhouse Memorial Trust Lecture, 23. Oxford: Oxford University Press, 1954.
MacKinnon, D. M. 'Reflections on Donald Baillie's Treatment of the Atonement'. In *Christ, Church and Society: Essays on John Baillie and Donald Baillie*, edited by David Fergusson, 115-22. Edinburgh: T&T Clark, 1993.
MacKinnon, D. M. 'Sacrament and Common Meal'. In *Burden*, edited by John C. McDowell, 77-82. London: T&T Clark, 2011.
MacKinnon, D. M. 'Some Reflection on Secular Diakonia'. In *Burden*, edited by John C. McDowell, 67-76. London: T&T Clark, 2011.
MacKinnon, D. M. '"Substance" in Christology: A Cross-bench View'. In *Burden*, edited by John C. McDowell, 237-54. London: T&T Clark, 2011.
MacKinnon, D. M. 'The Evangelical Imagination'. In *Burden*, edited by John C. McDowell, 189-99. London: T&T Clark, 2011.
MacKinnon, D. M. *The Stripping of the Altars: The Gore Memorial Lecture*. Fontana library. London: Collins, 1969.
MacKinnon, D. M. 'The Tomb Was Empty'. In *Burden*, edited by John C. McDowell, 255-60. London: T&T Clark, 2011.
Malcolm, Norman. 'Wittgenstein's Philosophical Investigations'. *The Philosophical Review* 64, no. 4 (1954): 530-59.
Mander, W. J. *British Idealism: A History*. Oxford; New York: Oxford University Press, 2011.
Marcel, Gabriel. *Men against Humanity*. London: Harvill Press, 1952.
Marcel, Gabriel. *The Mystery of Being 1, Reflection and Mystery*. Gifford lectures (University of Aberdeen). London: Harvill Press, 1950.
Marcel, Gabriel. *The Mystery of Being 2, Faith and Reality*. Gifford lectures (University of Aberdeen). London: Harvill Press, 1951.
Marion, Jean-Luc. *God without Being*. Religion and Postmodernism. Chicago, IL: University of Chicago Press, 1991.
Maritain, Jacques. *True Humanism* [in Translation of: Humanisme intégral.]. 4th ed. London: Centenary Press, 1946.

McCutcheon, Felicity. *Religion Within the Limits of Language Alone: Wittgenstein on Philosophy and Religion*. Aldershot: Ashgate, 2001.
McDowell, John C. 'Rend Your Speech a Little: Reading Karl Barth's das Nichtige Through Donald MacKinnon's Tragic Vision'. In *Conversing with Barth*, edited by John C. McDowell and Mike Higton, 142–72. Aldershot: Ashgate, 2004.
McDowell, John C., Kirkland, Scott A., and Moyse, Ashley J., eds. *Kenotic Ecclesiology: Select Writings of Donald M. MacKinnon*. Minneapolis, MN: Fortress Press, 2016.
Michalson, Gordon E. 'Re-Reading the Post-Kantian Tradition with Milbank'. *Journal of Religious Ethics* 32, no. 2 (2004): 357–83.
Milbank, John. '"Between Purgation and Illumination": A Critique of the Theology of Right'. In *Christ, Ethics and Tragedy: Essays in Honour of Donald MacKinnon*, edited by Kenneth Surin, 161–96. Cambridge: Cambridge University Press, 1989.
Milbank, John. *The Word Made Strange: Theology, Language, Culture*. Oxford: Wiley, 1997.
Mitchell, Basil. *Faith and Logic: Oxford Essays in Philosophical Theology*. London: Allen and Unwin, 1957.
Mitchell, Basil. *Morality Religious and Secular: The Dilemma of the Traditional Conscience*. Gifford lectures (University of Glasgow): 1974–1975. Oxford: Clarendon Press, 1980.
Moltmann, Jürgen. *The Crucified God: The Cross of Christ as the Foundation and Criticism of Christian Theology* [in Translation of: Der gekreuzigte Gott. 2. Aufl. München [Munich] : Christian Kaiser, 1973]. London: SCM Press, 1974.
Moore, Andrew. *Realism and Christian Faith: God, Grammar, and Meaning*. Cambridge: Cambridge University Press, 2003.
Moore, G. E. Principia *Ethica*. Cambridge: University Press, 1903.
Morgan, Robert. 'Non Angli sed Angeli: Some Anglican Reactions to German Gospel Criticism'. In *New Studies in Theology*, edited by Stephen Sykes and Derek Holmes, 1–30. London: Duckworth, 1980.
Moser, Paul K. *The Evidence for God: Religious Knowledge Re-examined*. Cambridge: Cambridge University Press, 2010.
Mulhall, Stephen. 'Wittgenstein on Religious Belief'. In *The Oxford Handbook of Wittgenstein*, edited by Oskari Kuusela and Marie McGinn, 755–74. Oxford: Oxford University Press, 2011.
Muller, André. 'Donald M. MacKinnon the True Service of the Particular, 1913-1959'. Unpublished PhD Thesis, University of Otago, 2010.
Murray, Paul D. 'Reason, Truth and Theology in Pragmatist Perspective: A Study in the Theological Relevance of Postfoundationalist Approaches to Human Rationality with Particular Reference to the Work of Richard Rorty, Nicholas Rescher and Donald MacKinnon'. University of Cambridge, 2003.
Nagel, Thomas. *The View from Nowhere*. New York: Oxford University Press, 1986.
Nielsen, Kai. 'Some Remarks on the Independence of Morality from Religion'. *Mind* 70, no. 278 (1961): 175–86.
Nussbaum, Martha 'Perceptive Equilibrium: Literary Theory and Ethical Theory'. In *A Companion to the Philosophy of Literature*, edited by Garry Hagberg and Walter Jost, 241–67. Oxford: Blackwell, 2010.
O'Donovan, Oliver. *A Conversation Waiting to Begin: The Churches and the Gay Controversy*. London: SCM Press, 2009.
O'Donovan, Oliver. *Resurrection and Moral Order: An Outline for Evangelical Ethics*. 2nd ed. Leicester: Apollos, 1994.
Pannenberg, Wolfhart. *Revelation as History* [in Translation of: Offenbarung als Geschichte.]. London: Sheed and Ward, 1969.

Parsons, Charles. 'The Transcendental Aesthetic'. In *The Cambridge Companion to Kant*, edited by Paul Guyer, xii, 482p. Cambridge: Cambridge University Press, 1999.
Pasternack, Lawrence. 'The *ens realissimum* and Necessary Being in "The Critique of Pure Reason"'. *Religious Studies* 37, no. 4 (2001): 467-74.
Peterman, James F. *Philosophy as Therapy: An Interpretation and Defense of Wittgenstein's Later Philosophical Project*. New York: State University of New York Press, 1992.
Phillips, D. Z. 'God and Ought'. In *Christian Ethics and Contemporary Philosophy*, edited by Ian T. Ramsey, 133-9. London: SCM Press, 1966.
Pigden, Charles. 'Russell's Moral Philosophy'. In *The Stanford Encyclopedia of Philosophy*, edited by Zalta Edward, 2014. https://plato.stanford.edu/entries/russell-moral/.
Platts, Mark de Bretton. *Ways of Meaning: An Introduction to a Philosophy of Language*. London: Routledge and Kegan Paul, 1979.
Quash, Ben. *Theology and the Drama of History*. Cambridge: Cambridge University Press, 2005.
Ramsey, Ian T. *Christian Ethics and Contemporary Philosophy*. London: SCM, 1966.
Ramsey, Michael. *From Gore to Temple: The Development of Anglican Theology Between Lux Mundi and the Second World War, 1889-1939*. London: Longmans, 1960.
Raphael, D. D. *The Paradox of Tragedy*. The Mahlon Powell lectures. Bloomington: Indiana University Press, 1960.
Read, Rupert J. 'Wittgenstein's Philosophical Investigations as a War Book'. *New Literary History* 41, no. 3 (2010): 593.
Rhees, Rush, ed. *Recollections of Wittgenstein*, Oxford paperbacks. Oxford: Oxford University Press, 1984.
Ritchie, Angus. *From Morality to Metaphysics: The Theistic Implications of Our Ethical Commitments*. Oxford: Oxford University Press, 2012.
Roberts, Richard. 'Theological Rhetoric and Moral Passion in Light of MacKinnon's Barth'. In *Christ, Ethics and Tragedy: Essays in Honour of Donald MacKinnon*, edited by Kenneth Surin, 1-14. Cambridge: Cambridge University Press, 1989.
Rose, Gillian. *The Broken Middle*. Oxford: Blackwell, 1992.
Ross, W. D. 'The Basis of Objective Judgments in Ethics'. *International Journal of Ethics* 37, no. 2 (1927): 113-27.
Russell, Bertrand. *History of Western Philosophy*. 2nd ed. London: Routledge, 1991. 1961.
Russell, Bertrand. 'On Verification: The Presidential Address'. *Proceedings of the Aristotelian Society* 38 (1937): 1.
Sands, Kathleen. *Escape from Paradise*. Minneapolis, MN: Fortress Press, 1994.
Sayre-McCord, Geoff. 'Moral Realism'. http://plato.stanford.edu/archives/sum2011/entries/moral-realism/.
Schultz, Bart. 'Bertrand Russell in Ethics and Politics'. *Ethics* 102, no. 3 (1992): 594-631.
Simon, Ulrich E. *A Theology of Auschwitz*. London: SPCK, 1978.
Smith, Christian. *Moral, Believing Animals: Human Personhood and Culture*. Oxford: Oxford University Press, 2003.
Sorley, W. R. *Moral Values and the Idea of God*. Cambridge: University Press, 1918.
Stanley, Timothy. *Protestant Metaphysics after Karl Barth and Martin Heidegger*. London: SCM, 2010.
Stead, Christopher. *Divine Substance*. Oxford: Clarendon Press, 1977.
Steiner, George. *Language and Silence: Essays 1958-1966*. London: Faber, 1967.
Steiner, George. 'Tribute to Donald MacKinnon'. *Theology* 98, no. 781 (1995): 2-9.
Stephenson, Alan. *Rise and Decline of English Modernism*. London: SPCK, 1984.

Stern, Robert. *Understanding Moral Obligation: Kant, Hegel, Kierkegaard*. Cambridge: Cambridge University Press, 2011.
Stevenson, Charles L. *Ethics and Language*. New Haven, CT: Yale University Press, 1944.
Stratton-Lake, Philip. 'On W.D. Ross's "The Basis of Objective Judgments in Ethics"'. *Ethics* 125, no. 2 (2015): 521–4.
Strawson, P. F. *The Bounds of Sense: An Essay on Kant's Critique of Pure Reason*. London: Routledge, 1989.
Surin, Kenneth, ed. *Christ, Ethics and Tragedy: Essays in Honour of Donald MacKinnon*. Cambridge: Cambridge University Press, 1989.
Surin, Kenneth, ed. 'Some Aspects of the "grammar" of "incarnation" and "kenosis": Reflections Prompted by the Writings of Donald MacKinnon'. In *Christ, Ethics and Tragedy: Essays in Honour of Donald MacKinnon*, edited by Kenneth Surin, 93–116. Cambridge: Cambridge University Press, 1989.
Swinburne, Richard. 'The Value and Christian Roots of Analytical Philosophy of Religion'. In *Faith and Philosophical Analysis: The Impact of Analytical Philosophy on the Philosophy of Religion*, edited by Harriet A. Harris and Christopher J. Insole, 33–45. Aldershot, Hants; Burlington, VT: Ashgate, 2005.
Sykes, Stephen, and Derek Holmes. *New Studies in Theology*. London: Duckworth, 1980.
Szabados, Béla. 'Introduction'. In *Wittgensteinian Fideism?*, edited by K. Nielsen and D.Z. Phillips, 1–15. London: SCM Press, 2005.
Taylor, A. E. *Does God Exist?* London: Macmillan, 1945.
Taylor, A. E. *The Faith of a Moralist: Gifford Lectures Delivered in the University of St Andrews, 1926-1928, Natural Theology and the Positive Religions*. 2 vols. Vol. 2, London: Macmillan, 1930.
Taylor, A. E. *The Faith of a Moralist: Gifford Lectures Delivered in the University of St Andrews, 1926-1928, The Theological Implications of Morality*. 2 vols. Vol. 1, London: Macmillan, 1930.
Taylor, A. E. 'The Right and the Good'. *Mind* 48, no. 191 (1939): 273–301.
Taylor, A. E. 'The Vindication of Religion'. In *Essays Catholic & Critical*, edited by Edward Gordon Selwyn, 29–82: London: Society for Promoting Christian Knowledge, 1929.
Taylor, A. E. 'Theism'. In *Encyclopædia of Religion and Ethics*, edited by James Hastings, John A. Selbie and Louis H. Gray, 261–86. Edinburgh: T&T Clark, 1908.
Tennant, F.R., and S. M. den Otter. 'Sorley, William Ritchie (1855-1935), Philosopher'. In *Oxford Dictionary of National Biography*. Oxford: Oxford University Press. https://doi.org/10.1093/ref:odnb/36197.
Thompson, C. 'Wittgenstein's Confessions'. *Philosophical Investigations* 23, no. 1 (01/2000 2000): 1–25.
Thompson, Caleb. 'Wittgenstein, Augustine and the Fantasy of Ascent'. *Philosophical Investigations* 25, no. 2 (01/2002 2002): 153–71.
Thompson, John. 'Was Forsyth Really a Barthian Beofre Barth?'. In *Justice the True and Only Mercy: Essays on the Life and Theology of Peter Taylor Forsyth*, edited by Trevor A. Hart, 237–55. Edinburgh: T&T Clark, 1995.
Torrance, Thomas F. *Karl Barth, Biblical and Evangelical Theologian*. Edinburgh: T&T Clark, 1990.
Vanheeswijck, Guido. 'Robin George Collingwood on Eternal Philosophical Problems'. *Dialogue: Canadian Philosophical Review / Revue canadienne de philosophie* 40, no. 3 (01/2001 2001): 555–69.
Vanhoozer, Kevin J. 'Once More into the Borderlands: The Way of Wisdom in Philosopy and Theology after the "Turn to Drama"'. In *Transcending Boundaries in Philosophy and*

Theology: Reason, Meaning and Experience, edited by Kevin J. Vanhoozer and Martin Warner, 31–54. Aldershot: Ashgate, 2007.

Via, Dan O. *The Hardened Heart and Tragic Finitude*. Eugene, OR: Cascade Books, 2012.

Virtue, Charles F. Sawhill. 'The Axiological Theism of A. E. Taylor'. *Philosophy* 27, no. 101 (1952): 110–24.

Waller, Giles. 'Freedom, Fate and Sin in Donald MacKinnion's Use of Tragedy'. In *Christian Theology and Tragedy: Theologians, Tragic Literature, and Tragic Theory*, edited by T. Kevin Taylor and Giles Waller, 101–18. Farnham: Ashgate, 2011.

Ward, G. 'Tragedy as Subclause: George Steiner's Dialogue with Donald Mackinnon'. *Heythrop journal* 34, no. 3 (01/1993 1993): 274–87.

Warnock, Mary. *Ethics since 1900*. 2nd ed. London: Oxford University Press, 1966.

White, Roger. 'MacKinnon and the Parables'. In *Christ, Ethics and Tragedy: Essays in Honour of Donald MacKinnon*, edited by Kenneth Surin, 49–70. Cambridge: Cambridge University Press, 1989.

White, Roger M. *Talking About God: The Concept of Analogy and the Problem of Religious Language*. Surrey: Ashgate, 2010.

Wignall, P.G. 'D.M. MacKinnon: An Introduction to His Early Theological Writings'. In *New Studies in Theology 1*, edited by S. Sykes and D. Holmes, 75–94. London: Duckworth, 1980.

Williams, Rowan. *The Edge of Words: God and the Habits of Language*. London: Bloomsbury, 2014.

Williams, Rowan. *The Tragic Imagination*. Oxford: Oxford University Press, 2016.

Williams, Rowan. 'Theology after Wittgenstein by Fergus Kerr'. *Philosophical Investigations* 10, no. 4 (1987): 343–7.

Williams, Rowan. 'Trinity and Ontology'. In *Christ, Ethics and Tragedy: Essays in Honour of Donald MacKinnon*, edited by Kenneth Surin, 71–92. Cambridge: Cambridge University Press, 1989.

Wittgenstein, Ludwig. 'A Lecture on Ethics'. *The Philosophical Review* 74, no. 1 (1965): 3–12.

Wittgenstein, Ludwig. *Notebooks, 1914-1916*. Oxford: Blackwell, 1961.

Wittgenstein, Ludwig. *Philosophical Investigations* [in Translation of: Philosophische Untersuchungen.]. 3rd ed. Oxford: Blackwell, 1968.

Wittgenstein, Ludwig. *Tractatus logico-philosophicus* [in Translation of: Logisch-Philosophische Abhandlung. - Parallel German text and English translation.]. London: Routledge, 1981.

Wittgenstein, Ludwig. *Zettel*. Oxford: Blackwell, 1981.

Wolterstorff, Nicholas, and Terence Cuneo. *Inquiring about God: Selected Essays*. 2 vols. Vol. 1, Cambridge: Cambridge University Press, 2010.

Wren-Lewis, J. 'A Study in Ethical Theory'. *Modern Churchman* 3, no. 2 (1960): 145–8.

INDEX

Absolute and Relative in History
    (MacKinnon)   163 n.54
abstraction   8, 57, 121, 171
Act and Being (Bonhoeffer)   186
Acts of the Apostles   130, 145
Adeimantus   32
Aeschylus   129
aesthetics   7, 73, 75–6, 125
agnosticism   12, 14, 14 n.29, 15–17,
    17 n.40, 19, 20 n.55, 21 n.58, 46,
    50, 54, 62, 76, 137, 141, 184, 189,
    189 n.22
Alexander, Samuel   49
analytical philosophy   8, 11, 34 n.123, 36,
    62–3, 74–6, 81, 92, 112
analytical theology   64 n.86
Anglo-American philosophy   121
Anglo-Catholicism   28–9, 48, 85
Anscombe, G. E. M.   34, 37, 50,
    166
anthropocentrism   14 n.29, 16–17,
    20 n.55, 31, 58
anthropomorphism   8, 14–16, 39, 150
Antigone (Sophocles)   142–3
anti-Semitism   145
Aquinas   1, 19 n.54, 35, 47, 179 n.124,
    188 n.20, 189
Aristotelian Society   77
Aristotle   3, 9, 23, 35, 47, 56, 78, 85, 111,
    111 n.137, 112 n.139, 122
Athalie (Racine)   141
atheism   76, 115, 117
atomism   6, 48, 63, 65, 67–8, 74, 85 n.15
atonement   98–107
Atonement and Tragedy (MacKinnon)
    145
Aufklärung   23
Axiarchism   184
Ayer, A. J.   36, 63–4, 66, 70, 72–4,
    73 n.129, 74 n.130, 77–8, 79, 151,
    153, 174

Bachelard, Sarah   176 n.111
Baillie, D. M.   109
Balthasar, Hans Urs von   2, 10, 61, 87, 88,
    90, 92, 92 n.46, 189
Barth, Karl   1–2, 8, 10, 32, 35–6, 39,
    61, 84, 86–7, 87 n.25, 88–9,
    89 nn.34, 36, 90, 92, 99, 102,
    106, 129, 131, 134–5, 135 n.64,
    137, 189
Battle of the Somme   49
Bauman, Zygmunt   145
Bentham, Jeremy   6, 47
Berkeley, George   63, 125, 162
Berlin, Isaiah   7, 9, 42, 63, 77, 147, 178
Bible   129, 130
Black, Rufus   34 n.123, 37
Blake, William   126
Bloor, David   166
Bonhoeffer, Dietrich   98, 131, 134, 139,
    149, 186
Borderlands of Theology, and Other Essays
    (MacKinnon)   2
Bostock, David   66
Bradley, F. H.   47, 48, 54, 67, 90
Braithwaite, R. B.   78
Brink, David   34 n.123, 38, 58 n.62
Britain   10, 28, 29, 63, 118
    Anglicanism   25, 105
    idealism in   63, 65–75
Broad, C. D.   38, 58 n.62, 61 n.75
Brook, Nicholas   126
Brunner, Emil   86, 90–1
Bultmann, Rudolf   83, 83 n.5, 84, 86, 98,
    106, 172
Burke, Edmund   175 n.106
Butler, Joseph   9, 24, 25–6, 33, 40, 47, 70,
    172, 175 n.106, 176, 177, 180
Byrne, Peter   19, 26, 45

Caird, Edward   112
Camus, Albert   126

Caputo, John   172
Cartesianism   170 n.79
Cascardi, Anthony   144
Categories and *Metaphysics* (Aristotle)   111
catholic humanism   4, 151, 187
causality   20 n.55, 23, 162, 178
Cavell, Stanley   10–13, 13 n.26, 14, 78, 138, 142, 149, 152, 152 n.6, 158, 165 n.59, 170, 186 n.11
Cell, Edward   68, 68 nn.103, 104, 69 n.106, 71
Cerbone, David R.   154, 156, 159
Chisholm, Roderick   177 n.115
Christ   1, 3, 17, 23, 27, 81–2, 88–9, 96, 98, 100, 101, 101 n.89, 102, 103 n.94, 104, 106, 106 n.111, 110–11, 112, 115, 118–20, 129, 135, 146, 190. *See also* Jesus
Christendom   1, 134, 163
Christenson, Anne-Marie S.   153, 156
Christian Faith and Communist Faith (MacKinnon)   114
Christianity   26–7, 35, 47, 51, 81, 91, 98, 115, 116, 141, 144, 190
Christians   6, 8, 24, 35, 87 n.25, 115, 136, 142, 146
Christian scripture   127, 129–37
Christian social radicals   29
Christology   2, 4, 19 n.52, 28, 32, 61, 77, 80, 81, 84–5, 87, 89 n.33, 90, 92, 93 n.53, 99, 100–1, 101 n.89, 102–4, 105 n.105, 107–9, 111, 113 n.146, 114–15, 118–20, 125, 135, 145, 148, 173, 183, 189
Church of England   29, 48
Church of God, The (MacKinnon)   2
Coakley, Sarah   89 n.36
Coleridge, Samuel Taylor   60, 125, 126, 128
Coliva, Annalisa   71 n.118
Collingwood, R. T.   7, 77–8, 78 n.154, 96–7, 111, 125 n.17, 128, 133, 172, 173, 183
Conant, James   12
Concept of Prayer, The (Phillips)   75
Confessions (St. Augustine)   12, 152
Confucius   9

Connor, Timothy   2, 102 n.94, 107
Conrad, Joseph   126
contemplation   11, 60, 89, 136, 179–80
Copernican revolution   15, 112
Corinthians   96
Corneille   141
Creed, J. M.   65 n.86
Crisp, Oliver   64 n.86
criticisms   11, 95, 100, 114, 133–4, 171, 187
Critique of Pure Reason (Kant)   14, 16–17, 73, 127–8, 162 n.52
Crossman, R. H. S.   126
crucifixion   53–4, 130, 136, 140, 145
Crucifixion-Resurrection (Hoskyns)   87 n.25
Cupitt, Don   75, 75 n.138, 109, 167

Dan, Theodore   115 n.154
Davaney, Sheila Greeve   91 n.43
Davies, Brian   109
Death of Tragedy, The (Steiner)   139
DeHart, Paul   1
deism   26
Demant, V. A.   179 n.124
deontology   25, 26
Descartes, René   34, 49, 162
determinism   117, 120
Deutscher, Isaac   115 n.154
dialectical theology   86, 135
Diamond, Cora   12, 154, 166
Dickens, Charles   126
Dilman, Ilham   166
Dilthey, Wilhelm   78 n.154, 91, 172
doctrine of analogy   96, 189
Dodd, C. H.   94, 124, 131, 132–3
'Does Faith Create its Own Objects?' (MacKinnon)   96
Does God Exist? (Taylor)   48, 50
D'Oro, Giuseppina   97 n.72
'Drama and Memory' (MacKinnon)   125 n.17
Drury, Maurice O'Connor   151
dualism   51, 52, 171
Dummett, Michael   162 n.52, 163, 167, 167 n.70, 168

ecclesiology   2, 29, 137
Electra (Sophocles)   142

Eliot, George 126
Eliot, T. S. 126
emotivism 12, 36, 70 n.109, 79, 174
empiricism 6–7, 12, 25, 31, 40, 42, 63, 85 n.15, 96, 97, 119, 127, 171, 177
Enlightenment 170, 179 n.124, 188
epistemology 39, 49, 66, 71, 74, 86, 92–3, 97, 107–8, 108 n.120, 109, 133, 155–7, 159, 161, 164, 172
Ernst, Cornelius 149
error theory 36, 70 n.109
eschatology 23, 92, 140
ethics 9, 25 n.80, 36, 39, 41, 55, 55 n.48, 58, 79, 151–60
Eucharist 136–7
Euclid 126
Euthyphro Dilemma 35, 38–9
'Evangelical Imagination' (MacKinnon) 127, 145
evil 24, 53–4, 61, 79, 139–41, 146 n.115, 147–8, 173, 185
Ewing, A. C. 61 n.75, 73, 174
existentialism 7, 11

fact value distinction 40–1, 54, 60
Faith of a Moralist, The (Taylor) 46, 48, 50
Farrer, Austin 64, 86–7, 86 n.20
Fiddes, Paul S. 125 n.15, 186 n.11
fideism 88, 88 n.31, 89, 92
finitism 167 n.70
Flew, Antony 64, 151
Foot, Philippa 1
formalism 26, 42–3, 58, 173, 177
Form Criticism 94–5
Forsyth, P. T. 83, 87, 88, 90, 99 n.80, 102, 104–5, 110, 110 n.132, 189
foundationalism 14, 39
freedom 3, 7, 20, 22, 24, 26, 27, 43, 45, 56, 61, 117, 120, 136, 147, 173, 177 n.115, 178, 184
Freud, Sigmund 11, 124

Gesinnungsethik 24
Getzler, Israel 115 n.154
Gibbard, Allan 36
Gibson, Arthur 149
Gifford Lectures 48, 50, 51, 54, 60, 61, 125 n.17, 139–40, 147, 149, 172

God 15, 18, 19 n.54, 22, 23, 25–7, 33, 35, 39, 45, 53, 57, 61, 66 n.92, 69, 75, 82, 85, 87, 88, 94 n.57, 100 n.88, 103, 104, 105 n.105, 107–10, 115, 117, 119, 129, 131, 132, 134, 137, 148, 150, 176, 181
  existence 17, 49, 52
  knowledge 16
  notion of 17, 19, 21, 31–2, 46, 48, 64, 73, 75
  righteousness 82
God the Living and True (MacKinnon) 2
Goldberg, S. L. 123–4
Good Friday 106, 108 n.123
Gore, Charles 119
Green, T. H. 54

Hare, John E. 30 n.104, 34 n.123, 38, 176 n.109, 188
Hare, R. M. 36
Hart, Trevor A. 185 n.9
Hauerwas, Stanley 1, 3, 34 n.123, 38–9, 189
Hedley, Douglas 125 n.17, 128, 170 n.79, 184, 188, 189
Hegel, Georg Wilhelm Friedrich 9, 23–4, 24 n.75, 47, 47 n.9, 58, 60, 67, 91, 91 n.43, 106 n.111, 108 n.123, 112, 125, 140, 143, 172, 185, 186, 187
Heidegger, Martin 75, 155
historicism 7, 78 n.154, 94, 96
Hobbes, Thomas 125, 177 n.115
holism 101 n.88, 169–70
Holland, Henry Scott 94 n.58, 106, 109
holocaust 30, 139, 141, 173
Holy Spirit 128–9, 130, 141
homoousion 83 n.5
Hoskyns, E. C. 83, 87, 87 n.25, 90, 94 n.58
humanism 16, 23, 150, 151, 173, 177, 177 n.116, 187
Humanism and Terror (Merleau-Ponty) 118
Humboldt, Alexander 91 n.43
Hume, David 37, 40, 47, 63, 127–8

idealism 6, 16, 54, 56, 67, 76, 90–1, 98, 119, 127, 150, 155, 156, 159, 162, 163, 166
  in Britain 65–75

realism and   1, 3–4, 10, 13–15, 33, 47, 70, 144, 151, 155, 162, 162 n.52, 181, 186, 190
Idealism and Realism: An Old Controversy Dissolved (Kerr)   151
Idea of History, The (Collingwood)   97
imagination   96, 115, 127, 128–9, 130, 133, 136, 184
incarnation   26, 29, 82, 84 n.10, 85–97, 101, 102, 106, 109–10, 112, 115, 118–20, 130, 131, 134, 173, 181, 188
Insole, Christopher J.   19, 22 n.62, 63–4, 186 n.13, 188, 189 n.22
'Intellect and Imagination' (MacKinnon)   127
intuition/intuitionism   18, 58, 62, 173–81, 177 n.116, 181, 185, 186
Inventing Right and Wrong (Mackie)   37

Janz, Paul D.   3, 3 n.8, 22 n.62, 101 n.88, 130 n.42, 135, 148, 162 n.52, 168–9, 185, 186, 186 n.13, 187, 188, 189
Jeremias, Joachim   124, 131, 132–3
Jesus   3, 9, 24, 26, 54, 65 n.86, 81, 83–5, 87, 88–9, 92, 94, 94 n.57, 95–6, 97 n.69, 98, 98 n.78, 99, 101 n.88, 102, 103, 105, 105 n.107, 106, 107, 107 n.115, 108–9, 110–11, 114, 117, 129, 130, 132, 133, 134, 135, 136, 137, 142, 145, 150, 181, 187. *See also* Christ
'Jesus of history'   82, 83
Jülicher, Adolf   131–2
Julius Caesar (Shakespeare)   122, 126, 143

Kant, Immanuel   3–4, 7, 9, 11, 14–16, 17–28, 18 n.44, 19 nn.51, 52, 20 n.55, 21 n.58, 21 n.60, 25 n.80, 30–2, 30 n.104, 31 n.109, 34, 34 n.123, 36, 40, 42–3, 45, 46–7, 47 n.9, 49–53, 55, 57, 60, 62, 65, 69, 73–4, 73 n.129, 74 n.130, 76, 80, 87, 90, 90 n.39, 96, 104, 105 n.105, 111, 112, 117, 122, 127–8, 137, 141, 147, 148, 150, 161–2, 162 n.52, 164, 164 n.59, 165, 165 n.59, 166, 167 n.69, 176, 177, 177 n.115, 178, 180, 186 n.13, 188, 188 n.20, 189, 189 n.22
transcendental illusion   15 n.30, 165 n.59
Kantian agnosticism   17, 17 n.40, 184
kenosis   4, 82, 108–10, 113, 113 n.146, 114, 118
Kermode, Frank   126
Kerr, Fergus   1, 63, 67, 88, 88 n.29, 151, 154–5, 157, 167, 170–1, 187
Kierkegaard, Søren   11, 24 n.80, 83, 149
King Lear (Shakespeare)   126
Kittel, Gerhard   86
Küng, Hans   92, 92 n.46

Lang, Cosmo   29
Lenin, Vladimir   116–20
Lenin and Theology (MacKinnon)   114
Leninism   115
Letter to the Romans (Barth)   87 n.25
Levinas, Emmanuel   40, 149 n.127
Lewin, M.   115 n.154
liberalism   28–9, 31, 35
liberal theology   26, 28, 30, 84, 93, 134
liberation theology   93
Lie Down in Darkness (Styron)   126
Lightfoot, Joseph   86, 94, 94 nn.56, 57, 95, 95 n.61
Lindbeck, George   114
linguistic philosophy   10–11
Lisbon earthquake (1755)   42 n.158
literature
    and moral philosophy   121
    and moral realism   122–37
Little Did I Know (Cavell)   12
Logic, Truth and Language (Ayer)   77
Long, Eugene Thomas   61, 61 n.75
Lovibond, Sabina   34 n.123, 36–7, 161, 164 n.59, 166
Lukacs, George   115 n.154
Luther, Martin   23, 111
Lux Mundi (Gore)   28, 119

McCutcheon, Felicity   167 n.69
McDowell, John   39, 166
Mach, Ernst   49, 74
MacIntyre, Alasdair C.   187, 189
Mackie, J. L.   36–7, 59, 70 n.109
Macquarrie, John   84, 98

Malcolm, Norman   166
Mander, W. J.   67, 69
Marcel, Gabriel   125, 126
Maritain, Jacques   23, 96, 135 n.64, 177
Marx, Karl   11, 172
Marxism   3, 35, 53, 115, 116–17, 173, 187, 190
Merleau-Ponty, Maurice   118
Metaphysical and Religious Language (MacKinnon)   163 n.54
metaphysics   7, 10, 14, 26–7, 28, 32, 47, 55, 58 n.62, 59–60, 62–3, 65, 67, 71–2, 74, 77, 84–5, 87, 91, 107, 112, 114, 157, 177, 185
　classical   31, 99 n.80
　language of   4, 31, 43, 47, 65–6, 69, 183
　monist   49, 68, 90–1
Michalson, Gordon E.   188, 188 n.20, 189
Midgley, Mary   1
Milbank, John   3–4, 17 n.40, 120, 146 n.115, 177 nn.114, 116, 185, 185 n.9, 186, 186 n.11, 187, 188, 188 n.20, 189, 190
Mill, J. S.   6–7, 9, 24 n.80, 47, 73, 77, 147
Milton, John   129, 141, 145
Minar, Edward   166
Mitchell, Basil   64, 79
modernist movement   83
modernist theology   77, 93
modernity   7, 47, 88, 90, 98, 116, 139
Modern Tragedy (Williams)   139
Moltmann, J.   83, 92–3, 108 n.123
monism   56, 60
monotheism   141
Moore, G. E.   10, 38, 39–40, 58 n.62, 61 n.74, 63, 66, 68, 68 n.102, 70–1, 71 n.118, 72, 74, 75 n.138, 85, 85 n.15, 86, 90, 90 n.39, 104, 150, 163, 168, 174, 176, 180, 183, 184
moral agency   24, 34, 137, 176, 178, 187
moral anthropology   51, 187
moral intuition   39–40, 176
moralism   105 n.105
moral law   16, 21 n.60, 26, 27 n.97, 30
moral philosophy   4, 9, 25, 31, 34 n.123, 39, 45, 47, 50, 54, 78, 79, 82, 104, 123, 139, 146, 150, 173–81, 179, 183, 185

moral realism   1, 3–4, 10, 13–14, 22, 31, 32–42, 34 n.123, 43, 60, 82, 101, 114, 121, 129, 151, 160, 173, 181, 183, 184–5, 190
moral struggle   24, 97, 121
Moral Values and the Idea of God (Sorley)   54–5
More, Henry   189
Morgan, Robert   94 n.56, 95 n.61
Moser, Paul K.   88 n.31, 108 n.120
Mulhall, Stephen   158, 158 n.35, 166
Muller, André   2, 47, 53, 63, 68 n.102, 85 n.15, 86 n.19, 93, 118 n.170, 163 n.54
Murdoch, Iris   1, 39–40, 121, 184
Murray, Paul D.   9 n.16, 43 n.161
Myth of God Incarnate (Hick)   84

Nagel, Thomas   154–6, 166, 186
naturalism   36, 54, 55, 62, 70
natural law   25, 36, 42, 62, 121, 173–81, 177 n.114, 179 n.124, 181, 185, 186, 188
natural science   47, 55, 55 n.48, 56, 69, 86
natural theology   48, 51, 89, 149
New Testament   82–3, 84, 86, 87 n.25, 93–4, 94 n.58, 95, 98, 102 n.94, 132, 145
　St. Matthew's Gospel   145
　St. Mark's Gospel   94, 132
　St. Luke's Gospel   129–30
　St. John's Gospel   94–5, 100, 127, 128, 145
'Nicene Creed'   83 n.5
Nielsen, Kai   35 n.127
Nietzsche, Friedrich   11, 36, 67, 140
nihilism   50
Nineham, Dennis   98
nominalism   164 n.57, 166
non-cognitivism   27, 36–7, 70 n.109
nonnaturalism   58 n.62
non-realism   13 n.26, 38, 50, 59, 66, 175
norm expressivism   36
Nostromo (Conrad)   126
nuclear proliferation   41
Nussbaum, Martha   121, 123 n.8

October Revolution 118
O'Donovan, Oliver 28, 31, 34 n.123, 38, 176 n.111
Oedipus the King (Sophocles) 126, 142, 144, 144 n.106
'On the Notion of a Philosophy of History' (MacKinnon) 126, 163 n.54
ontological argument 49, 52
onto-theology 31, 75
Orwell, George 126
Otto, Rudolph 50, 136

Pannenberg, Wolfhart 92, 92 n.46, 93, 93 n.53
'Parable and Sacrament' (MacKinnon) 131–2
parables 124, 131, 133, 134, 136, 137
Parables of Jesus (Jeremias) 133
Parables of the Kingdom, The (Dodd) 133
'Paradise Regained' (Milton) 145
Paradox and Discovery (Wisdom) 148
Paradox of Tragedy, The (Raphael) 139
Peterman, James F. 12, 154
Phédre (Racine) 141
Phillips, D. Z. 39, 75, 75 n.138, 167 n.69
Philosophical Investigations (Wittgenstein) 12, 152–4, 158
philosophy 3, 6, 12, 69, 71, 89, 158, 187
  analytical 8, 11
  of history 24, 91, 170
  of mathematics 168 n.70
  of religion 8, 39, 48, 63–4
  and theology 8, 10, 17, 27, 31, 54, 61, 63, 75–6, 89 n.36, 90, 125
  therapy 14–17
Pigden, Charles 70, 70 n.109
Plato 3, 7 n.8, 9, 14, 16, 23, 33, 47, 51, 60, 125, 138, 142, 144, 147, 154
pluralism 56, 60
Plutarch 126
pneumatology 130, 137
Polyeucte (Corneille) 141
Popper, Karl 64, 77–8
positivism 6, 10, 25, 42, 63–4, 76, 77, 86, 163, 187, 190
positivist realism 7, 13 n.26, 33
post-Enlightenment 83
Prall, D. W. 52

prescriptivism 36
Price, Richard 38
Prichard, H. A. 9, 38, 80, 174, 174 n.101
Principia Ethica (Moore) 71
Problem of Conduct, The (MacKinnon) 49
Problem of Metaphysics, The (MacKinnon) 12, 32, 126, 131
Prometheus Vinctus (Aeschylus) 129
Putnam, Hilary 169, 186

Quick, Oliver Chase 110
Quine, Willard Van Orman 111, 112 n.139

radical orthodox 8 n.15, 188
Radical Orthodox movement 8 n.15
Ramsey, Ian 35 n.127, 94 n.58, 119
Raphael, D. D. 116, 139–41, 142
rational religion 27 n.97, 30–1, 43, 161
Raven, C. E. 83 n.5
realism 6, 10, 16–17, 20 n.55, 25, 30, 33, 38, 61, 66–7, 77, 82–3, 92, 102 n.92, 104, 107, 111, 114, 121, 124–5, 127–8, 129, 132, 137, 146, 156, 169, 171, 173, 178, 185, 187. *See also* moral realism
  confessional 13
  and idealism 1, 3–4, 10, 13–15, 47, 70, 144, 151, 155, 162, 162 n.52, 181, 186, 190
  positivist 7, 13 n.26, 33
Redaction Criticism 95
redemption 83 n.5, 99, 99 n.83, 100, 101 n.88, 114, 122
reductionism 6, 8, 26, 31 n.109, 55, 58, 71, 72, 74, 79
'The Refutation of Idealism' (Moore) 70
relativism 50, 51–2, 156, 159
Religion Within the Limits of Reason Alone (Kant) 20
Religious Prospect, The (Demant) 179 n.124
Remarks on the Foundation of Mathematics (Wittgenstein) 167
resurrection 54, 81, 100, 103, 105, 105 n.107, 106, 106 n.113, 107, 120, 141, 142, 145, 176

revelation   17–19, 23, 26, 30–1, 30 n.104, 64, 75, 82, 85–97, 108, 119, 130, 131, 135, 147, 177 n.114, 187
Revelation as History (Pannenberg)   92 n.46
Richards, I. A.   141
Riddle of the New Testament, The (Hoskyns)   87 n.25
Ritchie, Angus   183, 184, 185
Ritschl, Albrecht   91, 134
Rose, Gillian   186
Ross, W. D.   38, 58 n.62, 174
Russell, Bertrand   10, 49–50, 63–4, 66–70, 70 n.109, 71, 73, 74, 77, 79, 86, 90, 90 n.39, 169, 173
Russian Peasants and Soviet Power (Lewin)   115 n.154
Ryle, Gilbert   121, 125

St. Augustine   12–13, 32, 35, 152
St. Paul   9–10, 24, 25–6, 176, 177, 180, 187
St. Thomas   96
Samson Agonistes (Milton)   141
Sartre, Jean Paul   180
Sayre-McCord, Geoff   34 n.123, 35
scepticism   10, 12, 15, 17, 24, 37, 38, 42, 49, 95–6, 136, 158, 162 n.52, 170
Schleiermacher, Friedrich   107 n.117, 134
Schlick, Moritz   66, 74
Schultz, Bart   70
Sea of Faith (Cupitt)   167
Second World War   29, 48, 64, 188
sense perception   56, 59–60, 97
Shakespeare, William   122, 126, 138, 142, 143
Shiner, Roger   11
Shub, David   115 n.154
Sidgwick, Henry   38, 58 n.62, 78
sociology   29–30, 145
Socrates   123
solifidianism   23
solipsism   154–5
'Some Reflections on Secular Diakonia' (MacKinnon)   119
Sophocles   126, 142, 144
Sorley, W. R.   41, 45–6, 54–62, 80, 81, 129, 184

soteriology   82, 99–100, 102, 102 n.93, 103–4, 114
Spinoza, Baruch   60, 67
State and Revolution (Lenin)   116
Stead, Christopher   87 n.25
Steiner, George   1, 7 n.13, 78 n.154, 101 n.89, 125, 125 n.17, 126, 130, 139, 141, 147
Stenius, Erik   164 n.59
Stern, Robert   21 n.60
Stevenson, Charles L.   174
Stone, Darwell   119
Strawson, P. F.   3, 15, 20 n.57
Stripping of the Altars, The (MacKinnon)   2
Study in Ethical Theory, A (MacKinnon)   9, 12–13, 17, 24, 126
Styron, William   126
subjectivism   58, 174
substance   17, 82, 84–5, 105, 110–14, 125, 145, 171
Surin, Kenneth   114
Swinburne, Richard   62, 64, 64 n.86
Szabados, Béla   5

Taylor, A. E.   3, 23, 40–1, 40 n.149, 45–54, 80, 81, 126, 129, 175, 184
Taylor, Charles   186
teleology   19, 23, 46, 49, 51, 58, 121
Temple, William   29–30
Tennant, F. R.   54
theism   17, 24, 26–7, 45, 48–9, 54–5, 60, 61–2, 75, 90, 183, 184–5, 190
Theism (Taylor)   48–50
theodicy   62, 82, 122, 146
'Theology and Tragedy' (MacKinnon)   139
The Rainbow (Lawrence)   126
'therapeutic' methodology   8–14
Thirlwall, Connop   84 n.10
Thompson, Caleb   11 n.21, 12–13, 152, 152 n.6
Tillich, Paul   75
Timaeus (Plato)   47
Trachiniae (Sophocles)   142
Tractatus Logico-Philosophicus (Wittgenstein)   74, 153, 163, 164 n.59, 165, 167 n.69

tragedy   17, 28, 43, 53, 82, 100–2, 106, 116, 118–19, 136, 138, 144, 146, 185
tragic literature   138–50
tragic realism   185, 187
transcendence   31, 62–3, 65, 88–9, 110, 136, 147, 149
'The Transcendence of the Tragic' (MacKinnon)   147
Trinity   81–2, 103, 105, 106, 108 n.123, 115

Under Western Eyes (Conrad)   126
universalism   39, 188
utilitarianism   8, 25, 26, 78, 79–80, 121, 174, 181

value judgements   55–6, 58, 148, 176, 178
Vellacott, Phillip   126, 144
'Verification and Experience' (Ayer)   77
verificationism   66
Vienna Circle   64, 66, 73, 74, 78
Vindication of Religion in *Essays Catholic and Critical* (Taylor)   48–50
Virtue, C. F.   51–3
Virtue, Charles   46
voluntarism   8, 36

Warnock, Mary   1, 67, 79, 174 n.101, 175
White, Roger   124, 131, 132, 190
Whitehead, A. N.   51, 111
Williams, Bernard   33, 113, 123–4, 166
Williams, Michael   166
Williams, Raymond   139
Williams, Rowan   1, 108 n.123, 148–50, 185–7
Wilson, Cook   77
Winch, Peter   121
Wisdom, John   11–14, 63–4, 75 n.138, 77, 100, 148, 163, 164 n.59, 168
Wittgenstein, Ludwig   3, 10–11, 11 n.21, 12–14, 14–15, 17, 39, 42, 63–4, 66, 68 n.104, 74–5, 75 n.138, 85, 149, 150, 151–73, 153 n.9, 157 n.30, 158 n.35, 163 n.54, 164 n.57, 175, 176, 183, 184, 190
Wittgensteinian Fideism? (Szabados)   5
Wren-Lewis, John   9